Consumer Rights and Protections

Recent Titles in Contemporary Debates

Media Bias
American Foreign Policy
Human Trafficking
Women's Equality in America
Political Control of America's Courts
America's National Debt
Energy Resources
Vaccination Sexual Assault and Harassment in America
LGBTQ+ Life in America
Public and Private Education in America
Guns in America
Race Relations in America
Voting in America
Poverty and Welfare in America
Free Speech and Censorship
American Journalism and "Fake News"
Prisons and Punishment in America
Muslims in America
Immigration
Marijuana
Climate Change
The Affordable Care Act

Consumer Rights and Protections

Examining the Facts

Nancy Hendricks

BLOOMSBURY ACADEMIC
NEW YORK • LONDON • OXFORD • NEW DELHI • SYDNEY

BLOOMSBURY ACADEMIC
Bloomsbury Publishing Inc, 1385 Broadway, New York, NY 10018, USA
Bloomsbury Publishing Plc, 50 Bedford Square, London, WC1B 3DP, UK
Bloomsbury Publishing Ireland, 29 Earlsfort Terrace, Dublin 2, D02 AY28, Ireland

First published in the United States of America 2025

Cover image: vayno/Adobe Stock

A catalog record for this book is available from the Library of Congress.

ISBN: HB: 978-1-4408-8130-5
ePDF: 978-1-4408-8131-2
eBook: 979-8-7651-1682-1

Series: Contemporary Debates

Typeset by Newgen KnowledgeWorks Pvt. Ltd., Chennai, India
Printed and bound in the United States of America

For product safety related questions contact
productsafety@bloomsbury.com.

Contents

How to Use This Book

Consumer Rights and Protections: Examining the Facts is part of ABC-CLIO's Contemporary Debates reference series. Each title in this series, which is intended for use by high school and undergraduate students as well as members of the general public, examines the veracity of controversial claims or beliefs surrounding a major political or cultural issue in the United States. The purpose of this series is to give readers a clear and unbiased understanding of current issues by informing them about falsehoods, half-truths, and misconceptions—and confirming the factual validity of other assertions—that have gained traction in America's political and cultural discourse. Ultimately, this series has been crafted to give readers the tools for a fuller understanding of controversial issues, policies, and laws that occupy center stage in American life and politics.

Each volume in this series identifies thirty to forty questions swirling about the larger topic under discussion. These questions are examined in individualized entries, which are in turn arranged in broad subject chapters that cover certain aspects of the issue being examined, for example, history of concern about the issue, potential economic or social impact, or findings of latest scholarly research.

Each chapter features four to ten individual entries. Each entry begins by stating an important and/or well-known **Question** about the issue being studied—for example, "How did politics impact the evolution of consumer rights and protections?" or "Do consumer rights and protections safeguard over-the-counter products?"

The entry then provides a concise and objective one- or two-paragraph **Answer** to the featured question, followed by a more comprehensive, detailed explanation of **The Facts**. This latter portion of each entry uses quantifiable, evidence-based information from respected sources to fully address each question and provide readers with the information they need to be informed citizens. Importantly, entries will also acknowledge instances in which conflicting data exists or data is incomplete. Finally, each entry concludes with a **Further Reading** section, providing users with information on other important and influential resources.

The ultimate purpose of every book in the Contemporary Debates series is to reject "false equivalence," in which demonstrably false beliefs or statements are given the same exposure and credence as the facts; to puncture myths that diminish our understanding of important policies and positions; to provide needed context for misleading statements and claims; and to confirm the factual accuracy of other assertions. In other words, volumes in this series are being crafted to clear the air surrounding some of the most contentious and misunderstood issues of our time—not just add another layer of obfuscation and uncertainty to the debate.

Introduction

In 1726, British author Jonathan Swift published *Gulliver's Travels,* a satirical novel chronicling trips to imaginary places. One was the fictitious land of "Lilliput." There, Gulliver discovers that in cases of fraud, Lilliputians believe that an honest person will not be looking for deceit and therefore, the villain has the advantage. Because trust is destroyed by deception, Lilliputians saw fraud as an offense punishable by the death penalty. Modern-day fraudsters in the United States are not subject to capital punishment, but American consumers are beneficiaries of a growing number of laws and regulations designed to advance consumer rights and protections. However, although a number of laws and regulatory agencies attempt to shield the citizens of the nation from devious—and sometimes deadly—practices, support for enforcing these measures often shifts with changes in the political atmosphere.

Through much of American history, there were very few remedies for deceptive business practices. The nation's economic system was primarily governed by the rule of *caveat emptor,* a Latin phrase usually translated as "buyer beware." According to some, anything could be sold by an enterprising vendor in order to make a profit, and it was up to consumers to decide whether or not to buy it. For many years, a consequence of *caveat emptor* was that Americans were being sold tainted food that often killed them. In addition, there were dangerous pharmaceuticals on the market that could be equally deadly. Sometimes the effect was financial, as in the case of consumers spending money on ineffectual products or being swindled out of their life savings. It is imperative to state that ethical manufacturers and honest businesses sell good products, and that abuses by the few are what led to greater consumer protections. Under *caveat emptor,* it was often a case of public health versus private wealth.

Consumer protection laws may be defined as rules that safeguard purchasers of goods and services against products that are defective, dishonest, or dangerous. They also guard people from being deceived by fraudulent business practices, including deceptive advertisements. In 1962, President John F. Kennedy made a speech to Congress in which he proposed a "Consumer Bill of Rights." According to his declaration, every American consumer has four fundamental rights: the right to safety, the right to choose, the right to be heard, and the right to be informed. In later years, a fifth element was added: the right to redress, or compensation to consumers who were harmed.

The path of consumer rights and protections in America roughly followed the nation's trajectory from a small country in the 1700s and 1800s with an agriculture-based economy, through the industrial age of the late 1800s and early 1900s and the growth of large, impersonal corporations. The prosperous late twentieth century saw the rise of materialism in which unrestrained buying was considered patriotic, accompanied by the concept of consumerism to protect the people who were doing all that buying. Finally, the computer age of the twenty-first century has seen an astronomical rise in new technology, including cryptocurrency and artificial intelligence, for which it is said that there are currently few regulatory controls because few lawmakers completely understand it.

For the most part, there was little demand in the early days of the nation for governmental control over consumer goods, food, fraudulent schemes, and health-related concoctions. *Caveat emptor* remained prevalent so as not to stifle the growing economy. However, a situation far from home began to tip the scales. During the Mexican War in 1848, stories filtered back that US soldiers fighting in the conflict were dying in large numbers, not in combat, but because ineffective medicines were used to treat wounds and disease. This led to Congress passing the Drug Importation Act of 1848, an early attempt at federal regulation of pharmaceuticals in America. It was widely felt at the time that the culprits selling useless medications had to be foreigners; therefore, the legislation only covered imports. Still, it was a first step in the regulation of consumer products in the United States, establishing a precedent. At the time, however, many people continued to feel that the government had no place involving itself in commerce—in short, business was none of the government's business.

In the past, many companies generally opposed rules on consumer protection, preferring a "hands-off" policy for the free market. Arguing that the government had no place regulating private enterprise, they claimed that legislative oversight could be considered un-American. Furthermore, opponents declared that regulating business would result in lower profits for the producer, because the way to keep prices down often involved cutting corners.

Their position was that increased costs of production would have to be passed along to consumers, who would balk at paying higher prices.

Another factor in the lack of consumer protections was that inferior products, whether food or retail goods, were often marketed to such groups as Blacks and other minorities, immigrants, women, and the elderly. Those marginalized segments of the population were rarely in a position to demand consumer rights.

Things began to change in 1898 with a highly publicized scandal involving tainted meat being provided for US troops fighting in the Spanish American War that year. Public outrage led to a few changes, such as inspections of meat factories. Bills were periodically introduced in Congress around this time to protect American consumers from abuses in what they were being sold, but few laws had much impact until the Progressive Era of the early 1900s.

Caveat emptor and its "hands-off" policy toward business faced off against the sweeping legislation of America's Pure Food and Drug Act of 1906. Some felt that with a shift toward consumer protection in the Progressive Era, there was an emerging spirit of *caveat venditor*, Latin for "seller beware." Under *caveat venditor*, consumers had greater protections by making food processing companies, manufacturers, and service providers accountable for what they sold.

Consumer rights and protections are not without controversy. Some claim that they lead to a "nanny state" perpetrated by an overly protective government. Others claim that advisements, no matter how dubious, are covered by the provision for freedom of speech under the First Amendment in the Constitution. There are some who argue on both sides of consumer protections regarding the "pink tax"—charging more to women—as well as whether or not it even exists. Arguments over consumer rights and protections have persisted for decades through such episodes in American history as the fertilizer boom, the "Margarine Wars," and the battle over "Pure Ketchup." Books such as Upton Sinclair's *The Jungle* (which exposed poor conditions in meat-processing facilities) and displays like the *American Chamber of Horrors* (an exhibit put together for Congress presenting problem products) were eye-opening to many people but scorned by others.

In recent times, the Savings and Loan Scandal of the 1980s–1990s played a part in consumer protections, as did the "housing bubble" in the 2000s and the recession of 2007–8. In response, a new federal agency called the Consumer Finance Protection Bureau (CFPB) arose in 2010 to protect money-related transactions of the public, although it became politically controversial.

Many Americans generally do not think about consumer protections, expecting that their food and pharmaceuticals are kept safe by such entities as the Food and Drug Administration (FDA). Still, outbreaks of food-borne illnesses and deaths continue to occur along with questionable practices by a few in the pharmaceutical industry. Some consumer issues are as current as today's headlines with emerging technology like cryptocurrency and artificial intelligence on the rise.

The story of how consumer rights and protections evolved in America is stocked with a colorful cast of characters. Some of the names may be familiar, including activist Ralph Nader, author Upton Sinclair, and US Presidents Franklin Roosevelt and Theodore Roosevelt, as well as Charles Ponzi, for whom the Ponzi Scheme was named. Other individuals may be little known, but they left an impact on Americans for generations. These included Sarah Howe, Harvey Washington Wiley, and an intrepid group known as the Poison Squad who ingested common food additives to see if the substances were harmful—which they often were. Beginning in a time when the concept of consumer protection in the United States was both unfamiliar and strongly opposed by powerful forces, many Americans today owe the safety of the food they eat and the products they buy to such pioneers.

1

Historical Overview of Consumer Rights and Protections in America

Through most of early American history, consumer rights and protections were rare. In the colonial society that developed in what became the United States, most people earned their living on small farms through agriculture and by raising livestock. Families provided many of their own essentials such as food, clothing, and small household goods like soap and candles, which were made at home and often could be traded with neighbors. For other items, consumers generally knew the local shopkeepers whom they patronized because they were usually close to home. If there were problems with a product that a consumer bought, it was not difficult to contact the merchant responsible—face-to-face.

During the colonial era, a number of goods and products such as tea arrived by ship from England. Many were heavily taxed, which eventually became one of the root causes of the American Revolution. After the War of Independence, as the United States continued to grow, the rise of steam-powered ships and railroads enabled goods to be transported over long distances. Especially in the burgeoning cities, there were fewer close relationships between consumers and the makers of the products they bought.

The Industrial Revolution of the 1800s transformed much of life in the United States. To find jobs, many people moved from farms to urban areas where they were joined by immigrants from other countries. The populations of these sprawling cities of factories and crowded neighborhoods did not have the space or resources to raise their own food, so they became increasingly dependent on distant farms and grocery stores. When shocking sanitary and workplace safety conditions in the meatpacking industry and other industries became known, the first meaningful government regulations covering consumer rights and protection were enacted, such as the Pure Food and Drug Act of 1906. However, *caveat emptor*, or "buyer beware," remained the prevailing system. That is, it was the consumers' responsibility to evaluate the worthiness of a product (and any risks involved) before deciding whether or not to buy it.

Throughout the evolution of consumer rights and protections in America, there were opponents who believed that the government had no business interfering with private enterprise, no matter how unsavory or unethically sellers of goods or services behaved. Others countered that the federal government was the only entity strong enough to protect consumers from powerful industrial forces. The wisdom and effectiveness of consumer protections quickly became a source of polarizing political disputes.

During the twentieth and early twenty-first centuries, there were individuals and organizations who strove to safeguard people from what they considered to be abuses in the marketplace. Some early consumer advocates, like Harvey Washington Wiley, were well known in their day but have faded from the modern consciousness. More recent crusaders for consumer rights, like Ralph Nader, may be more familiar.

Q1: How did industrialization affect the rise of consumer rights and protections?

Answer: There have been sporadic attempts to implement consumer rights and protections in America since its early days. However, for much of the nation's history, the guiding economic principle was *caveat emptor*. Following the arrival of the Industrial Revolution and the outbreak of several scandals related to product quality and food safety in the late 1800s, some consumer safeguards were enacted, changing the nature of the American economy in which the marketplace grew less immune from government regulation. Industrial development in the United States altered traditional patterns of how people lived, eventually leading to changes in the ways consumers were protected.

The Facts: During the 1700s, most families grew their own food crops and raised their own livestock. Almost all goods, from clothing to candles, were made by hand, either at home or by local craftsmen. Consumer goods such as clocks were an expensive luxury beyond the reach of most people. Industrialization, which developed through most of the nineteenth century, affected virtually all aspects of American life. The Industrial Revolution spurred the transition from handmade goods to those manufactured by machines in factories, often on large-scale assembly lines. Industrialization transformed the economy from one that had been based on small farms and local artisans to one that was dominated by machine-driven manufacturing at factories in distant locations.

Most historians state that the Industrial Revolution began in the textile industry of Great Britain during the mid-eighteenth century, after which it quickly made its presence felt in the United States and other parts of the world. Industrialization coincided with the growth of America's railroads, which were capable of transporting food products and manufactured goods across long distances that were far from their place of origin. As more industries became mechanized, manufacturers were able to produce more goods. They could make a higher profit, even while selling their goods at lower prices, because more consumers started to be able to afford to buy them, which in turn increased the volume of sales. Goods in the general marketplace became more plentiful, affordable, and accessible.

Before the Industrial Revolution, consumer items were generally made and sold based on daily orders. Small businesses usually stocked goods that would sell promptly, having neither the willingness nor the space to build up a large inventory. That changed with industrialization, as it was more efficient to make many of the same products all at once, store them in a warehouse, and wait for them to be sold. Advertising was required to create demand and attract buyers for the unsold inventory.

A far-reaching byproduct of the Industrial Revolution "was a fundamental shift in cultural attitudes towards women" (National Women's History Museum 2017). Before industrialization, for example, women hand-sewed garments for their family, often after spinning their own wool. The advent of textile mills and garment factories allowed Americans to purchase ready-made clothing, freeing women from this type of work, to some extent, and transforming them instead into consumers and therefore targets for advertising campaigns.

While the Industrial Revolution brought enhancements in the quality of life for many Americans, there were also downsides to industrialization, including rising levels of pollution, unsustainable consumption of natural resources, overcrowded cities resulting in unsanitary conditions, and a growing divide between America's richest and poorest citizens. During the rise of industrialization, waves of immigrants from other countries arrived in the United States. Often desperately poor, uneducated, and not able to speak English, they had little experience with being consumers. Many workers of all kinds were exploited as cheap labor, living in filthy slums and working up to sixteen hours a day, six days a week. In general, men were not paid well but often received at least twice as much as women, particularly "factory girls," a term that generally refers to young women who left rural homes to work in urban factories during the Industrial Revolution.

Along with a lack of protection for workers, consumer rights were not in vogue. In the realm of such necessities as food, consumers were now at the mercy of others. For example, before the Industrial Revolution, people living in rural areas might have caught their own fish from a nearby lake to cook for dinner. With so many newcomers flocking to urban centers, people quickly became consumers dependent on others for their food, and sellers did not always have the buyer's best interest at heart. In one case, "the New York City inspector called the famous Washington and Fulton fish markets 'a singular agglomeration of … collected filth'" (Strasser 2000, 19).

With continuing industrialization in the late 1800s, there came a growing trend toward consumerism—the acquisition of goods as a way to exhibit social and economic status. Even considering the meager wages offered by industrialization, many average Americans managed to find themselves with small amounts of spending money to purchase goods and services that were unavailable to earlier generations of Americans. Some historians see the rise of industrialization in the 1800s through the end of the twentieth century as the time when consumer culture came to the forefront of life in the United States. It affected "how people made their livings, how people got their clothes, how people got their furniture, how people got all of the material of daily life" (National Women's History Museum 2017).

In the past, many early Americans had displayed themselves modestly, both out of necessity and through a desire to practice humility, which was sometimes mandated under the law in places such as the Puritan colonies. The citizens of colonial New England, for example, "were not to dress in a manner unsuitable for their social station" (Johnson 2017, 177). Women in New England "did not wear billowing skirts, headdresses, or jewelry, including a wedding ring" (Johnson 2017, 180). That changed as decades passed and a new era emerged in the late 1800s, often called the Gilded Age. With industrialization came increased social acceptance—even whole-hearted encouragement—of consumerism. Shoppers "first became known as consumers in 1897 when Sears, Roebuck & Company identified us as such in a section of its catalog titled 'Consumer's Guide'" (Larson 1992, 18).

By that time, the phenomenon of consumerism had become prevalent enough to attract criticism in the form of a book published in 1899, *The Theory of the Leisure Class* by Thorstein Veblen (1857–1929). Veblen, an American sociologist, was a critic of what he called "conspicuous consumption," defined by the *Merriam-Webster* dictionary as lavish or wasteful spending for the purpose of enhancing one's social prestige. Veblen's arguments against consumerism were refuted by proponents of capitalism whose businesses benefited from such spending. Industrialists tended to protest against any policies that might restrict those profits, including proposals for consumer rights and protections.

After the First World War ended in 1918 and as the twentieth century progressed, consumerism rose to new heights. The growth of department stores and mail-order catalogs allowed average Americans to be tempted by items that they had not even known they wanted. Until this point in America's economic history, buying more than what was needed for daily life was generally a luxury reserved only for the wealthy or those who wanted to appear that way. However, starting in the 1920s, several factors combined to produce the kind of consumerism for average Americans that continues to characterize modern society.

First, in the 1920s, while much of Europe had been decimated by the war, the United States enjoyed unparalleled prosperity. The nation's postwar economic boom was greatly augmented by the widespread growth of electricity across the country at that time. The American marketplace was flooded with previously unimaginable electronic marvels such as phonographs, radios, refrigerators, vacuum cleaners, and washing machines. American consumers wanted them all.

Second, by the 1920s, many companies of all kinds began to offer customers the opportunity to obtain items on credit or to make their purchases through installment plans consisting of small, regular payments. Although sizeable interest charges were not always taken into account by the purchaser, it became easier for average Americans to join the rage for consumerism under the banner of slogans such as "Buy Now, Pay Later" and "A Dollar Down and a Dollar a Week."

Another factor was the invention of the automobile. During the 1920s, mass-produced autos transformed America in almost every way. Produced on assembly lines, "cars roared into society and revolutionized modern life [creating] a consumer craze for automobiles" (McGreevy 2021). In the beginning, many autos were fairly standard machines for basic transportation, often available only in black. But soon, automakers started to paint their cars in different colors and design new styles. "In 1927, General Motors began making annual changes in body styles, a practice that came to be known as 'planned obsolescence.' The stated mission of GM's research division was 'the organized creation of dissatisfaction'" (Larson 1992, 20). Planned obsolescence involves the designing of products to have "a limited useful life or to become outdated rapidly. This strategy encourages consumers to purchase new products more frequently, boosting sales and ensuring continuous revenue for manufacturers" (Automotive American 2024). That dissatisfaction took hold among consumers. Automakers were happy to provide the solution to their discontent, helping consumers avoid the embarrassment of being seen in "last year's model" by offering sparkling new styles to choose from each year. By the time Thorstein Veblen died in 1929, he could no doubt see evidence of his theory of conspicuous consumption on every street.

Also during the 1920s, there was a tremendous expansion in the field of advertising. In order to please the manufacturers who were their clients, ad agencies had to create promotions to stimulate demand. Manufacturers and their ad agencies were under pressure to catch the attention of consumers and differentiate their product from others on the market. One way to accomplish this was to exaggerate or even lie, if need be, in order to give advertising clients the sales boosts they desired. In 1927, the president of the American Association of Advertising Agencies stated, "It may be necessary to fool people for their own good. … Average intelligence is surprisingly low" (Larson 1992, 21).

Newspapers and magazines flourished during this era, providing fertile ground in which to place advertisements. Even illiterate people who could not read and immigrants who were unable to speak English could look at the attractive pictures of consumer goods, creating the desire to own them. Another factor was a marvel of the time—radio. It connected average people to the wider world and provided a cornucopia of entertainment. Along with music and news programs, radio in the 1920s brought comedy, drama, serials, and science fiction into American homes. Programming was paid for and therefore determined by corporations and their advertising agencies. Prime examples were daytime dramas aimed at women. These ongoing serials came to be known as "soap operas" due to the fact that they were initially sponsored by companies that made household cleaning products.

In the industrial age, advertising took on a life of its own, one that did not necessarily place the welfare of the consumer first. According to author and professor of communications Inger Stole, it "became not only an adjunct to the 'real business of manufacturing;' it became as vital as the steel, the workers and the machinery because it created its own by-product: the loyal consumer" (Stole 2005, 5). Showing what a product could do was not the prime directive. Advertisers had to provide a reason for potential consumers to purchase their product over its competitors. "This led to advertising strategies that attempted to capture and exploit consumers' emotions" (Stole 2005, 5). By the end of the 1920s, more observers started adopting Thorstein Veblen's viewpoint in condemning conspicuous consumption as wasteful and even damaging to the soul of average Americans. However, according to historian and best-selling author Erik Larson, "marketers countered with an argument they would dust off again in the 1990s … [that] they were merely exercising their constitutional right to 'freedom of speech'" (Larson 1992, 21).

Even amid the economic devastation of the Great Depression in the 1930s and the rationing that took place during the Second World War in the 1940s, advertising in the industrial age retained its hold on consumers. Ads for products such as automobiles, radios, refrigerators, and luxurious clothing often reminded people of what they might not be able to have at the moment but offered the promise of what they would be able to buy in a brighter and more prosperous future—one that was realized with the wartime awakening of America's still-mighty industrial capacity. Long-slumbering steel plants, automotives lines, airplane makers, and clothing manufacturers roared back to life during the Second World War, infused with financial support from the federal government to support the Allied war effort against the Axis powers of Nazi Germany, Japan, and Italy. Demand for workers of all kinds soared, as did career opportunities for women. By the time the war ended with an Allied victory in spring 1945, America had finally shaken off the last of the Depression and looked poised for healthy economic growth and opportunity.

For the average American consumer, that long-awaited future arrived in the form of a postwar economic boom driven by the return of Americans who had served in the military during the war and the pent-up demand for products that promised good value or high social approval. The onslaught of new consumer goods was accompanied by the advent of television, which provided an extraordinary medium for advertising products to the American people. The whole family, including children, could see the products right before their eyes, stimulating the desire to have them. Rolling off assembly lines, the dazzling array of consumer items of the 1950s, from toys to TV dinners, set the stage for the kind of conspicuous consumption that has characterized the modern world. To increase consumer demand, businesses and their advertising agencies devised new means of attracting buyers for their wares through merchandising, packaging, and image-making. Targeting women as primary consumers became the cultural vogue in advertising, based on portraying the feminine role as guardian of the family, providing their loved ones with a better life through consumerism.

In addition, Cold War political developments in the 1950s and the years that followed equated consumerism with patriotism. In the optimism of the postwar era, many people tended to believe what they were told by the government as well as by well-known, successful corporations. Democracy and capitalism were presented as being intertwined, with the freedom of entrepreneurship promoted as "The American Way." Postwar consumers were told they were contributing to maintaining a strong American industrial economy and enjoying the benefits of capitalism. Consumer advocates who questioned deceptive marketing or critics such as labor leaders faced potential accusations of having communist ties, which weakened their position in both public opinion and in negotiations between labor and management.

Throughout the late twentieth century, as more products were manufactured, more advertisements tempted buyers. False advertising became a growing problem, prompting a move toward greater consumer rights and protections. Some advertisements of the 1950s touted sugar for weight loss, adding soft drinks to babies' milk, and serving donuts for their nutritional value in raising healthy children. According to historian Susan Strasser, there was little protection for consumers in the face of abuses other than "obviously fraudulent practices like short-weighting [providing a weight less than what was charged for] which could be brought to the attention of municipal officials" (Strasser 2000, 19). Some consumers may have been able to attain such remedies, but many were not.

By the dawn of the twenty-first century, the Industrial Revolution was giving way to the Information Age. Still, the consumerism that was ushered in by industrialization did not diminish; in fact, it grew even larger in the face of a constant flow of new technological gadgets (such as cell phones) and emerging social media. Fresh challenges arose for average consumers, ranging from the food they ate and beverages they drank to the industries surrounding pharmaceuticals and finances, as well as the rapid obsolescence of constantly emerging new technologies. The move from the Industrial Age to the Information Age generated calls for greater consumer rights and protections in the face of increasing globalization in the twenty-first century.

Further Reading

Automotive American. 2024. "GM and the Dawn of Planned Obsolescence in the Automotive Industry." May 30, 2024. Accessed November 28, 2024. https://automotiveamerican.com/2024/05/30/gm-and-the-dawn-of-planned-obsolescence-in-the-automotive-industry/.

Johnson, Claudia Durst. 2017. *Daily Life in Colonial New England*. Santa Barbara, CA: ABC-CLIO, 177, 180.
Larson, Erik. 1992. *The Naked Consumer: How Our Private Lives Become Public Commodities*. New York: Henry Holt, 18, 20, 21.
McGreevy, Nora. 2021. "How the Automobile Changed the World, for Better or Worse." *Smithsonian*. Accessed November 28, 2024. https://www.smithsonianmag.com/smart-news/how-automobile-changed-world-cars-history-art-design-vehicles-180978109/.
National Women's History Museum. 2017. "Shop 'Til You Drop: Creating a Feminized Consumer Culture." Accessed November 28, 2024. https://www.womenshistory.org/articles/shop-til-you-drop.
Stole, Inger. 2005. *Advertising on Trial: Consumer Activism and Corporate Public Relations in the 1930s*. Urbana: University of Illinois Press, 5.
Strasser, Susan. 2000. *Never Done: A History of American Housework*. New York: Henry Holt, 5, 19.

Q2: How did politics impact the evolution of consumer rights and protections?

Answer: According to the *Merriam-Webster* dictionary, "politics" may be defined as pertaining to government, guiding governmental policy, and winning or holding control over a government. In terms of consumer rights and protections, however, the nuance of politics is more specific. It is the basic ideology of how much—if any—government control or regulation should there be over private enterprise.

The Facts: Historian Lawrence Glickman states that "consumer politics is as American as apple pie. Throughout American history, consumer activists have sought to employ consumer power" (Glickman n.d.). He cites the famed Boston Tea Party of 1773 as a means of claiming the individual rights of the consumer to express displeasure with their purchasing choices. In this case, colonial consumers chose not to buy goods from England that were shipped to America with prohibitive taxes attached. Their protests took the form of dumping imported British tea into Boston Harbor. Similarly, as a political statement, proponents of America's antislavery movement in the mid-1800s urged consumers not to buy goods that had been produced by the labor of enslaved people.

By 1880, the act of refusing to buy certain goods in order to support a greater purpose had its own name: "boycott." The term evolved from usage in Ireland when the agent for an absentee British landlord tried to increase rents and evict tenant farmers. His Irish laborers refused to work for him or comply with his demands, leaving the agent's crops to rot in the fields. Word spread about how the tenant farmers were rebelling against the agent, whose name was Charles Boycott. His name became synonymous with a refusal to buy certain goods or support certain businesses in order to express a social or political sentiment. Boycotts became a significant element of consumer rights. Consumers have the power of boycotting certain items or companies to register displeasure at questionable products or a way of doing business that might be considered unfair.-

Over the years, as American consumers were victimized by deceptive, dangerous, and abusive business practices, there were periodic calls for greater government regulation in the marketplace. However, conservatives generally favored a hands-off policy in favor of free enterprise. Glickman wrote that "advocates of free enterprise focused on a compelling set of fears about government power [that] constrained and transformed politics in the United States" (Glickman 2019, 4). For example, British writer C. S. Lewis (1898–1963) spoke for many opponents of business regulation when he wrote in 1948 that "of all tyrannies, a tyranny exercised for the good of its victims may be the most oppressive. It may be better to live under robber barons than under omnipotent moral busybodies" (Lewis 2014, 324). He claimed that "those who torment us for our own good will torment us without end for they do so with the approval of their own conscience," reducing consumers who need governmental protection to the level of "infants, imbeciles, and domestic animals" (Lewis 2014, 324).

Brian Johnson, former deputy director of the US Consumer Financial Protection Bureau, took issue with that sentiment, stating that "the fundamental purpose of government is protecting the rights of its citizens. And that means protecting the vulnerable and less fortunate among us. It means making sure consumers aren't taken advantage of" (Johnson 2018). Johnson also asserted the right of consumers to take legal action for breach of contract or fraud. However, he said that the cost of bringing a private suit has become "increasingly prohibitive because the cost of litigation [has] dwarfed whatever damages the consumer could likely demonstrate" (Johnson 2018). He believed that only a strong institution such as the federal government has the power as well as the obligation to protect its citizens. Opponents disagree, believing that consumers should be free to make decisions without interference from a government agency.

Political opposition to government regulation in consumer affairs intensified during the early Cold War era of the 1950s and 1960s. That time period corresponded with a tremendous growth in American consumerism.

A cornucopia of products flooded the marketplace, with their producers attempting to attract millions of America's affluent consumers. Historians Naomi Oreskes and Erik Conway state that opponents to consumer rights and protections expressed fears that government regulation of the marketplace, even pertaining to dangerous products, "would be the first step on the slippery slope to socialism, communism or worse" (Oreskes and Conway 2023, 2). Oreskes and Conway refute that theory by stating that the United States implemented "environmental, workplace, and public health safeguards both before and during the Cold War and we had not succumbed to communism. Many European countries had even stronger regulations—particularly with respect to consumer products—and they were still democracies too" (Oreskes and Conway 2023, 3).

However, those claims did little to assuage opposition to the government having a role in regulating the marketplace. For example, after the US surgeon general declared that secondhand smoke (smoke inhaled due to proximity to people who are smoking) was hazardous to anyone exposed to it, the US Environmental Protection Agency (EPA) indicated that there is no known safe level of exposure to secondhand tobacco smoke, considering it passive smoking. Subsequently, Fred Singer, a professor of environmental science, coauthored a paper in 1993 claiming that the EPA's work "was rigged, and that the EPA review of the science—done by leading experts from around the country—was distorted by a political agenda to expand government control over all aspects of our lives" (Oreskes and Conway 2011, 5–6). According to Oreskes and Conway, Singer's report was funded by a grant from the Tobacco Institute, a tobacco industry trade group.

The political elements of consumer rights and protections continue being debated. They are grounded in the basic argument of how much governmental regulation in the marketplace is too much, as well as whether the government should have any role in the free market at all.

Further Reading

Glickman, Lawrence. n.d. "The American Tradition of Consumer Politics." *The American Historian*. Accessed September 10, 2024. https://www.oah.org/tah/issues/2017/may/the-american-tradition-of-consumer-politics/.

Glickman, Lawrence. 2012. *Buying Power: A History of Consumer Activism in America*. Chicago: University of Chicago Press.

Glickman, Lawrence. 2019. *Free Enterprise: An American History*. New Haven, CT: Yale University Press, 4.

"How Can We Base an Economy on Consumption?" 2010. PBS News. Accessed November 28, 2024. https://www.pbs.org/newshour/economy/how-can-we-base-an-economy-on.

Johnson, Brian. 2018. "Toward a 21st Century Approach to Consumer Protection." Consumer Financial Protection Bureau. Accessed November 28, 2024. https://www.consumerfinance.gov/about-us/newsroom/toward-21st-century-approach-consumer-protection/.

Lewis, C. S. 2014. *God in the Dock: Essays on Theology and Ethics*. Grand Rapids, MI: Eerdmans Publishing, 324.

Oreskes, Naomi, and Erik Conway. 2011. *Merchants of Doubt: How a Handful of Scientists Obscured the Truth on Issues from Tobacco Smoke to Global Warming*. New York: Bloomsbury, 5, 6.

Oreskes, Naomi, and Erik Conway. 2023. *The Big Myth: How American Business Taught Us to Loathe Government and Love the Free Market*. New York: Bloomsbury, 2, 3.

Q3: Who were early leaders in efforts to secure increased consumer protections?

Answer: With the advent of the Industrial Revolution, consumer rights and protections in America gained more attention, both by individuals and from organized groups. One reason was that, starting in Massachusetts in 1852, more states began passing laws to make education compulsory. Greater literacy heralded the creation of more newspapers in the United States. As the primary source of mass communication, newspapers carried news of scandals, such as tainted food provided to American troops during the Spanish American War, which appalled many citizens. In addition, newspaper advertisements were sometimes characterized by exaggerations if not falsehoods. More individuals and organizations began calling for consumer rights and protections, with their demands reaching a large audience. At the same time, opponents who supported an unregulated marketplace made their objections to consumer protections widely known. Such opposition was generally based on businesses protecting their bottom line and the belief that government had no place interfering with private enterprise, even to protect the health and well-being of the public.

The Facts: Although calls for greater consumer rights and protections increased during the Industrial Revolution, an early example exists in colonial America. As a basic operating principle in the marketplace, standardizing weights and measures was an early form of consumer protection. The concept of "measure for measure" dates back to the ancient Greek and Roman civilizations. Recognizing that vendors could make any claim as to what constituted a full ounce, pound, gallon, and so forth, the Connecticut colony established a statute in 1637 to determine uniform standards in order to avoid potential strife among colonists who felt they were being cheated by local merchants. The colonial government of Connecticut ordered that "there shall be a measure of each [village] brought to Hartford on the next particular Court and then there will be a settled course for a measure in each" (Connecticut State Department of Consumer Protection n.d.). The statute was put in place to make sure all consumers could enjoy the same standard of weights across the Connecticut colony and not feel short-changed. In that way, "righteousness and justice may be maintained amongst us in our commerce and dealings each with other" (Connecticut State Department of Consumer Protection n.d.). This early example of government intervention in the marketplace was implemented as much to keep peace in the Connecticut colony as to protect the consumer rights of its citizens.

Around the time of the American Revolution, a new book called *An Inquiry into the Nature and Causes of the Wealth of Nations* (1776) was published that would become a foundational text in political economics. The book's main concepts involved a free market (with little or no government interference) and an invisible hand, by which people's self-interest benefits them, which, in turn, eventually benefits larger society. Its author, who is often called the "Father of Capitalism," was Scottish economist Adam Smith (1723–1790). Capitalism is defined by the *Merriam-Webster* dictionary as an economic system characterized by private ownership of capital goods for personal profit via the free market, unencumbered by governmental regulation.

After America won its independence, the new nation was striving to strengthen its economy and cultivate prosperity among its citizens. *Caveat emptor* reigned supreme as nineteenth century America "gained a reputation for being a bastion of *laissez-faire*" (Balleisen 2017, 46). The latter phrase, from the French, essentially translates as "leave it alone" and is the cornerstone of economic theories that oppose any government intervention in the operations and activities of private business.

In 1879, the first known proposal supporting large-scale federal consumer rights and protections came when Hendrick B. Wright (1808–1881), a US representative from Pennsylvania, introduced the first bill in Congress to prohibit food and drink "adulteration"—the practice of reducing the quality of a product by diluting it with other substances. However, the bill died in committee. That same fate would befall almost 200 subsequent proposals during the next three decades, designed to protect consumers from adulteration and misbranding of food and drugs (Diamond 2002). The bills died in every session of Congress until 1906 when the Pure Food and Drug Act was ultimately passed, a quarter century after the pioneering Congressman Wright had died.

Women, in their role as guardians of the family, played their part in early attempts to provide consumer rights and protections. In 1884, the Ladies Health Protective Association was created to organize a campaign to rid New York City of horrific stockyards and slaughterhouses. As the first group to take a stand, they were enraged not only by the blight on their neighborhoods from the vermin and stench of Manhattan's stockyards, but also by callous business owners and city officials who refused to do anything about it. This brush-off caused the women to step up their crusade against the offenders, which finally succeeded after ten years of effort, at least in curtailing some of the worst offenses. Beyond cleaning up unhealthy public nuisances, the organization also extended their mission to investigating the city's water supply. Even though American women did not have the vote until 1920, the Ladies Health Protective Association was able to influence the passage of local laws in New York during the late 1800s that covered basic consumer-related issues. In addition, branches of the organization began to be formed in other locations. In 1897, delegates from forty similar protective associations attended a national convention in Philadelphia, Pennsylvania. From that conference, the Woman's Health Protective Association of the United States was formed, putting its faith in the power of women to effect change to protect both their own families and the general public.

Ella Reeve Bloor (1862–1951) of Louisiana took individual action. In 1905, she helped author Upton Sinclair (1878–1968) gather information on the scandalous state of Chicago's meatpacking operations. Her investigative reporting was an important contribution to Sinclair's novel *The Jungle* (1906), which described shocking working and sanitary conditions in America's meatpacking industry. Sinclair's book changed the trajectory of consumer rights and protections in America by bringing a previously unseen level of public awareness to the issue. The novel portrays the lives of workers, who are primarily immigrants in desperate need of work and therefore particularly vulnerable, as an endless cycle of being mistreated by employers, cheated by conmen, exploited by human traffickers, and scorned by the wealthy. Along with depicting the inhumane treatment suffered by the workers and their families, Sinclair vividly described revoltingly unsanitary conditions inside the packing plant, which shocked readers. The nation was stunned by his reports of vermin such as rats, along with their droppings, finding their way into the packed meat that consumers had been buying. In addition, Sinclair revealed that the meat products on the nation's dinner tables might also include severed human body parts of injured workers.

After sales of meat fell, meatpackers announced that they would clean up the plants. However, the continued public outcry led to a demand for Congress to pass federal legislation mandating government regulation of the industry. It culminated in the enactment of both the Pure Food and Drug Act of 1906 and the Meat Inspection Act that same year. Author Jack London once stated publicly that *The Jungle* "did for the 'wage slaves' of today what *Uncle Tom's Cabin* had done earlier for black slaves" (quoted in Arthur 2006, 65), but Sinclair, whose primary motivation in writing the book had been to arouse public sympathy for meatpacking industry workers, stated that he had "aimed at the public's heart and accidentally hit it in the stomach" (Arthur 2006, 83).

During the late 1800s and early 1900s, the Women's Christian Temperance Union (WCTU) fought to protect families and communities by initiating what they felt would be a pure and sober world by moderating the use of alcohol. Eventually, the WCTU came to be synonymous with Prohibition, or outlawing the sale and manufacture of alcohol in America through the Eighteenth Amendment. However, when the group was founded in 1874, some of its members urged temperance, or restraint in the use of alcohol, not necessarily total abstinence. Part of their mission was to target patent medicines, which often contained heavy doses of alcohol along with opiates and narcotics. Addiction was a common result among people who unwittingly consumed patent medicines. Many WCTU members began to equate adulterated medicines and foods with alcohol, arguing that they all harmed families and communities. They felt this was especially true in poverty-stricken communities, leading to malnutrition, violence, and other social problems. "The Women's Christian Temperance Union crusaders were among the most avid pure food, drink and drug advocates," wrote historian Lorine Goodwin. "To them, the crusade against adulterated foods and dangerous drugs was an integral part of temperance" (Goodwin 1999, 11).

In 1899, social worker Jane Addams (1860–1935) became a cofounder of the National Consumers League (NCL). Today, Addams is best known for her work among the poor at Hull House in Chicago, providing social services to the destitute. In her travels, what she saw first-hand convinced her of the need for a nationwide group to protect all consumers, including—or perhaps *especially*—the poor. At one market, she saw decaying meat alongside rotten fruit and vegetables being sold to the poor. Addams saw "people dressed in rags, their hands thin, white and empty, clutching to reach the food that was already unfit to eat" (Knight 2010, 49). More than a century after its founding, the NCL remains a significant nonprofit advocacy group for consumer rights and protections.

The first general secretary of the NCL was Florence Kelley (1859–1932), who held the position for thirty years. Under Kelley's leadership, one of the main goals of the NCL was to assist consumers in demanding safety and reliability in the goods and services they bought. Eventually becoming director of the NCL, Kelly played an important role in building public support for the Pure Food and Drug Act of 1906. She not only fought for consumer rights and protections but also saw the power that consumers could use to influence other kinds of reforms, including unfair labor conditions such as sweatshops and child labor. According to Jon Grinspan, curator of political history at the Smithsonian National Museum of American History, having "major leverage as head of the National Consumers League ... she organized the buying power of thousands of working- and middle-class shoppers to punish abusive employers" (Grinspan 2022).

Ellen Swallow Richards (1842–1911), the first woman to be admitted to the Massachusetts Institute of Technology (MIT), was also the founder of the American Home Economics Association in 1908, a group that later changed its name to the American Association of Family and Consumer Sciences to reflect its mission. Richards wrote extensively on consumer issues, including books such as *Food Materials and Their Adulterations* (1885) and *Air, Water, and Food from a Sanitary Standpoint* (1900). She conducted experiments to demonstrate how women could check for adulterated food in their own kitchen. In doing so, "Ellen Swallow Richards applied chemistry to the home to advocate for consumer safety" (McNeill 2018). Many consumer laws "that continue to protect people from manufacturers and corporations can trace their beginnings to Richards" (McNeill 2018). In a study of common kitchen staples in Massachusetts, she discovered that food such as sugar was adulterated with chloride. She began speaking on the topic of tainted food to women's groups as a consumer issue, stating that "the woman must know something of chemistry in self-defense. ... It is for women to institute reform" (McNeill 2018). At speaking engagements, hundreds of women generally attended her speeches. Still, the federal Food and Drug Act of 1906 would not become law until more than twenty years later. In 2011, honoring her work for consumer safety, Richards was in the top ten on the "MIT150" list of top 150 innovators published by the *Boston Globe* in honor of MIT's 150th anniversary.

Chemist Harvey Washington Wiley (1844–1930) spent his early career conducting experiments on different types of fertilizers before focusing his attention on adulterated food and drug products. Wiley taught for several years at Indiana's Purdue University but expanded his concerns beyond academia, arguing vehemently against the practice of adulteration not only in fertilizers but also in food. Beginning in 1881, he served as Indiana's state chemist to analyze the contents of commercial fertilizers. At that time, he also experimented on adulterated food products at Purdue, where one trustee "declared publicly that scientific progress was 'the devil's tool'" (Blum 2018, 20). After being appointed to the Bureau of Chemistry at the US Department of Agriculture as chief chemist in 1883, Wiley published the agency's first major study of food products in 1887. His reports might have gone unnoticed if he had not begun using human volunteers in 1902 to test chemical additives in consumer food products. After a reporter noticed what he and his volunteers were doing, the word went out that Wiley was conducting experiments that were "dubbed 'The Poison Squad' studies by the nation's newspapers" (Blum 2018, 5). The name "Poison Squad" caught the public's attention.

For years, Wiley fought to develop a national anti-adulteration law, starting with products such as fertilizer and evolving into the realm of consumer items such as food and drugs. He submitted a proposal to the US Congress in 1899, but no action was taken. The bill was reintroduced the following year, but sustained opposition from corporate interests derailed his "fight to bring order to a lawless food industry" (Science History Institute n.d.). Finally, with public support, the Pure Food and Drug Act of 1906—sometimes known as the Wiley Law—was passed into law. According to the Science History Institute, "a pure food and drug bill would probably not have passed in 1906 without Wiley's unceasing commitment" (Science History Institute n.d.).

It was US President Theodore Roosevelt (1858–1919) who signed the Pure Food and Drug Act of 1906, which most historians mark as the first significant federal consumer protection law in America. Facing off against forces who believed that governmental entities had no business interfering with private enterprise, Roosevelt took a public stand that "the government needed to intervene more actively on behalf of the general public" (Milkis n.d.). Even before he read Upton Sinclair's book *The Jungle*, Roosevelt had first-hand knowledge of what was being sold by the unregulated meatpacking industry. As a military officer in Cuba during the Spanish American War in 1898, Roosevelt saw the kind of tainted food that was being sold by meatpackers to the Army for American troops. There were allegations that the "shoddy meat supplies had killed more soldiers than the Spanish had killed with gunfire. … Both officers and foot soldiers accused the Army of feeding them 'embalmed beef'" (Blum 2020), which became known nationwide as a term for rotting meat preserved with formaldehyde, a chemical used in funeral homes to embalm the dead. When the federal government held hearings after the war, the good news/bad news was that "the beef served in Cuba was no worse than the beef sold in American grocery stores" (Blum 2020). After becoming president, Roosevelt supported the Meat Inspection Act of 1906 and the Pure Food and Drug Act of 1906. "Roosevelt hardly needed to be reminded of the bill, having initiated it himself" in his 1905 State of the Union address to Congress (Morris 2002, 436).

However, not all parties were in favor of federal consumer protection laws. Congressional opponents included "those who objected on the grounds of constitutional interpretation, those who were not aware of the seriousness of the problem and believed there were more pressing questions, and those who were personally interested in the perpetuation of frauds that would be illegal under a pure food statute" (Bailey 1930). When pure food and drug proposals were presented in Congress, "the opposition was more silent than outspoken, making its weight felt through parliamentary obstructionism. Some Southern conservatives did openly challenge the constitutionality of such legislation. 'The Federal Government,' opined a Georgia congressman, 'was not created for the purpose of cutting your toe nails or corns'" (Young n.d.). Even after the "embalmed beef" scandal shocked the nation, Congressional leadership balked.

To help Roosevelt push through the proposal, Harvey Washington Wiley of the US Department of Agriculture "energized his coalition to a last burst of pressure. Committees engaged in a final flurry of compromise. And the bill became law" (Young n.d.). With its enactment in 1906, American consumers saw history being made on their behalf. Despite opposition from powerful forces, with the passage of the Pure Food and Drug Act of 1906, the traditional business practice of *caveat emptor* began to give way. That year, through the efforts of a number of groups and individuals, the era of demand for consumer rights and protections in America was underway.

Further Reading

American Chemical Society. n.d. "Ellen H. Swallow Richards." Accessed September 10, 2024. https://www.acs.org/education/whatischemistry/women-scientists/ellen-h-swallow-richards.html.

Arthur, Anthony. 2006. *Radical Innocent: Upton Sinclair*. New York: Random House, 65, 83.

Bailey, Thomas. 1930. "Congressional Opposition to Pure Food Legislation, 1879–1906." *American Journal of Sociology* 36, no. 1. Accessed November 28, 2024. https://www.journals.uchicago.edu/doi/abs/10.1086/215284.

Balleisen, Edward. 2017. *Fraud: An American History from Barnum to Madoff.* Princeton, NJ: Princeton University Press, 46.

Blum, Deborah. 2020. "Gloom and Horror Unrelieved." *The American Experience.* Accessed November 27, 2024. https://www.pbs.org/wgbh/americanexperience/features/poison-squad-gloom-horror-unrelieved/.

Blum, Deborah. 2018. *The Poison Squad: One Chemist's Single-Minded Crusade for Food Safety at the Turn of the Twentieth Century.* New York: Penguin, 5, 20, 23.

Bowman, John S. 1995. *The Cambridge Dictionary of American Biography.* New York: Cambridge University Press, 72.

Connecticut State Department of Consumer Protection. n.d. "The Roots of Consumer Protection in America." Accessed September 10, 2024. https://portal.ct.gov/DCP/Agency-Administration/About-Us/History/The-Roots-of-Consumer-Protection-in-America.

Diamond, Jenny Ann. 2002. "Who Shall Meet the Foe If Not She? Women's Participation in the Movement Leading Up to the Federal Food and Drug Act of 1906, as Seen Through the Pages of 'Good Housekeeping.'" Digital Access to Scholarship at Harvard. Accessed November 27, 2024. https://dash.harvard.edu/bitstream/handle/1/8889492/Diamond.pdf.

Goodwin, Lorine. 1999. *The Pure Food, Drink, and Drug Crusaders, 1879–1914, New Edition.* Jefferson, NC: McFarland, 11.

Grinspan, Jon. 2022. "The Father-Daughter Team Who Reformed America." *Smithsonian.* Accessed November 27, 2024. https://www.smithsonianmag.com/history/father-daughter-duo-reformed-america-180981016/.

Knight, Louise. 2010. *Jane Addams: Spirit in Action.* New York: W. W. Norton, 49.

McNeill, Leila. 2018. "The First Female Student at MIT Started an All-Women Chemistry Lab and Fought for Food Safety." *Smithsonian.* Accessed November 27, 2024. https://www.smithsonianmag.com/science-nature/first-female-student-mit-started-women-chemistry-lab-food-safety-180971056/.

Milkis, Sidney. n.d. "Theodore Roosevelt: Domestic Affairs." Miller Center, University of Virginia. Accessed September 10, 2024. https://millercenter.org/president/roosevelt/domestic-affairs.

Morris, Edmund. 2002. *Theodore Rex.* New York: Random House, 436.

National Consumers League. n.d. "About Us." Accessed September 20, 2024. https://nclnet.org/about-ncl/about-us/.

Science History Institute. n.d. "Harvey Washington Wiley." Accessed September 10, 2024. https://sciencehistory.org/education/scientific-biographies/harvey-washington-wiley/.

Sklar, Kathryn Kish. 1995. *Florence Kelley and the Nation's Work: The Rise of Women's Political Culture, 1830–1900.* New Haven, CT: Yale University Press.

Swallow, Pamela C. 2014. *The Remarkable Life and Career of Ellen Swallow Richards: Pioneer in Science and Technology*. Hoboken, NJ: Wiley.
Virginia Commonwealth University Libraries. 2008. "Florence Kelley (1859–1932)." *Social Welfare History Project*. Accessed November 27, 2024. https://socialwelfare.library.vcu.edu/people/kelley-florence/.
Young, James Harvey. n.d. "The Long Struggle for the Law." U.S. Food and Drug Administration. Accessed September 10, 2024. https://www.fda.gov/about-fda/changes-science-law-and-regulatory-authorities/long-struggle-law.

Q4: Who were the leading advocates for consumer rights and protections after 1906?

Answer: The year 1906 was a watershed in America. When Upton Sinclair's *The Jungle*, about filthy conditions in the meatpacking industry, was published in February of that year, it enraged the nation's citizens, who demanded action from their elected officials. Four months later, the US Congress passed the landmark Meat Inspection Act of 1906 and the Pure Food and Drug Act of 1906, leading to the creation of the federal Food and Drug Administration, which was authorized in 1906 to enforce the Pure Food and Drug Act. These pieces of federal legislation marked the first challenge to America's longstanding tradition of *caveat emptor* in the free marketplace and paved the way for the establishment of other consumer safeguards in the twentieth and early twenty-first centuries, pursued by various individuals and organizations.

The Facts: For many people today, it is difficult to envision our nation without the consumer rights and protections that they now take for granted. Most do not realize that it was not until 1906, about three hundred years after the nation's founding, that the traditional concept of *caveat emptor* was challenged. The effort was made by the federal government in order to protect the American people, and it came about in the face of powerful opposition.

Although the NCL had been established in 1899, during the early years of the twentieth century, there was still the kind of strong opposition to government regulation that was prevalent throughout the nation's history to that time. However, through the years, a move toward consumer protection gained strength. "After World War II, advocates focused on food safety, product design, clear labeling, lending practices, and environmental regulation. Backed by consumer frustration, they achieved significant legislative victories" (Smithsonian n.d.).

After 1906 some business interests recognized that support for increased government intervention in business and industry might continue to grow unless steps were taken to mitigate public concerns through a form of self-regulation. In 1912, a private organization called the Better Business Bureau (BBB) was created to help build consumer confidence in the marketplace without government controls. The BBB created a ratings system to help consumers identify dependable businesses. The organization has aspired to set standards for ethical business behavior and monitor compliance to help consumers identify trustworthy businesses and avoid those that engage in unethical practices.

After America's entry into the First World War in 1917, the US Food Administration was created to control food production and distribution in the United States. This new federal agency, which was led by future US president Herbert Hoover (1874–1964), marked a significant expansion of governmental authority, giving Hoover a free hand to "fix prices, seize factories, ban uneconomical practices ... and do whatever else necessary to ensure sufficient food supplies and fair prices for producers and consumers" (Whyte 2018, 186). Under Hoover, the agency aimed to prevent monopolies (companies with significant control over an industry—an absence of competition) and hoarding by imposing government controls where needed. After the war, Hoover served as the US Secretary of Commerce from 1921 to 1929. Although he was considered a conservative, Hoover sought to mitigate unrestrained capitalism in order to dampen public interest in socialism, which was gaining popularity in other countries. Hoover advocated for product testing and standardization of consumer goods like automobile tires. Much of Hoover's historical reputation was dimmed by his single term as president from 1929 to 1933, when America sank into the depths of the Great Depression. Yet, it was his leadership in previous posts that loosened the hold of *caveat emptor* on the marketplace, helping to counteract it by providing governmental protections for American consumers.

The authors of two popular books published during the late 1920s and early 1930s focused on consumer issues, advocating for change. *Your Money's Worth: A Study in the Waste of the Consumer's Dollar* by Stuart Chase and Frederick Schlink was published in 1927. The writers protested against marketing practices that made it difficult for consumers to judge the value of the products they bought. The book aroused interest in moving toward the demand for widespread product testing in order to provide greater protections for American consumers. In 1929, Chase and Schlink founded Consumers' Research, an organization with a mission of educating and protecting consumers from harmful products.

In 1933, Frederick Schlink and Arthur Kallet coauthored a book titled *100,000,000 Guinea Pigs: Dangers in Everyday Foods, Drugs, and Cosmetics*. It alleged that Americans were being used as unwitting test subjects, or "guinea pigs," by producers of foodstuffs and patent medicines. The book's cover proclaimed that " 'Pure Food' laws do not protect you. "This book names names and describes scores of typical 'standard' products that are either dangerous or worse than useless for the purposes advertised" (Kallet and Schlink 1933). The authors claimed that the Pure Food and Drug Act of 1906 was not effective against such abuses because powerful business entities with ties to the government obstructed greater consumer protection.

A magazine called *Consumer Reports*, first published in 1936, presented itself as an objective source of information that consumers could use to help assess the safety and performance of products. Remaining a popular publication into the twenty-first century, it dedicates itself to independent product testing and consumer-oriented research.

During his presidential campaign in 1960, John F. Kennedy (1917–1963) pledged to support American consumers. As president, he sought inputs from consumer advocates, leading to his speech to Congress on March 15, 1962, in which he urged lawmakers to act on behalf of the American people by increasing consumer rights and protections. In his speech, he proposed a Consumer Bill of Rights, which included the right to safety, the right to information, the right to be heard, and the right to make choices.

A book appeared in September of that same year that approached the level of impact in 1962 that *The Jungle* had in 1906. Written by biologist Rachel Carson (1907–1964), *Silent Spring* described the harmful effects of pesticides not only on the environment but also on American consumers. For example, Carson charged that "the common salad bowl may easily present a combination of organic phosphate insecticides. Residues well within the legally permissible limits may interact" (Carson 2002, 31–2). Not only were fruits and vegetables affected, but also milk and meat. The fields where dairy cows grazed "were of course contaminated also … and [their products] should not be marketed. This situation is unfortunately typical of the lack of consumer protection that is all too common" (Carson 2002, 159–60). Carson also cited animals slaughtered for meat after grazing in contaminated fields or having eaten pesticide-ridden grain, finally asking "Who is safeguarding the consumer?" (Carson 2002, 169).

In 1964, Esther Peterson (1906–1997) was named by President Lyndon Johnson to the newly created position of assistant for consumer affairs. She held that position in the Johnson administration until 1970 and was later appointed by President Jimmy Carter as director of the US Office of Consumer Affairs, where she served from 1977 to 1981. Peterson had been involved with the NCL since the 1940s, dedicating herself to consumer protections such as accurate food labeling and truth in advertising. However, hoping to bridge any perceived divide, she also worked with big businesses such as the grocery industry on advances such as standardized packaging and other improvements that would benefit both business and consumers.

Virginia Knauer (1915–2011) was appointed as President Richard Nixon's special assistant for consumer affairs and was the first director of the US Office of Consumer Affairs. Serving from 1969 to 1977 and again from 1981 to 1989, she promoted such consumer-based concepts as nutritional labeling, recycling, and unit pricing of groceries. Knauer also correctly predicted that if American automakers did not begin to install safety improvements and environmental advances, foreign manufacturers would increase imported auto sales in the United States.

Just as Harvey Washington Wiley had been a household name in the early twentieth century for his efforts, Ralph Nader (1934–) became a famous consumer advocate in the 1960s and 1970s. Nader originally became synonymous with consumer protections in the American automotive industry due to his bestselling book *Unsafe at Any Speed* (1965), which asserted that American car makers prioritized profits over safety in their manufacturing operations. However, Nader also addressed other issues such as flammable clothing and unsanitary food preparation. According to biographer Justin Martin, Nader "became a fierce proponent of openness on the part of government and corporations—in fact, he is the primary architect of the Freedom of Information Act," which provides public access to certain government records (Martin 2002, xv). Nader has also been credited with being integral to the passage of a host of important consumer protection laws in the 1970s and 1980s, including the Occupational Safety and Health Act (OSHA) (1970), Clean Water Act (1972), Consumer Product Safety Act (1972), Foreign Corrupt Practices Act (1977), and the Whistleblower Protection Act (1989), as well as being instrumental in creating the Environmental Protection Agency in 1970.

As a US senator, Elizabeth Warren (1949–) chaired the Congressional Oversight Panel, a government entity that was created in 2008 to monitor the implementation of the $700 billion Troubled Asset Relief Program (TARP) when the US economy was in distress due to the bursting of a housing "bubble" that was instrumental in causing a national financial meltdown. TARP was aimed at stabilizing the nation's financial system and reviving economic growth. In response to that crisis, Warren proposed creating a federal Consumer Financial Protection Bureau (CFPB) to safeguard the rights of Americans in financial matters, stating that banks "were making fortunes by misleading people about interest rates, fees, and other snares built in home mortgage documents [thereby driving] millions of people deep into debt" (Warren 2021, 6). In addition, existing laws were "so spread out that no single agency felt any urgency about actually enforcing them" (Warren 2021, 6). Warren asserted that a rising bankruptcy rate among average citizens was caused not by their irresponsible overspending but by unscrupulous lenders. The CFPB was established as a federal entity in 2010.

With the rise of individuals and organizations promoting consumer rights and protections in the late twentieth and early twenty-first centuries, there also arose complaints among conservative opponents that, with an increased number of regulations being enacted to protect consumers, the American people were being coddled as if they were children. These critics were concerned with government overreach and overregulation.

Further Reading

Carson, Rachel. 2002. *Silent Spring Updated Edition*. New York: Mariner Books, 31–2, 159–60, 169.

"Consumer Bill of Rights." n.d. Commonwealth of Massachusetts. Accessed September 10, 2024. https://www.mass.gov/service-details/consumer-bill-of-rights.

Kallet, Arthur, and F. J. Schlink. 1933. *100,000,000 Guinea Pigs: Dangers in Everyday Foods, Drugs and Cosmetics*. Vanguard Press. Cover accessed on Amazon.com, September 11, 2024. https://www.amazon.com/100-000-Guinea-Pigs-Cosmetics/dp/B0008560Y2.

Krauthammer, Charles. 1997. "Challenge to the Nanny State." *Washington Post*. Accessed November 27, 2024. https://www.washingtonpost.com/archive/opinions/1997/01/17/challenge-to-the-nanny-state/e6acf692-9310-4433-9d0d-da4f27b2340b/.

Martin, Justin. 2002. *Nader: Crusader, Spoiler, Icon*. New York: Basic Books, xv.

Smithsonian National Museum of American History. n.d. "Consumer Advocacy." Accessed September 10, 2024. https://americanhistory.si.edu/american-enterprise-exhibition/consumer-era/consumer-advocacy.

Warren, Elizabeth. 2021. *Persist*. New York: Metropolitan Books, 6.

Whyte, Kenneth. 2018. *Hoover: An Extraordinary Life in Extraordinary Times*. New York: Vintage, 186.

2

Federal Laws and Agencies Overseeing Consumer Rights and Protections

In America's early years, there was a general feeling among industrial leaders and conservative groups that the government had no right to interfere in business matters. The rationale was that it was up to consumers to determine what might be good or bad for them in the products they bought. This widely publicized viewpoint meant that there was little public support for passing laws or establishing agencies authorizing any regulations on business operations or practices.

This state of affairs remained in place until the 1906 publication of Upton Sinclair's book *The Jungle*, which described appalling practices in America's meatpacking industry. The public outcry about the revelations in Sinclair's muckraking book became so great that Congress passed the Pure Food and Drug Act later that same year. In 1932, with the country gripped by the economic crisis known as the Great Depression, President Franklin Roosevelt introduced a number of programs that inserted the government into private enterprise in ways that had never before been seen. Many of those programs benefitted consumers by helping them obtain enough money to purchase food and necessities.

After America's entry into the Second World War in 1941, many of the nation's idle factories sprang into life producing war materials. Employment soared, with women in particular benefitting because so many American men were serving in the nation's armed forces. When the war ended in 1945, factories sent a dazzling array of peacetime consumer goods rolling off assembly lines. After years of deprivation, American consumers had money to buy what they wanted, and they wanted *everything*. The postwar years were the beginning of the age of consumerism, the name for an inclination toward increased acquisition of goods and services. In that atmosphere, there came calls for greater consumer rights and protections, such as banning deceptive advertising and outlawing toys that were dangerous to children.

In 1962, President John F. Kennedy introduced a Consumer Bill of Rights. During subsequent presidential administrations, consumer protection laws were passed that dealt with things such as greater food safety as well as consumer finance protection such as truth in lending. The number of consumer rights and protections that were enacted in the late twentieth and early twenty-first centuries led opponents of business regulation to complain that the United States was turning into a "nanny state" with a government that treated consumers like children. But supporters—including many American consumers—described these laws and reforms as vital in protecting them from unethical and fraudulent business practices.

Q5: What were the first American laws pertaining to consumer rights and protections?

Answer: Although *caveat emptor* was the predominant force in the American economy through the nation's early history, a few consumer protections evolved in the nineteenth and early twentieth centuries. Far-reaching laws were put in place in the second half of the nineteenth century during the presidential administrations of Abraham Lincoln and Benjamin Harrison. However, nothing in America's early years surpassed a consumer protection law enacted by Theodore Roosevelt: the Pure Food and Drug Act of 1906. Later, America's entry into the First World War led to government intervention and consumer protections under Woodrow Wilson in the name of patriotism. Slowly, the grip of *caveat emptor* on American consumers began to unravel.

The Facts: In the midst of the nation's Civil War, Abraham Lincoln (1809–1865) made one of the first ventures by government into the free marketplace. Lincoln, who was president from 1861 to 1865, signed the National Currency Act of 1863 and the National Bank Act of 1864 (essentially a revised version of the 1863 law) in order to help finance the Union's war effort and stabilize the economy. These laws allowed the federal government to create a nationwide banking system at a time when a majority of financial institutions were state-chartered. "Numerous banks and other businesses issued quantities of their own paper currency [and] counterfeiting abounded" (American Numismatic Society n.d.). In a footnote to history, the US Secret Service was established in 1865 not to protect the president but to fight counterfeiters because such criminals undermined public confidence in the national system of currency. In addition, unregulated "wildcat" banks were issuing unsecured loans to consumers, fueling land speculation. To avoid destabilizing the American economy during wartime, the legislation passed by Congress and signed by Lincoln also provided for the creation of the Office of the Comptroller of the Currency to regulate federal currency. Passed by Congress during the Civil War era more than 150 years ago, the National Bank Act still constitutes the basic governing framework for America's national banking system.

After the Civil War, industrialization swept across the nation, bringing about practices such as monopolies to drive competitors out of business and then to charge consumers whatever the monopoly desired. There was rising public hostility to this kind of price-fixing during the presidential administration of Benjamin Harrison (1833–1901), who took office in 1889. In a near-unanimous vote, Congress passed the Sherman Anti-Trust Act in 1890. This federal act outlawed monopolistic business practices, encouraging free competition in commerce. Although it turned out to be enforced only sporadically, it was the first federal law designed to aid consumers by regulating price-fixing by big corporate entities.

According to the US Census Bureau, the nation's population in 1870 was about 38 million people. By 1900, that number had virtually doubled, reaching over 76 million, a number that included about ten million immigrants who came from outside the United States. In 1901 Theodore Roosevelt (1858–1919) assumed the presidency after the death of President William McKinley, serving until 1909. He recognized the vast changes taking place in American society with industrialization, waves of new immigrants from Europe and other parts of the world, and rising rates of natural resource development and consumption. Roosevelt had a pro-business orientation, but "he often stated that there must be reform in order to stave off socialism; if government did not act, the people would turn to more extreme measures to seek remedies" (Milkis 2022).

Roosevelt believed that the federal government had the right to regulate big business in order to protect the welfare of American consumers as well as to curtail the appeal of socialism. In what was called the Progressive Era of the early twentieth century, he used the power of the presidency to bust the "trusts"—corporate monopolies that made their own rules and forced consumers to pay the price. Because so many consumers and businesses were dependent on the railroads, he supported two early laws aimed at railroad conglomerates that had a tendency toward price-fixing. The Elkins Act of 1903 and the Hepburn Act in 1906 were notable not only for authorizing government intervention in the operations of big business but also by Roosevelt's direct appeal to the American people through a speaking tour supporting the acts after there was resistance by conservatives in Congress. Specifically, the Elkins Act of 1903 made it illegal for companies that shipped large quantities of goods to receive special treatment, discounts, or rebates. Three years later, the Hepburn Act granted the Interstate Commerce Commission (ICC) the power to regulate railroad rates to make them more reasonable after the full hearing of a complaint.

Many historians consider the most significant consumer protection laws passed during the presidential administration of Theodore Roosevelt to be the Meat Inspection Act of 1906 and the Pure Food and Drug Act of 1906. Roosevelt used newspapers, the predominant media of the time, to communicate his support for these laws to the American people directly, answering criticism from big business and conservative political blocs that opposed government intervention in private enterprise. As a colorful speaker, he aimed to generate news items that were guaranteed to get the attention of the average consumer. One way was showing his support for consumers when the public became repulsed and angry about descriptions of filthy conditions in the meatpacking industry in Upton Sinclair's 1906 book *The Jungle*. People were shocked by reports of vermin, rat poison, animal excrement, and the severed human body parts of injured workers finding their way into meat products that were sold to consumers for dinner.

In a speech to Congress, Theodore Roosevelt called for legislation mandating both federal inspection of all plants engaging in interstate commerce and an accurate statement of content on food labels. In language that could be printed by newspapers to catch the attention of the public, he described conditions in stock yards as "revolting. It is imperatively necessary in the interest of health and of decency that they should be radically changed" (Roosevelt 1906). Instead of relying on private businesses to regulate themselves, he called for strong federal laws giving the US Department of Agriculture the power to inspect meat products, to supervise production, and "to prescribe the sanitary conditions under which the work shall be performed" (Roosevelt 1906). There was opposition by business-related lobbying associations as well as members of Congress who resisted government intervention in private enterprise in any form. However, Congress passed the legislation, and Theodore Roosevelt quickly signed the Meat Inspection Act of 1906 and the Pure Food and Drug Act of 1906. His support of such laws for the good of the public endeared him to many American consumers.

Woodrow Wilson (1856–1924) served as US president from 1913 to 1921. Building on the Bureau of Corporations, a government entity established under

Theodore Roosevelt in 1903, Wilson supported the passage of the Federal Trade Commission Act in 1914. The Bureau of Corporations had been a federal agency that was tasked with investigating monopolies by big business. Its report on the petroleum industry was used in the successful prosecution that broke up the Standard Oil monopoly in 1911. Under Wilson, the establishment of the Federal Trade Commission (FTC) as a successor to the Bureau of Corporations strengthened the government's capacity to protect consumers by promoting competition and preventing unfair practices.

The United States entered the First World War in 1917. That year, Wilson supported the expansion of governmental powers into private enterprise by signing the Food and Fuel Control Act, which created the US Food Administration and the US Fuel Administration. Taking control of the nation's food production and fuel supply to aid the war effort, this federal entity set fair prices for consumers, not relying on the businesses themselves to do so. Wilson appealed to the public's sense of patriotism, framing this form of government intervention as a voluntary act by individuals for the good of the war effort. Governmental controls and the support of the public allowed American consumers to make it through the First World War without food rationing.

As the United States entered the 1920s, some consumer advocates felt that having set a precedent of government intervention, there was more work to be done in protecting the nation's consumers. Opposing forces felt the government had gone too far. In any case, these early laws proved to be a wedge in the seemingly intractable wall of *caveat emptor* that had traditionally dominated the American marketplace.

Further Reading

American Numismatic Society. n.d. "A History of American Currency." Accessed September 10, 2024. https://numismatics.org/a-history-of-american-currency/.

Federal Trade Commission. n.d. "Our History." Accessed September 20, 2024. https://www.ftc.gov/about-ftc/history.

Milkis, Sidney. 2022. "Theodore Roosevelt: Domestic Affairs." Miller Center, University of Virginia. Accessed November 27, 2024. https://millercenter.org/president/roosevelt/domestic-affairs.

Office of the Comptroller of the Currency. n.d. "Founding of the OCC and the National Banking System." US Department of the Treasury. Accessed September 10, 2024. https://www.occ.treas.gov/about/who-we-are/history/founding-occ-national-bank-system/index-founding-occ-national-banking-system.html.

Roosevelt, Theodore. 1906. "June 4, 1906: Message Regarding Meatpacking Plants." Miller Center, University of Virginia. Accessed November 27, 2024. https://millercenter.org/the-presidency/presidential-speeches/june-4-1906-message-regarding-meatpacking-plants.
Woodrow Wilson Presidential Library and Museum. n.d. "Food Administration." Accessed September 10, 2024. https://presidentwilson.org/items/show/34084.

Q6: How did the New Deal affect consumer rights and protections?

Answer: Franklin Delano Roosevelt (1882–1945) was a distant cousin of President Theodore Roosevelt. When Franklin Roosevelt, also commonly known as FDR, was elected president in 1932, he faced the worst economic crisis in the nation's history: the Great Depression. The catastrophe had begun in 1929 with the collapse of the stock market. Shock waves from that disaster resulted in soaring unemployment and financial insecurity. In his 1933 inaugural speech, Roosevelt promised a "new deal for the American people" in the form of a host of new laws and programs designed to combat the Depression. Roosevelt's "New Deal" was harshly criticized by some for the muscular ways in which he inserted the federal government into private enterprise; others complained he did not do enough. Despite opposition, a number of FDR's programs, such as Social Security, continue to this day.

The Facts: After the collapse of the stock market in 1929, a ripple effect decimated the nation. Banks failed, destroying people's life savings. Unemployment soared, leaving consumers with no money for food and other necessities. Families were left homeless due to foreclosure on their houses and farms; renters who fell behind on payments to the landlord often found themselves on the street.

Franklin Roosevelt saw robust federal intervention as essential to rescue the American economy and provide desperately needed support to the people of the nation. Part of that effort was to help Americans become consumers again. Doing so would allow factories to reopen, putting laborers back to work. Then, more people could become consumers, more factories would reopen, and so on, lifting the nation out of economic depression.

He also saw his mandate as implementing safeguards to prevent another national economic catastrophe in the future. In doing so, he inserted the government into the free market in ways that had never before been seen, becoming harshly criticized by some. However, during Roosevelt's unprecedented four terms in office, the New Deal gained the support not only of most Americans but also from Congress, which churned out a vast amount of legislation designed to address the country's economic ills.

During the Depression, there was a sense of anger and desperation among Americans. Some observers feared that the nation would turn to the rising tide of socialism that was taking place in other countries. Roosevelt tried to avert that inclination because, as one historian wrote, he "believed in the premise of American capitalism, but he also saw that American capitalism circa 1932 required reform in order to survive. … FDR was neither a die-hard liberal nor a conservative" (Leuchtenburg n.d.). In seeking a remedy, the question of reform that was always inherent in the New Deal was a matter of how much and what kind.

Some New Deal programs "came into being by law, some by executive order; some are well known, some are not; some changed names or were amended in mid-course; some lasted only a few years, some still exist" (McKee and Walker n.d.). In 1933 alone, important New Deal initiatives included the Agricultural Adjustment Act to stabilize prices for consumers of food and to support the purchasing power of farmers; the Emergency Banking Relief Act to try salvaging people's savings, and the Glass-Steagall Banking Act, which created the Federal Deposit Insurance Corporation (FDIC) to insure people's bank accounts. Also in 1933 came the Home Owners' Loan Act, providing financial assistance to home buyers; Federal Emergency Relief Act, giving financial aid to states in support of local relief programs, and the Public Works Administration to create jobs, putting people back to work and paying them for their labor in order to stimulate buying power.

Efforts to ease the Depression continued in 1934. Among New Deal programs that year were the Frazier-Lemke Farm Bankruptcy Act to restrict the ability of banks to repossess farms; the Electric Home and Farm Authority, which helped American consumers purchase electrical appliances; Federal Credit Unions to offer cooperative savings and loan opportunities so that consumers could borrow money without resorting to usury (unreasonably high interest rates); and the National Housing Act, which enabled guaranteed mortgages from banks for home buyers. When the stock market had collapsed in 1929, there were no safeguards in place to protect consumers of financial instruments such as stocks and bonds. In 1934, the Securities Exchange Act created the Securities and Exchange Commission (SEC) to oversee stock market activities, curb abuses, and regulate stock trading in public corporations that could prove disastrous to individual consumers and the country as a whole if the system failed.

As the Depression kept its grip on the nation in 1935, that year's New Deal programs included the Public Utility Holding Company Act, which protected consumers from utility rate increases. That same year, the Works Progress Administration (WPA) was put into effect, employing millions of unemployed Americans in a variety of ways, such as construction of public buildings and roads. A noted portion of the WPA was Federal Project Number One, which was created in 1935 to help more than 10,000 actors, artists, dancers, musicians, and writers. They were put to work on such projects as painting murals on the walls of public buildings, performing plays through the Federal Theatre Project, and collecting oral histories via the Historical Records Survey. Some individuals employed by the WPA endured to become American icons. "Painter Jackson Pollock was stealing food from pushcarts before he was hired by the WPA's famed murals division," observed journalist Neda Ulaby. "And writer Ralph Ellison used language from the oral histories he recorded for the WPA in Harlem in his later groundbreaking novel *The Invisible Man*" (Ulaby 2020). Further, "in communities such as Harlem or the South Side of Chicago, unprecedented opportunities opened up for African American artists" thanks to the WPA (Wilkinson 2020). The WPA took many Americans from joblessness to becoming consumers. For example, country singer Loretta Lynn has stated that by putting her father to work, the WPA enabled her to have her first store-bought dress as a child instead of the flour sacks she had been wearing.

Another New Deal landmark in 1935 was the Social Security Act, which created a national system of old-age pensions, unemployment insurance, aid to mothers with children, and assistance for the disabled. Despite criticism, Social Security continues to provide benefits to more than 67 million Americans as of 2024. "Although some factions in Congress have attempted to privatize or dismantle Social Security in recent years, it remains one of the most popular and effective New Deal programs" (Hadley 2020).

Programs such as pensions and unemployment insurance so that people would not be left without buying power were all the more remarkable because of the person who championed them: a member of Roosevelt's inner circle named Frances Perkins (1880–1965). She was the first woman appointed to a presidential cabinet in the nation's history. FDR had known that naming a woman as Secretary of Labor would provoke criticism and that her proposals "would stir heated opposition, even among his loyal supporters" (Downey 2010, 2). Yet, almost a century later, her plans for pensions and unemployment insurance remain popular among most Americans.

New Deal programs with direct benefits to consumers include the Robinson-Patman Act (1936), also called the Anti-Price Discrimination Act, which strengthened rules against fixed pricing and control by monopolies. The Bankhead-Jones Farm Tenant Act (1937) provided aid to tenant farmers and sharecroppers, allowing some of the nation's poorest people to become consumers. Safeguarding consumers from unfair or deceptive practices, including false advertising, was the Wheeler-Lea Act in 1938.

That same year, the Food, Drug, and Cosmetic Act of 1938 brought the manufacture of cosmetics and medical devices under government regulation. A response to dangerous products such as a coal-tar based brand of mascara that caused impaired vision and even blindness, this law required cosmetics to be labeled with adequate directions for safe use and removed dangerous products from the marketplace altogether. One such product was Koremlu, which was sold as a lotion for removing unwanted body hair but which in reality contained rat poison that caused neurological damage, respiratory problems, blindness, and baldness among some users. According to the FDA, this act "forever altered the landscape of consumer protection in America. For the first time, the Food and Drug Administration (FDA) had authority to regulate medical devices and cosmetics, and to establish standards for foods" (Food and Drug Administration 2018). In addition, new drugs had to be proven safe for their labeled use before they could be marketed. Today, this New Deal-era program continues to safeguard the nation's consumers.

New Deal programs were subjected to scathing opposition by those who felt it was too much government intrusion into private enterprise. Franklin Roosevelt was also condemned by others who felt he was not doing enough. However, most of the public responded positively, electing FDR to an unprecedented four terms as president. A number of New Deal consumer protection initiatives, such as Social Security, the Federal Deposit Insurance Corporation, and the Food, Drug and Cosmetic Act, remain highly popular in today's world.

Further Reading

Downey, Kirstin. 2010. *The Woman Behind the New Deal: The Life and Legacy of Frances Perkins—Social Security, Unemployment Insurance, and the Minimum Wage.* New York: Anchor, 2.

Food and Drug Administration. 2018. "80 Years of the Federal Food, Drug, and Cosmetic Act." Accessed November 27, 2024. https://www.fda.gov/about-fda/fda-history-exhibits/80-years-federal-food-drug-and-cosmetic-act.

Hadley, Debbi. 2020. "7 New Deal Programs Still in Effect Today." *ThoughtCo*. Accessed November 27, 2024. https://www.thoughtco.com/new-deal-programs-still-in-effect-today-4154043.

Leuchtenburg, William. n.d. "Franklin D. Roosevelt: Domestic Affairs." Miller Center, University of Virginia. Accessed September 10, 2024. https://millercenter.org/president/fdroosevelt/domestic-affairs.

McKee, Brent, and Richard A. Walker. n.d. "New Deal Programs." *The Living New Deal*. Accessed September 10, 2024. https://livingnewdeal.org/what-was-the-new-deal/programs/.

Ulaby, Neda. 2020. "Art of the New Deal: How Artists Helped Redefine America During the Depression." NPR. Accessed November 27, 2024. https://www.npr.org/2020/05/25/854864293/art-of-the-new-deal-how-artists-helped-redefine-america-during-the-depression.

Wilkinson, Alissa. 2020. "Artists Helped Lift America out of the Great Depression. Could That Happen Again?" *Vox*. Accessed November 27, 2024. https://www.vox.com/culture/21294431/new-deal-wpa-federal-art-project-coronavirus.

Q7: What are the most significant consumer protection laws of the post-Second World War era?

Answer: After the Second World War, the American economy rose to become arguably the most prosperous and dynamic the world had even seen. From the late 1940s and beyond, the watchword of America was *consumerism*, the concept of acquiring goods in ever-increasing amounts. However, consumer spending did not simply mean satisfying material desires on an individual level. The US government vigorously promoted consumerism as a form of patriotism in order to show that the American way of life was superior to deprivation under Communism. Enjoying healthy paychecks, more Americans had the ability to become enthusiastic consumers. With people purchasing more products, there came a greater interest in making sure consumers were protected from items that were dangerous or ineffective as well as from deceptive advertising. From the late 1940s to the present day, a flurry of contemporary consumer rights and protections emerged.

The Facts: In the 1930s, as an aftershock of the 1929 stock market crash, factories across the country sat idle. Unemployment plagued the nation, triggering a cascade of severe economic problems. People had no money to buy consumer goods, so more factories closed; when factories closed, more people were laid off and had no money to buy consumer goods. During the Great Depression of the 1930s, consumerism gave way to survival.

However, when America was fighting the Second World War from 1941 to 1945, factories came to life building weapons. Jobs were plentiful and pay was good. However, there were few consumer items available to buy because most resources went into manufacturing equipment for the war effort. When the war ended in 1945, factories retooled for the peacetime world. Instead of bombers, tanks, and machine guns, consumer goods such as televisions, washing machines, and dazzling new automobiles rolled off the assembly lines.

Starting in the late 1940s, America experienced an astounding revival in consumerism. Certainly, many Americans were left behind, especially minorities and those in pockets of poverty. But for the burgeoning middle class, it began to seem as if every day was Christmas. Manufacturers did everything possible to maintain the holiday atmosphere by introducing new styles of existing products every year. They also employed advertising strategies that implied that people who resisted making such purchases were underprivileged and/or unpatriotic. Along with new styles of big-ticket items such as television sets, this tactic was seen most conspicuously in America's automotive industry. New car lines with a few differences in styling were released every year. Parking a new car in front of the house was a very noticeable way of showing the world that your household and family were thriving.

This "conspicuous consumption," or ostentatiously displaying signs of wealth to gain status in society, was not new. During the Gilded Age of the late 1800s, this concept was highlighted by sociologist Thorstein Veblen in his 1899 book, *The Theory of the Leisure Class*. Veblen believed that buying lavish consumer items was wasteful and did not hold any practical value for people apart from showing off their material wealth. Veblen also claimed that advertising plays a direct role in conspicuous consumption. By promoting a must-have brand, many consumers will want to associate themselves with the product to "keep up with the Joneses."

With the juggernaut of television in the postwar years, advertisers found the new entertainment medium to be a godsend, having the ability to entice consumers via both sight and sound. Soon abuses began to occur, as some advertisements crossed the line into deception. The Lanham Act took effect in 1947 to fight false advertising if ads "exaggerated benefits, denied side effects, and blatantly lied in order to sell their products or services" (Truth in Advertising 2012).

In 1959, Tennessee Senator Estes Kefauver (1903–1963) began leading the Senate's Antitrust and Monopoly Subcommittee to hearings on the pharmaceutical industry. The focus included manipulation of consumers by advertisements that promoted prescription drugs, a field that had grown tremendously in the postwar years. For example, Diuril treated high blood pressure and Miltown was a tranquilizer. In their advertising campaigns, "companies spent millions of dollars to make Miltown and Diuril household names" (American Institute of the History of Pharmacy n.d.). Through legislation proposed in 1961, the Kefauver-Harris Amendment to the Federal Food, Drug, and Cosmetic Act gave the Food and Drug Administration authority to require drug advertising to disclose accurate information about side effects.

In 1962, President John F. Kennedy (1917–1963) made a speech to Congress concerning what he called the Consumer Bill of Rights. He declared that the federal government must play a role in guaranteeing protections to America's buying public. Kennedy said that "if consumers are offered inferior products, if prices are exorbitant, if drugs are unsafe or worthless, if the consumer is unable to choose on an informed basis, then his dollar is wasted, his health and safety may be threatened, and the national interest suffers" (Kennedy 1962). Kennedy proposed four basic consumer rights:

(1) The right to safety—to be protected against the marketing of goods which are hazardous to health or life.
(2) The right to be informed—to be protected against fraudulent, deceitful, or grossly misleading information, advertising, labeling, or other practices, and to be given the facts he needs to make an informed choice.
(3) The right to choose—to be assured, wherever possible, access to a variety of products and services at competitive prices; and in those industries in which competition is not workable and Government regulation is substituted, an assurance of satisfactory quality and service at fair prices.
(4) The right to be heard—to be assured that consumer interests will receive full and sympathetic consideration in the formulation of Government policy, and fair and expeditious treatment in its administrative tribunals. (Kennedy 1962)

Kennedy's speech was noteworthy by underscoring how far the nation had moved from the tradition of *caveat emptor*, with its custom of discouraging any government intervention in the free marketplace. According to law professor Anne Fleming, Kennedy's speech was a "call for the federal government—'the highest spokesman for all the people'—to act on behalf of consumers" (Fleming 2019).

President Lyndon Johnson (1908–1973) did not hesitate to deploy the federal government into areas of the free market where it had not previously gone.

After winning office by a landslide in 1964, Johnson felt that he had a mandate from the American people to implement his domestic program, which he called the Great Society. One commitment was assisting American consumers by providing them "with some protection against shoddy goods and dangerous products" (Germany 2023).

One of Johnson's first acts as president was aimed at consumers of health care. In 1965, Johnson signed the Medicare and Medicaid Act, also known as the Social Security Amendments of 1965. One of his predecessors, Harry Truman (1884–1972), who served as president from 1945 to 1953, had tried to pass some form of medical insurance for older citizens, "but he had been beaten down by the medical lobby. Johnson took the legislation creating Medicare to Independence, Missouri, to sign it in Truman's presence" (Middleton 2008). Johnson enrolled Truman as Medicare's first beneficiary, presenting the former president with the first Medicare card.

Consumer protection laws came rapidly under Lyndon Johnson's administration. The Child Protection Act of 1966 mandated federal control over hazardous substances, requiring a warning label on many household items, including medicine bottles. The law restricted toys and children's items that could be considered hazardous due to containing dangerous substances, such as eyes on a doll that were made of poisonous beans. Signing the bill, Johnson stated, "Now there is a law that says what looks like candy will not be deadly firecracker balls. Now there is a law that says Johnny will not die because his toy truck was painted with a poison" (*Washington Post* 2014).

The Cigarette Labeling and Advertising Act, which became effective in 1966, required that every pack of cigarettes must contain the now-common warning to consumers: "Caution: Cigarette Smoking May Be Hazardous to Your Health." The Fair Packaging and Labeling Act of 1966 was part of Johnson's consumer protection program by directing manufacturers to disclose information completely and truthfully on labels and packaging. Signing the bill into law, Johnson said it meant that "the American family will get full and fair value for every penny, dime and dollar that that family spends" (*Washington Post* 2014).

Lyndon Johnson considered the air we consume by breathing to be part of what Americans should expect their government to protect. When he signed the Air Quality Act of 1967, guaranteeing the government increased authority to control air pollution, he asked, "Don't we really risk our own damnation every day by destroying the air that gives us life?" (*Washington Post* 2014).

More consumer protection laws followed before Johnson's presidency ended in 1968. The Wholesome Meat Act of 1967 prohibited the sale of meat that had not been inspected by the USDA. The Wholesome Poultry Products Act of 1968 required dirty processing plants to clean up or close down. To protect consumers of financial products, the Truth in Lending Act of 1968 required full disclosures by financial services about their products, also guarding against inaccurate billing and unfair credit card practices.

After Johnson left office in 1969, President Richard Nixon (1913–1994) led the country through 1974. During that time, he asked Congress to pass legislation for consumer protection while also recognizing the role of private enterprise. Nixon delivered a message to Congress in 1969 with the opening sentence, "Consumerism—[as] Upton Sinclair and Rachel Carson would be glad to know—is a healthy development that is here to stay" (Nixon 1969). During his speech, he echoed John F. Kennedy's 1961 Consumer Bill of Rights with what Nixon called the Buyer's Bill of Rights. Nixon's proposition was that the buyer has the right to accurate information on which to make a free choice, to expect that health and safety are taken into account, and to have complaints "heard and weighed, when his interests are badly served" (Nixon 1969).

In a 1971 speech, Nixon credited the role of big business by saying, "The history of American prosperity is the history of the American free enterprise system" (Nixon 1971). However, in that same speech, he added that the marketplace confronted the public with what he called "impenetrable complexity in many of our consumer goods." This, he stated, was due to inflated advertising claims, dubious product quality, and questionable merchandising, abuses that he hoped to mitigate.

One of the first acts passed under the Nixon administration challenged the American automobile industry via the Highway Safety Act of 1970, which set the first mandatory federal safety standards for motor vehicles. By creating the Consumer Product Safety Commission (CPSC) in 1972, the Consumer Product Safety Act was far-reaching in its scope. It enabled the government to develop safety standards and to pursue recalls for products that presented risks of injury or death to consumers. It empowered the government to ban a product if there was no feasible alternative. The Fair Warranty Disclosure Act of 1975 required that consumers receive detailed information about warranty coverage, providing clearer warranties and prohibiting deceptive ones.

Gerald Ford (1913–2006) took office as president in 1974 and served through 1977. He expressed his position on government intervention in free enterprise as part of his 1976 State of the Union speech by referring to "the petty tyranny of massive government regulation" (Ford 1976). Still, several important consumer protection measures became law during his administration. One, officially called

Public Law 93–495, was informally known as the Federal Deposit Insurance Increase Act. Ford signed the act into law, doubling the amount of FDIC-insured bank deposits for consumers from $20,000 to $40,000. It also protected consumers with charge accounts from the effects of billing errors and prohibited discrimination based on sex or marital status in applications for credit. In 1976, Ford signed the Equal Credit Opportunity Act Amendments to address equality in business transactions and the Consumer Leasing Act to cover fairness in leases for items like cars or furniture. That same year, Ford signed the Consumers Product Safety Commission Improvements Act of 1976 to protect consumers from unreasonable risk of injury from the use of hazardous products.

Jimmy Carter (1924–2024) was president from 1977 to 1981. A bill that Carter supported to establish an independent Office of Consumer Representation was defeated by lawmakers in Congress. However, his administration saw some successes in rights and protections for consumers. The Fair Debt Collection Practices Act, which was signed by Carter in 1977, prohibited collectors from abusing, harassing, or oppressing consumers and from using unfair means to collect debts such as making deceptive, false, or misleading representations. Under Carter, the Airline Deregulation Act of 1978 marked "the first time in US history that an industry was deregulated" (Strong n.d.). By removing federal control over such matters as fares and routes, new lower-cost airlines scrambled to entcr the market, typically lowering many ticket prices for consumers. In 1980, Carter signed the Federal Trade Commission Improvement Act, which he said strengthened the FTC's role in protecting the nation's consumers.

The term "Reaganomics" came to encapsulate the economic policies of the presidential administration of Ronald Reagan (1911–2004), which ran from 1981 to 1989. Reagan's consumer-related actions took the form of mandates, such as an executive order requiring the end of price controls on oil (which was reflected by lower prices at the gas pump for a time) and lowering the oil windfall profits tax. In addition, Reagan supported foreign imports that would help American consumers "by lowering the cost of goods and keeping inflation down" (Cannon n.d.). He also signed the Toy Safety Act of 1984 giving the CPSC the power to recall dangerous toys from the marketplace.

George H. W. Bush (1924–2018) was president from 1989 to 1993. When he took office after Reagan, the federal budget debt was three times larger than it had been under Carter in 1980. According to Stephen Knott, a professor of national security affairs, "This financial situation severely limited the President's ability to enact major domestic programs" (Knott n.d.). However, one piece of consumer protection legislation passed under Bush was the Telephone

Consumer Protection Act of 1991, which aimed to protect privacy rights of telephone users. That same year, he signed the Truth in Savings Act as part of an improvement package for the Federal Deposit Insurance Corporation, which required financial institutions to make consumers aware of the annual percentage yield on savings accounts.

During the presidency of Bill Clinton (1946–), whose term of office ran from 1993 to 2001, a major piece of consumer-related legislation was the 1994 enactment of the North American Free Trade Agreement (NAFTA). By eliminating most tariffs on products traded among Canada, Mexico, and the United States, lower prices in many areas benefited consumers, especially imported oil from Canada and Mexico that reduced the price of gasoline. In 1999, Clinton signed the Gramm-Leach-Bliley Act, also known as the Financial Services Modernization Act of 1999. It affected financial institutions by requiring them to describe how they collect private information and with whom they share it as well as explaining what measures they take to safeguard sensitive data.

George W. Bush (1946–) was US president from 2001 to 2009. One consumer-related law signed by Bush was 2003's American Dream Downpayment Initiative, which was aimed at helping qualified consumers with down payments and closing costs, enabling more consumers to buy homes. The Consumer Product Safety Improvement Act of 2008 amended existing consumer protection statutes to focus on products for children and infants. By defining what constitutes a children's product, it addressed such provisions as all-terrain vehicles (ATVs), cribs, toys, and the presence of lead in infant or toddler products. It also mandated applicable children's products to be tested by an accredited laboratory and companies to provide written evidence of compliance.

Serving as president from 2009 to 2017, Barack Obama (1961–) took measures toward dealing with identity theft, improving privacy for consumers who shop online, and striving to enhance the security of Americans who become victims of a security breach. The Student Digital Privacy and Parental Rights Act of 2015 prevented certain advertisements targeting students ranging in age from kindergarten to twelfth grade. The Personal Data Notification and Protection Act of 2017 required businesses that collect sensitive personal information to notify consumers when a security breach has been discovered. However, the prime consumer protection law of the Obama administration is generally considered by historians to be the Dodd-Frank Wall Street Reform and Consumer Protection Act, which was enacted in 2010 in response to "Great Recession" of 2008–9. This economic downturn was caused primarily by risky and excessive mortgage lending practices. Calling the two-year recession the worst financial crisis since the Great Depression, Obama pledged the federal resources offered by the law to "crack down on abusive practices in the mortgage industry … and that's not just good for consumers; that's good for the economy" (Obama 2010). The Dodd-Frank law made sweeping changes across the nation's financial services industry by granting additional powers to federal financial regulatory agencies.

Donald Trump (1946–) was president of the United States from 2017 to 2021. In 2018, he signed the Economic Growth, Regulatory Relief, and Consumer Protection Act, which rolled back some of the financial regulations that were put in place by the Dodd-Frank Wall Street Reform and Consumer Protection Act. One of its most significant elements was raising the threshold from $50 billion to $250 billion under which banks are deemed "too big to fail."

Joseph Biden (1942–) served as president from 2021 to 2024. During his administration, the No Surprises Act was signed into law in 2020. It affected consumers enrolled in health insurance plans to prevent and/or limit unexpected health care billing for patients following emergency and some nonemergency medical services, such as out-of-network providers or air ambulance services. The Inflation Reduction Act in 2022 aimed to place a limit on out-of-pocket drug costs to consumers at pharmacies and reduce the price of pharmaceutical products. It acted to lower the cost of insulin and recommended adult vaccines for Medicare clients with the goal of making essential medication more accessible to consumers. The 2022 Debt Collection Rule updated the definition of harassment in the twenty-first-century world by restricting how often debt collectors can contact a consumer through text, email, and social media. Also reflecting the modern world, a 2022 executive order directed a number of federal agencies, such as the Consumer Financial Protection Bureau (CFPB) and the Securities and Exchange Commission to study cryptocurrency in order to "report on regulatory gaps and propose future financial regulations that could mitigate risk to financial stability and financial market integrity" (Brookings Institution 2023).

From a way to finance the Civil War to the modern universe of cryptocurrency, and from Abraham Lincoln to Joe Biden, the number and types of consumer protection laws have grown as the nation progressed. By the twenty-first century, *caveat emptor* was no longer in total control.

Further Reading

American Institute of the History of Pharmacy. n.d. "Remembering Pharmacy's Past: Looking Back at Pharmacy and the Kefauver Hearings." Accessed September

10, 2024. https://aihp.org/remembering-pharmacys-past-looking-back-at-pharmacy-and-the-kefauver-hearings/.

Brookings Institution. 2023. "Tracking Regulatory Changes in the Biden Era." Accessed November 27, 2024. https://www.brookings.edu/articles/tracking-regulatory-changes-in-the-biden-era/.

Cannon, Lou. n.d. "Ronald Reagan: Domestic Affairs." Miller Center, University of Virginia. Accessed September 10, 2024. https://millercenter.org/president/reagan/domestic-affairs.

The Consumer Product Safety Improvement Act (CPSIA). n.d. United States Consumer Product Safety Commission. Accessed September 10, 2024. https://www.cpsc.gov/Regulations-Laws--Standards/Statutes/The-Consumer-Product-Safety-Improvement-Act.

Fleming, Anne. 2019. "Consumer Rights are Worthless without Enforcement." *The Conversation*. Accessed November 27, 2024. https://theconversation.com/consumer-rights-are-worthless-without-enforcement-113244.

Ford, Gerald. 1976. "President Gerald R. Ford's Address Before a Joint Session of the Congress Reporting on the State of the Union, 1976." Gerald R. Ford Presidential Library and Museum. Accessed November 27, 2024. https://www.fordlibrarymuseum.gov/the-fords/gerald-r-ford/key-speeches-and-writings-gerald-r-ford.

Germany, Kent. 2023. "Lyndon B. Johnson: Domestic Affairs." Miller Center, University of Virginia. Accessed November 27, 2024. https://millercenter.org/president/lbjohnson/domestic-affairs.

Kennedy, John F. 1962. "John F. Kennedy Special Message to the Congress on Protecting the Consumer Interest." University of California, Santa Barbara. Accessed November 27, 2024. https://www.presidency.ucsb.edu/documents/special-message-the-congress-protecting-the-consumer-interest.

Knott, Stephen. n.d. "George H. W. Bush: Domestic Affairs." Miller Center, University of Virginia. Accessed September 10, 2024. https://millercenter.org/president/bush/domestic-affairs.

Lazarus, David. 2018. "56 Years Later, Kennedy's Call for a Consumer Bill of Rights Is Forgotten Under Trump." *Los Angeles Times*. Accessed November 27. 2024. https://www.latimes.com/business/lazarus/la-fi-lazarus-kennedy-consumer-bill-of-rights-20180315-story.html.

Middleton, Harry. 2008. "LBJ: Still Casting a Long Shadow." *Prologue Magazine* 40, no. 2. Accessed November 27, 2024. https://www.archives.gov/publications/prologue/2008/summer/lbj.html.

Nixon, Richard. 1969. "Richard Nixon Special Message to the Congress on Consumer Protection." University of California, Santa Barbara. Accessed November 27. 2024. https://www.presidency.ucsb.edu/documents/special-message-the-congress-consumer-protection-0.

Nixon, Richard. 1971. "Presidential Statement to Congress: Nixon's Consumer Message." *CQ Almanac*. Accessed November 27, 2024. https://library.cqpress.com/cqalmanac/document.php?id=cqal71-869-26707-1255015.

Obama, Barack. 2010. "Remarks on Signing the Dodd-Frank Wall Street Reform and Consumer Protection Act." National Archives. Accessed November 27, 2024. https://obamawhitehouse.archives.gov/the-press-office/remarks-president-signing-dodd-frank-wall-street-reform-and-consumer-protection-act.

Riley, Russell L. n.d. "Bill Clinton: Domestic Affairs." Miller Center, University of Virginia. Accessed September 10, 2024. https://millercenter.org/president/clinton/domestic-affairs.

Strong, Robert A. n.d. "Jimmy Carter: Domestic Affairs." Miller Center, University of Virginia. Accessed September 10, 2024. https://millercenter.org/president/carter/domestic-affairs.

Truth in Advertising. 2012. "A Brief History of Deceptive Advertising." Accessed November 27, 2024. https://truthinadvertising.org/articles/timeline/.

Washington Post. 2014. "Evaluating the Success of the Great Society." Accessed November 27, 2024. https://www.washingtonpost.com/wp-srv/special/national/great-society-at-50/.

Q8: Which federal agencies currently oversee consumer rights and protections?

Answer: In 1862, President Abraham Lincoln signed legislation to establish the United States Department of Agriculture (USDA) to help win the Civil War by supporting farmers who provided food for the Union army. This incursion by the federal government into the free market was generally not opposed since it was for a patriotic cause—winning the war. Across 150 years of American history, from the USDA in the nineteenth century to the CFPB in the twenty-first, about a dozen federal regulatory agencies were established to protect consumers, despite opposition from those who believed government had no place in meddling with private enterprise. Some of the most highly esteemed agencies by consumers, such as the Food and Drug Administration and the Federal Deposit Insurance Corporation, were established in a world quite different from our own but remain important in the present day.

The Facts: For many years, the United States operated without federal controls on the marketplace. Gradually, agencies were created to enforce the consumer protection laws that were passed by Congress. The predominant forces guiding the American economy from the time of the nation's founding were based on two concepts: (1) the buyer should beware and (2) the government should not intervene in private enterprise. That began to change with the coming of the Civil War in 1861.

It appears that even before the war, Abraham Lincoln had been thinking about protections related to agriculture, as at least half the population of the United States was involved in farming. In 1859, he made a speech in which he called farmers the "most numerous class [and] it follows that their interest is the largest interest. It also follows that … if there be inevitable conflict between that interest and any other, that other should yield" (Lincoln 1859). If he was thinking in terms of counteracting *caveat emptor*, he proved it in 1862 as the Civil War was raging. That year, there were between one and two million Union soldiers to feed. With their menfolk gone to war, untold numbers of wives, mothers, and sisters had to take over the family farm. Recognizing the vital importance of agriculture to the survival of the nation, Lincoln felt that farmers needed support, and the only entity strong enough to do so was the federal government. In 1862, he signed the US Department of Agriculture (USDA) into existence and was pleased enough with its work that in his final address to Congress before being assassinated in 1865, Lincoln called USDA "The People's Department" (US Department of Agriculture n.d.).

As decades passed, the USDA responded to mechanization in farming and the steady industrialization of the nation that was reducing the number of farmers while the number of food consumers grew. Today, the USDA consists of about 100,000 employees. Its goal continues to be protecting the nation's consumers by overseeing food processing and distribution. Its mandate includes "inspection of domestic product, imports, and exports; conducting risk assessments; and educating the public about the importance of food safety" (US Department of Agriculture n.d.). The USDA is authorized to ensure the safety of meat and poultry products by inspecting hundreds of plants across the nation. In addition, the agency became responsible for overseeing farm equipment, the fertilizer industry, and the nation's stockyards among other duties, including such twenty-first-century concerns as bringing broadband to underserved rural areas. Periodically, the USDA has faced opposition by those who consider the agency to be overzealous in its inspection regulations. Occasionally, an incoming political administration will claim the need to "trim the fat" from the USDA by mandating a cut in the number of inspectors and frequency of inspections, only to have them restored under the next administration—with both actions said to be in the name of consumer protection.

After decades of opposition, the Pure Food and Drug Act of 1906 was passed during the presidential term of Theodore Roosevelt. One of its provisions was establishing the Food and Drug Administration (FDA), the federal agency charged with overseeing what American consumers eat and prohibiting adulterated and/or misbranded food and drugs. Restricting impure food was a relatively new concept after years of *caveat emptor* when it was the consumer's duty to determine what was safe to put on the family dinner table. Roosevelt had experienced the effects of tainted food first-hand among his troops during the "embalmed beef" scandal in the Spanish American War of 1898, during which American soldiers were sickened or died from the poor quality meat they were provided.

With today's FDA claiming about 18,000 employees, the agency's mission continues to be protecting the health of American consumers by ensuring the safety of the nation's "food supply, cosmetics, and products that emit radiation [as well as] human and veterinary drugs, biological products, and medical devices" (US Food and Drug Administration n.d.). In addition, the FDA is also responsible for "regulating the manufacturing, marketing, and distribution of tobacco products to protect the public health and to reduce tobacco use by minors" (US Food and Drug Administration n.d.). Throughout its history, there have been accusations from business owners that the FDA exceeds its authority by overregulating. However, there are also those who do not feel it goes far enough to protect consumers, blaming the agency's food division for being under-resourced. "The CDC (Centers for Disease Control) estimates that more than 128,000 people are hospitalized and 3,000 people die from foodborne illnesses each year" (Evich 2022).

When the Federal Trade Commission (FTC) was established under Woodrow Wilson in 1914, it was part of an ongoing effort that started under Theodore Roosevelt to bust the "trusts" by breaking up monopolies. The huge conglomerates that arose under the "robber barons" of the late nineteenth and early twentieth centuries tended to set their own prices, undermining competition. The FTC's original mission was to prevent barriers to competition, with additional powers being granted by Congress over the years for the agency to regulate unfair business practices that can affect the consumer.

Today, the Federal Trade Commission claims that it is responsible for "issues that touch the economic life of every American. The FTC is the only federal agency with both consumer protection and competition jurisdiction in broad sectors of the economy" (Federal Trade Commission n.d.). To put it more succinctly, the FTC aims to promote competition and protect consumers. With about

1,100 employees today, the FTC has authority to prevent unfair or deceptive business practices not only in the traditional consumer marketplace, but also through the power to regulate internet commerce, which has become hugely popular with American consumers. The FTC is also involved with ensuring that tobacco companies follow specific regulations about how cigarettes, cigars, and smokeless tobacco products can be marketed to consumers in advertisements, especially those targeting young people.

After the First World War ended in 1918, the United States roared into the 1920s. It was a decade of good times for many, based on a level of prosperity that was previously unknown in the nation's history. Many average people invested in the stock market, putting profits in banks for safekeeping. In the "Jazz Age," the music stopped suddenly in 1929 when the stock market crashed. Thousands of banks failed, taking the life savings of millions of people with them. In 1933, President Franklin Roosevelt signed the Federal Deposit Insurance Corporation (FDIC) into existence. With about 5,000 employees, today's FDIC maintains stability and confidence in the American financial system. It insures deposits, examines banks for safety, and supervises their level of consumer protection. Today, the standard insurance amount is $250,000 per depositor. "Since the start of FDIC insurance on January 1, 1934, no depositor has lost a penny of insured funds as a result of a failure" (Federal Deposit Insurance Corporation n.d.).

During the financial catastrophe of the 1930s called the Great Depression that followed the stock market crash, a number of federal consumer protection agencies in addition to the FDIC were put into place to try to safeguard people in the future. In 1934, the Securities and Exchange Commission (SEC) was established in order to protect consumers who invest in financial products by maintaining the safety of financial markets. With about 4,500 employees, today's SEC is organized to ensure that consumers receive proper information so as to make informed investment decisions. It regulates major securities markets, determines risk analysis, and enforces rules and guidelines. The agency essentially maintains the relationship between the average consumer and the financial marketplace; or to put it another way, the SEC connects Main Street with Wall Street.

Also in 1934, the Federal Communications Commission (FCC) was created to oversee governmental regulation of the nation's radio, telegraph, and telephone communications, which were rapidly expanding at that time. Today, its 1,500 employees also supervise television, cable, and satellite systems by enforcing laws involving America's communications. In addition, the agency attempts to regulate emerging technology such as little-known corners of the internet along with devices such as mobile phones. As the FCC puts it, our phones "know a lot about us and the data generated by our devices is increasingly being used in unexpected ways" (Federal Communications Commission n.d.). At the time it was created in 1934, the FCC assumed responsibilities that had been divided between several other governmental agencies such as the Department of Commerce, Federal Radio Commission, Interstate Commerce Commission, and the US Post Office. The FCC's charge was to oversee the orderly development of broadcast communications, which began burgeoning in the 1920s, and to ensure that rates were reasonable for the average customer. Along with consumer-related matters, the FCC also supervises the Emergency Alert System nationwide.

There was initial opposition to the creation of the FCC, charging that with its formation, a governmental agency—not competitive market forces—would allocate airwaves. Today, there are periodic charges that the FCC practices censorship and that it restricts competition by being beholden to business interests. In 1987, the FCC was in the spotlight regarding its decision about the Fairness Doctrine, also known as "equal time." The Fairness Doctrine had been introduced as an FCC policy in 1949, requiring that holders of broadcast licenses present controversial issues in a way that reflected differing viewpoints. In 1987, amid the rise of cable TV, the FCC abolished the Fairness Doctrine. Some have cited the death of "equal time" as a contributing factor in the growth of political polarization in America.

Responding to the increase in aircrafts taking to the skies in the years following the Second World War, the Federal Aviation Agency (FAA) was established in 1958 to replace the old Civil Aeronautics Authority (CAA), which had been created under the New Deal in 1938. The FAA's immediate mission was to ensure the safe, efficient use of the nation's airspace, although in recent years, it has also become attuned to the rights and protections of air travel customers. A focus on consumer issues became more essential after 1978 when airlines were deregulated. This action not only increased the workload of FAA employees dramatically, but also opened the doors for a greater number of consumer-related matters. According to its website, the FAA employs around 40,000 workers, including about 14,000 air traffic controllers. With almost 20,000 airports in the United States and about 45,000 flights daily, the FAA keeps busy with those responsibilities in addition to regulating more than 800,000 drones and over 300,000 remote pilots. In recent years, the FAA has also had to oversee more than 550 licensed commercial space launches. That workload is unlikely to be reduced, since "the number of aircraft flying in US airspace is expected to double within the next 20 years" (Katz 2023). Along with those roles, the agency's Office of Aviation Consumer Protection is concerned with consumer issues ranging from flight delays to minimum seat size.

The Department of Housing and Urban Development (HUD) was created in 1965 as part of Lyndon Johnson's "War on Poverty." With about 7,000 employees, today this agency continues its mission of assisting consumers in lower economic brackets to obtain the benefits of home ownership along with helping those with issues that arise in rental units. HUD programs help consumers through block grants to develop affordable housing for low-income residents; public or subsidized housing for low-income individuals and families; inspections to ensure that housing is decent, safe, and sanitary; mortgage insurance on approved loans; rental assistance/rent relief; and resources for filing consumer complaints.

The Environmental Protection Agency (EPA), established in 1970, can be considered a consumer protection agency, as all Americans consume air, food, and water. Today the agency employs about 17,000 workers. It oversees the nation's environmental elements, including how such factors touch on areas like agriculture, energy, health, and natural resources such as water. The EPA administers and enforces federal laws such as those that were enacted to oversee contaminated lands and toxic sites. It also reviews chemicals in the consumer marketplace for their safety.

The EPA often finds itself in an uncertain position, depending on the political administration in power at the time. It occasionally faces opposition from those who believe the EPA exceeds its authority. For example, US Congressman Mike Simpson of Idaho has said, "I am fighting against the EPA's efforts to regulate certain industries out of existence and working to beat back a costly political agenda that harms Idaho farmers, energy developers, and families, all of whom bear the brunt of overregulation" (Simpson 2023). The lawmaker goes on to accuse the EPA of attempting "to regulate every puddle, ditch, and stream in this country" (Simpson 2023). The EPA periodically finds its budget being cut or restored as various political administrations come and go. According to a poll sponsored by the Harvard School of Public Health, although there is often a claim by opponents that EPA rules result in jobs being lost by hampering employers, opposition is likely based "on a more general distaste for government regulation overall" (Datz 2017).

With about 750 employees, the National Highway Traffic Safety Administration (NHTSA) was also founded in 1970. Its task was to help reduce death, injury, and financial losses that result from motor vehicle crashes. According to the US Department of Transportation's Bureau of Transportation Statistics, there were almost 54,000 deaths in auto-related crashes in 1969. The bureau adds that the number of highway fatalities continued to increase into the 1970s, "until the effects of new regulations [enforced by the NHTSA] ... finally kicked in" (Bureau of Transportation Statistics 2016). By 1989, the number of fatalities dropped to around 45,000. In 2019, the number was around 36,000 despite increased traffic on America's roads and highways. Much of the decrease in fatalities could be attributed to NHTSA's backing of safety systems such as mandatory airbags, antilock brakes, and seat belts. In addition to its pursuit of safety, the NHTSA helps automotive consumers by investigating and prosecuting odometer fraud, providing theft prevention standards, promoting programs to reduce impaired driving, and regulating the fuel economy program.

With a permanent workforce of fewer than 500 federal employees, the Consumer Product Safety Commission (CPSC) was established in 1972. Its mission is to protect consumers by "reducing the unreasonable risk of injuries and deaths associated with consumer products" (US Consumer Product Safety Commission n.d.). The agency is responsible for issuing and enforcing mandatory standards, banning consumer products if no feasible standard would adequately protect the public, and requiring a recall of products along with arranging for repair, replacement, or refund for the recalled products. It investigates potential product hazards as well as developing voluntary standards with manufacturers and businesses. Its task is also to inform consumers about product safety issues. CPSC holds jurisdiction "over thousands of types of consumer products, from coffee makers to toys to lawn mowers" (Consumer Product Safety Commission n.d.).

Periodically, the CPSC comes under scrutiny by governmental and political entities who claim that it either overreaches its authority to regulate manufacturers or does not do enough to protect consumers. In a 2019 hearing by the Congressional Subcommittee on Consumer Protection and Commerce, it was noted that the CPSC must monitor "over 15,000 products that are sold to and used every day in our homes, our schools, businesses, and elsewhere" (House Committee on Energy and Commerce 2019). During the hearing, it was also stated that "unfortunately for consumers ... the number of incidents reported in children's products [has] increased." Attorney David Oddo, who investigates wrongful death cases, claims that in one situation, there were "200 consumer reports citing dangerous stroller defects" (Oddo 2019). Following a lobbying campaign by the manufacturer, "the company was simply instructed to offer broader educational resources to consumers about proper use" (Oddo 2019). Some observers feel that the CPSC is hampered by limited authority. "Although there are regulations and safety standards in place, many are voluntary, leaving it up to manufacturers whether to adhere to recommendations on an array of products, from bedrails to amusement park rides" (Gibson 2022).

The most recent federal consumer protection agency to be established is the Consumer Financial Protection Bureau (CFPB), which was created in 2010. With about 1,600 employees, it is responsible for consumer protection in the financial sector. The impetus for its creation began in 2007, with a severe financial crisis in the United States precipitated by risky mortgage lending practices and a "housing bubble," which is a rapid increase in real estate prices that eventually becomes unsustainable. At that point, home prices plummet when the bubble bursts. Across the nation, millions of Americans were stunned as their home values plunged along with a drop in their savings when small businesses lost financing and jobs were eliminated. "Credit dried up, and countless consumer loans—many improperly made to begin with—went into default" (Consumer Financial Protection Bureau n.d.). According to the CFPB, many Americans had taken on loans that they could not afford and that they did not fully understand.

Before the CFPB was created, responsibility for enforcing federal law in financial matters was divided among several agencies. Today, they are consolidated under the CFPB as the singular "umbrella" agency, focusing directly on consumer financial protection. The agency's mandate is to enforce laws outlawing discrimination in consumer finance and to investigate abusive, deceptive, or unfair practices. It is tasked with scrutinizing payday lenders, supervising suspect financial companies, monitoring financial markets to determine if there are new risks to consumers, and serving as a clearinghouse for consumer complaints about the financial field. According to the CFPB, in the twelve years between 2011 and 2023, it put $17.5 billion "back in Americans' pockets in the form of monetary compensation, principal reductions, canceled debts, and other consumer relief" (Consumer Financial Protection Bureau 2023). In addition, it claims to have imposed $4 billion in penalties for violations of the law. The agency said it has sent four million consumer complaints to companies for response on behalf of customers and states that it handles 3,000 consumer complaints every day. The CFPB is also looking to the future "as tech giants and artificial intelligence reshape the industry" (Consumer Financial Protection Bureau 2023). The CFPB is not without opposition. "Critics say the CFPB, which has forced misbehaving banks to return more than $12 billion to consumers, is the epitome of government overreach and wields too much unchecked power" (Wattles and Egan 2017).

Consumer protection agencies have evolved in the years between trying to save the Union in 1862 and curtailing predatory lenders in the twenty-first century. As they were created, there was often criticism that such regulatory entities represented the government forcibly inserting itself into private enterprise. In addition to federal agencies, innumerable state and local bureaus contribute to a significantly higher number of consumer protection agencies than has ever before existed in the nation's history.

Further Reading

Bureau of Transportation Statistics. 2016. "A Half Century of Highway Safety Innovations–1966 to 2016." Accessed November 27, 2024. https://www.bts.gov/archive/publications/passenger_travel_2016/tables/half.

Consumer Financial Protection Bureau. n.d. "On Your Side through Life's Financial Moments." Accessed September 20, 2024. https://www.consumerfinance.gov/.

Consumer Financial Protection Bureau. 2023."Twelve Years of Protecting Consumers and Honest Businesses." Accessed November 27, 2024. https://www.consumerfinance.gov/about-us/blog/twelve-years-of-protecting-consumers-and-honest-businesses/.

Datz, Todd. 2017. "Poll: Majority of Americans Oppose President Trump's Proposed Cuts to EPA's Budget, Withdrawing from Paris Climate Treaty." Chan School of Public Health, Harvard University. Accessed November 27, 2024. https://www.hsph.harvard.edu/news/press-releases/poll-majority-americans-oppose-president-trumps-proposed-cuts-epas-budget-withdrawing-paris-climate-treaty/.

David, Marc. 2022. "A Short History of the U.S. Federal Trade Commission (FTC)." *Investopedia*. Accessed November 27, 2024. https://www.investopedia.com/articles/financial-theory/10/the-us-federal-trade-commission.asp.

Evich, Helena Bottemiller. 2022. "The FDA's Food Failure." *Politico*. Accessed November 27, 2024. https://www.politico.com/interactives/2022/fda-fails-regulate-food-health-safety-hazards/.

Federal Aviation Administration. n.d. "A Brief History of the FAA." Accessed September 20, 2024. https://www.faa.gov/about/history/brief_history.

Federal Communications Commission. n.d. "Consumer Help Center." Accessed September 20, 2024. https://www.fcc.gov/consumers.

Federal Deposit Insurance Corporation. n.d. "About the FDIC." Accessed September 20, 2024. https://www.fdic.gov/about.

Federal Trade Commission. n.d. "About the FTC." Accessed September 20, 2024. https://www.ftc.gov/about-ftc.

Gibson, Kate. 2022. "People Mistakenly Assume Consumer Products Are Safe, Top Regulator Says." *CBS News*. Accessed November 27, 2024. https://www.cbsnews.com/news/consumer-product-safety-commission-regulator/.

House Committee on Energy and Commerce. 2019. "Protecting Americans from Dangerous Products: Is the Consumer Product Safety Commission Fulfilling Its Mission?" US Government Publishing Office. Accessed November 27, 2024. https://www.govinfo.gov/content/pkg/CHRG-116hhrg39670/html/CHRG-116hhrg39670.htm.

Katz, Eric. 2023. "FAA Is Facing a Looming Staffing Crisis as Post-Pandemic Needs Grow." *Government Executive*. Accessed November 27, 2024. https://www.govexec.com/management/2023/03/faa-facing-looming-staffing-crisis-post-pandemic/384104/.

Lincoln, Abraham. 1859 [1953]. "Address before the Wisconsin State Agricultural Society, Milwaukee, Wisconsin." In *Collected Works of Abraham Lincoln, Volume 3*. New Brunswick, NJ: Rutgers University Press. Accessed November 27, 2024. https://quod.lib.umich.edu/l/lincoln/lincoln3/1:144.1?rgn=div2;view=fulltext.

National Highway Traffic Safety Administration. n.d. "NHTSA." Accessed September 10, 2024. https://www.nhtsa.gov/about-nhtsa.

Oddo, David. 2019. "Consumer Product Safety Commission Is Politicized and Buyers Face Safety Risks." *The Hill*. Accessed November 27, 2024. https://thehill.com/opinion/healthcare/438982-consumer-product-safety-commission-is-politicized-and-buyers-face-safety/.

Simpson, Mike. 2023. "My Continued Fight Against EPA Overreach." United States Congressman Mike Simpson. Accessed November 27, 2024. https://simpson.house.gov/news/documentsingle.aspx?DocumentID=400077.

US Consumer Product Safety Commission. n.d. "What We Do." Accessed September 20, 2024. https://www.cpsc.gov/.

US Department of Agriculture. n.d. "Health and Safety." Accessed September 20, 2024. https://www.usda.gov/topics/health-and-safety.

US Department of Housing and Urban Development. n.d. "Helping You Meet Your Housing Needs." Accessed September 20, 2024. https://www.hud.gov/.

US Environmental Protection Agency. n.d. "Our Mission and What We Do." Accessed September 20, 2024. https://www.epa.gov/aboutepa/our-mission-and-what-we-do.

US Food and Drug Administration. n.d. "About FDA." Accessed September 20, 2024. https://www.fda.gov/about-fda.

US Securities and Exchange Commission. n.d. "About the SEC." Accessed September 20, 2024. https://www.sec.gov/about.

Wattles, Jackie, and Matt Egan. 2017. "Why Wall Street and Republicans Hate the CFPB." CNN. Accessed November 27, 2024. https://money.cnn.com/2017/11/25/news/wall-street-elizabeth-warren-consumer-financial-protection-bureau/index.html.

3

Controversial Issues Involving Consumer Rights and Protections

For many Americans, consumer rights and protections are considered to be an essential element of society in order to safeguard the people of the nation. However, consistent with the ethos of the early history of the United States, the concept of *caveat emptor* has often come into direct conflict with the goal of protecting consumers.

One objection to consumer protection laws is that they deprive people of the right to decide for themselves what they want to purchase or place penalties on them for making certain purchasing decisions. A case in point involves tobacco products, as the government, in an attempt to address associated health issues, has made these products very expensive to dissuade people from purchasing them. Critics argue that adults have the right to choose what they wish to put into their bodies without government oversight or interference. Another example is the banning of children's toys that can be dangerous. Opponents claim that parents should be able to determine what is good or not good for their families. A familiar argument against consumer protection laws and agencies is that they lead to what is referred to as a "nanny state," in which the government takes on the role of caretaker for the welfare of adults who should be trusted to make their own decisions. Critics of the nanny state object to government limiting people's freedom to choose by interfering in private enterprise.

Another controversial issue involves free speech in the advertising industry and claims that the government has no right to restrict freedoms guaranteed by the First Amendment to the Constitution. Advertising is used to persuade consumers to purchase a particular product, and some argue that it is up to individual consumers to decipher whether an ad is an exaggeration and/or is promoting false claims before they decide whether or not to purchase the item. In judicial terms, advertising is considered "commercial speech," which has been determined by the courts to enjoy certain protections under the right to free speech. However, interpretations of the First Amendment by various courts can differ as to the admissible degree of exaggerated or untrue claims as well as whether the ads are targeting vulnerable groups such as children.

The "pink tax" refers to the higher pricing of products marketed toward women and girls than those marketed toward men and boys. (The "pink" comes from the fact that, traditionally, the color pink is associated with girls and blue with boys.) Not literally a tariff (such as sales tax) for which proceeds would go to a city or state, the pink tax is a tendency for manufacturers to charge females more than males for the products they purchase. Whether or not this apparent upcharge is attributable to pricing discrimination or to other market forces (such as gender-based differences in demand for products) has been debated. While a few states have initiated legislation to counteract the pink tax, the federal government has not enacted any consumer rights and protections in this area.

Q9: Does government involvement in consumer protection lead to a "nanny state"?

Answer: A "nanny" is a person, generally a woman, who is employed as a caregiver for young children. Beginning in the 1960s, the term "nanny state" emerged among conservatives who criticized what they felt were overly protective and restrictive government laws and agencies that intruded on private enterprise as well as on people's freedom of choice. Sometimes also called "paternalism," it indicates a parental-like limitation of individual freedoms presumably for people's own good. The concept often pertains to consumer protection laws. Opponents of these laws object to government intervention regarding products and services being sold by private enterprise, particularly regarding eating, smoking, drinking alcohol, or manufacturing toys that are said to be dangerous. Critics of nanny state regulations argue that the government has no right to decide what is best for individuals.

The Facts: In 2009, First Lady Michelle Obama planted a vegetable garden on the South Lawn of the White House. She said the move was intended to demonstrate healthy nutrition to help combat childhood obesity. Subsequent protests accused the First Lady of fostering a nanny state by telling the American people what to eat. The vegetable garden weathered the criticism and has remained in place through subsequent administrations. It provides fresh produce for food banks in Washington, DC, as well as for state dinners at the White House.

In 2012, in an attempt to curb obesity, New York City's mayor, Michael Bloomberg, supported a proposal to restrict the sale of soft drinks larger than 16 ounces by imposing a city ordinance to ban "super-size" sugary drinks. This proposal led to widespread outrage and ridicule of the mayor. He was called Nanny Bloomberg and was portrayed in caricatures costumed in a dowdy woman's dress.

Critics compared New York's proposed ban to the Prohibition era, when the government outlawed the manufacture and sale of alcohol in the United States. The Prohibition law, passed in 1920 in the form of the Eighteenth Amendment to the US Constitution, was hailed by supporters as a moral victory, a "noble experiment." It was intended to cure society of problems attributed to alcohol, such as family violence and desertion. However, Prohibition had unintended consequences, including the rise of organized crime, increased smuggling, loss of jobs, and a major drop in tax revenues. And despite the government's efforts, alcohol consumption did not decrease significantly, as many people obtained illegal liquor through various means before Prohibition was repealed in 1933.

In 2012, the proposed New York City super-size soda ban seemed unlikely to succeed in its goal to promote better health. Dr. Aaron Carroll, writing in the *Journal of the American Medical Association*, noted the comparison to Prohibition in the 1920s, calling the results then to be "disastrous." He indicated that the failures of government regulation at that time may be why there has been no prohibition on smoking, despite its well-known health effects. "We still haven't tried to make cigarettes illegal. We may make it difficult to smoke, and we may make it expensive, but it's still legal, and you can still do it" (Carroll 2021). In any case, the super-size soda ban was approved by the New York City's Board of Health in 2012 only to be repealed in 2014. The reversal came when the New York Court of Appeals, the state's highest court, determined that the Board of Health had "exceeded the scope of its regulatory authority" with the ban. The soda ban went away, but the mayor carried the "Nanny Bloomberg" label for a long time.

When the first national consumer protection effort, the Pure Food and Drug Act of 1906, was passed, public opinion tended to favor keeping consumers safe from tainted foods and adulterated pharmaceuticals. Many had been repulsed by the idea of what went into food products being sold to the public by unscrupulous meatpackers such as those spotlighted in Upton Sinclair's 1906 book, *The Jungle*. Although there was opposition to government interference in private enterprise via the Pure Food and Drug Act of 1906, something that worked in its favor was having a strong president like Theodore Roosevelt supporting the law. He could testify first-hand to the disastrous effects that adulterated meat had inflicted on troops during the Spanish American War in 1898. Untold numbers of soldiers became violently ill, and some died after eating food that had been provided to the Army by American meatpackers, who sold tainted beef products containing formaldehyde, a chemical used to embalm dead bodies.

As the years passed, more consumer protection laws evolved. By the early twenty-first century, laws were being proposed and/or implemented in various states. The bans included cooking with trans-unsaturated fatty acids ("trans fats"), junk food ads aimed at children, smoking outdoors in public places, and texting while jaywalking. Some states have called for requiring life jackets on rivers, regulating online gambling, and prohibiting toys in fast-food children's meals unless the food meets stringent nutritional standards. When the proposals were introduced, many were met with opposition by critics of the nanny state. Occasionally, there has been a legislative backlash to restrictions on individual freedom. In 2013, for example, the Mississippi Legislature passed "a ban on bans—a law that forbids municipalities to place local restrictions on food or drink" (Conly 2013b).

Some critics, such as economists James Bennett and Thomas Di Lorenzo, claim that a "nanny" sees the world in constant crisis, with public health being at risk from "profit-hungry corporations which carelessly expose us to the 'dangerous' products. ... All we ask is that the nannies permit us to go our own way, design our own diets, and ingest what we choose to ingest" (Bennett and Di Lorenzo 1999, 12). Many see the nanny state as a danger to their freedom of choice as consumers. As one commentator put it, "As individuals, we are each responsible for our own decisions and the corresponding consequences. ... Why should the state decide how I live? Am I not free to make my own decisions?" (Blanco 2017). Consumer choice advocate Bill Wirtz noted that "The idea of consumer protection remains important for governments because consumers have been taught to perceive themselves as victims" (Wirtz 2018).

On the other hand, there are those who consider consumer-related laws involving such issues as smoking to promote the well-being of the public at large, not just the individual smoker. They cite increased healthcare costs and higher medical insurance rates for everyone due to the burden of treating diseases caused by smoking and second-hand smoke. Opponents believe this is not justification for government interference. For example, economics professor Donald Boudreaux stated that "allowing government (in the name of taxpayers) to sue tobacco companies because smoking increases taxpayers' burdens is not itself sufficient grounds for penalizing tobacco companies" (Boudreaux 1997).

Conservative columnist David Harsanyi believes that there is a lack of consistency among policies claiming to protect consumers. He cites examples such as a ban in some states on mini-motorbikes, despite the fact that these bikes cause far fewer deaths than skiing, which is not banned. He also sees laziness on the part of politicians, government officials, and those whom he calls "do-gooders," stating that "creating alarm over trans fats, for example, is far easier than convincing consumers to eat less french fries" (Harsanyi 2007).

Author Sarah Conly has studied why some elements of the alleged nanny state cause such controversy, particularly when the infringement on personal freedoms are fairly minimal. For example, New York's ban on giant-size sugary drinks was not a ban on all soda. Consumers were still free to purchase as much soda as they wanted, after all. Conly notes that Americans often have a hostile response to being told what to do as well as a fear that laws like New York's are only the beginning, a slippery slope that will lead to more government control over their lives and restrictions on their freedoms. She states, however, that "banning a law on the grounds that it might lead to worse laws would mean we could have no laws whatsoever" (Conly 2013b). Suggesting that objections to these types of proposals have a basis in how they are presented, Conly cites the relative success of the campaign to make tobacco products more expensive so that many people cannot afford them. The government could have chosen to simply make tobacco products illegal, but increasing prices was a more palatable approach than an outright ban. According to Conly, "the former is thought of as a 'soft' method, and thus relatively unobjectionable, and the latter as a 'hard' method, and thus disrespectful of autonomy" (Conly 2013a, 6).

Some critics note that government intervention may be more about maintaining and increasing wealth than promoting societal well-being. Economist Dean Baker applied the nanny state label to policies that protect not the health of consumers but the profits of the rich. He cited support by some lawmakers for government intervention into "the inner workings of the economy to make sure the money flows in the direction they like" (Baker 2006, 2), such as using taxpayer funds for billions of dollars in bank bailouts.

The labels "nanny state" and "paternalistic government" provide insights into gender stereotypes and sexism in the United States. "The term 'nanny state' was created and continues to be used by conservatives, who have long opposed government interference. ... Because of its proximity to femininity and womanhood, the term 'nanny' has become an insult in politics"

(Jáquez 2022). Although related to the concept of the nanny state, the term "paternalism" is not used as often as an insult. Paternalism "suggests the view that the state stands to its citizens as a parent (or perhaps a male parent) stands to his children" (Feinberg 1989, 4). Calling the mayor of New York "Nanny Bloomberg" could be construed not only as opposition to his policy but also an assault on his masculinity, an indicator of weakness that is risky in the political arena.

To some, consumer protection laws play an important role in safeguarding average Americans in the marketplace. To the opponents of such statutes, however, these laws represent unwelcome government intervention that restricts the freedom of those same average Americans to make their own choices.

Further Reading

Baker, Dean. 2006. *The Conservative Nanny State: How the Wealthy Use the Government to Stay Rich and Get Richer*. Washington, DC: Center for Economic and Policy Research, 2.

Bennett, James, and Thomas Di Lorenzo. 1999. *The Food and Drink Police: America's Nannies, Busybodies, and Petty Tyrants*. New York: Routledge, 12.

Blanco, Bernardo. 2017. "Why Liberty and the Nanny State Are Incompatible." Foundation for Economic Education. Accessed November 27, 2024. https://fee.org/articles/why-liberty-and-the-nanny-state-are-incompatible/.

Boudreaux, Donald. 1997. "The Nanny State." Foundation for Economic Education. Accessed November 27, 2024. https://fee.org/articles/the-nanny-state/.

Carroll, Aaron. 2021. "Prohibition Won't Work for Soft Drinks Any More Than It Did for Alcohol." *JAMA Forum*. Accessed November 27, 2024. https://jamanetwork.com/channels/health-forum/fullarticle/2760298.

Conly, Sarah. 2013a. *Against Autonomy: Justifying Coercive Paternalism*. Reprint edition. New York: Cambridge University Press, 6.

Conly, Sarah. 2013b. "Three Cheers for the Nanny State." *New York Times*. Accessed November 27, 2024. https://www.nytimes.com/2013/03/25/opinion/three-cheers-for-the-nanny-state.html.

Feinberg, Joel. 1989. *Harm to Self*. New York: Oxford University Press, 4.

Harsanyi, David. 2007. *Nanny State: How Food Fascists, Teetotaling Do-Gooders, Priggish Moralists, and Other Boneheaded Bureaucrats Are Turning America into a Nation of Children*. Kindle edition, n.p.

Jáquez, Alannis. 2022. "The Nanny State: A Conservative Concern or a Misogynistic Myth?" *Columbia Political Review*. http://www.cpreview.org/articles/2022/4/the-nanny-state-a-conservative-concern-or-a-misogynistic-myth.

Lerner, George. 2012. "New York Health Board Approves Ban on Large Sodas." CNN. Accessed November 27, 2024. https://www.cnn.com/2012/09/13/health/new-york-soda-ban/index.html.
Wirtz, Bill. 2018. "Why Is the Nanny State So Popular?" Foundation for Economic Education. Accessed November 27, 2024. https://fee.org/articles/why-is-the-nanny-state-so-popular/.

Q10: Is advertising exempt from consumer protection laws under the First Amendment?

Answer: From ancient times to our own, consumers have been confronted with advertising. In order to convince the consumer to buy a particular product, claims about the item's superiority over others have sometimes been exaggerated. In other cases, advertising goes beyond exaggeration to the point of deception, such as hawking alleged health tonics (also known as "snake oil") as a cure for cancer, colic in babies, loss of virility in men, and reproductive problems in women. Some advertisers in the United States have claimed constitutional protection under the First Amendment right to free speech. While this protection exists to some degree, not all advertisements that consumers face are covered by the First Amendment. The difference between what is protected and what is not often depends on a court's interpretation of the advertiser's intent, the degree of perceived deception, and the type of potential consumers who are targeted, such as children.

The Facts: Along with freedom of assembly, freedom of the press, and the freedom to petition the government over grievances, the First Amendment to the US Constitution protects freedom of speech. When the United States was founded, the right of free speech was written into the Constitution because as British subjects, American colonists had been prohibited from criticizing the King, Parliament, or other government officials. Such criticism was considered to be sedition, a treasonous act against lawful civil authority. "In the American colonies before 1700, there were 1,244 prosecutions for seditious speech—a crime for which punishments included confinement to the stocks, public whippings, and worse" (Reynolds 2015), including the offenders' ears being cut off. Before the American Revolution, the colonists who would become the Founding Fathers had been forbidden to criticize what they felt were unjust laws, such as the Stamp Act of 1765. After winning independence, these men wrote the right of free speech, both public and private, into the new nation's governing document. The First Amendment conferred the right to express ideas and opinions without governmental restrictions or retribution.

What exactly qualifies for constitutional protection in the sphere of advertising? In terms of the marketplace, advertising is designed to persuade consumers to take some form of action, generally by purchasing the product or service being promoted. Under the judicial system, advertisements are considered to be commercial speech, which is "a form of protected communication under the First Amendment, [although] it does not receive as much free speech protection as forms of noncommercial speech, such as political speech" (Schultz 2009). In general, there has historically been significant regulation of commercial advertising to protect consumers and prevent fraud. "Beginning in the 1970s, however, the Supreme Court gradually recognized this type of speech as deserving some First Amendment protection" (Schultz 2009). Determining the degree of protection under the right of free speech is a relatively recent concept for advertising, including deceptive advertising. "From 'health tonics' that claim to cure baldness to cigarette companies denying the link between smoking and cancer, marketers throughout history have exaggerated benefits, denied side effects, and blatantly lied in order to sell their products or services" (Truth in Advertising 2012).

Advertising is an ancient practice. In the Middle Ages, before the invention of the printing press, "with literacy being rare, town criers, or 'professional loudmouths' would stand in public venues and yell about events and products, promoting them" (Richards 2022, 26). Going further back in time, excavations at ancient Greek and Roman sites have revealed ads that were painted on the sides of buildings. Some Roman merchants advertised themselves to consumers via elaborate mosaics, such as one that read, "Garum of Scaurus, the best quality of mackerel" (Imperium Romanum 2023). In the city of Carthage around the year 500 BCE, criers were dressed in garments emblazoned with images front and back, "which might well be the first example of advertising that appealed to two senses simultaneously" (Richards 2022, 27). Ancient advertisers would have been envious of the times to come when appealing to these two senses would reach a pinnacle with the introduction of television in the late twentieth century.

Before that time, in the late nineteenth and early twentieth centuries, print advertising had been the primary means of communication. Advertising practices in this medium caught the attention of the public as well as governmental authorities, as supporters of the era's progressive spirit were taking a long look at the concept of *caveat emptor*. In 1905, a series of articles in *Collier's* magazine revealed an investigation into the patent medicines that had been widely advertised to American consumers for decades. Many of these ads promised that the potions were soothing for babies suffering from such maladies as unexplained crying fits called colic. The main ingredient in many of these so-called health tonics was a heavy dose of alcohol. Other mixtures for babies were laced with hallucinogens, opiates, or toxic substances that could be deadly and/or cause a lifelong tendency toward addiction. Public outrage after the publication of the *Collier's* articles prompted Congress to pass the Pure Food and Drug Act of 1906.

A new form of entertainment arose in the early 1900s in the form of moving pictures (movies), expanding the format and reach of advertisements. Along with movie stars came celebrity endorsements, a popular mode of advertising that caught the eye of a star-struck public. In 1905, a beloved silent screen star of the day "launched the age of the celebrity endorser when he promoted Murad cigarettes in print ads, declaring that it was 'the natural preference of men of cultivated taste'" (Truth in Advertising 2012). The influencer in that case was comedian Roscoe "Fatty" Arbuckle, who later became notorious after being indicted in an infamous scandal involving alleged rape and murder. There is no documented evidence that advertisers sought Arbuckle's services as a celebrity endorser after the scandal.

A watershed event in consumer rights and protections came when the Federal Trade Commission (FTC) was established in 1914. Along with serving as an antitrust watchdog and upholding its mandate to prevent unfair methods of competition, the FTC ultimately became responsible for protecting consumers from deceptive advertising. In 1916, the first challenge to the newly formed FTC came in the form of a direct conflict between the First Amendment right to free speech and the usage of a misleading term in advertisements. According to FTC files, "the very first case published in Volume 1 of *Federal Trade Commission Decisions* proves that the intertwined roots of consumer protection and competition run deep" (Fair 2014). The case involved the Circle Cilk Company, a Philadelphia thread manufacturer that advertised one of its popular products as "Circle Cilk Embroidery Floss." National literacy rates were not high at the time, and many consumers failed to recognize the alternate spelling of the word "cilk" to describe cotton thread, as it was pronounced the same as the much more expensive product, silk. The FTC "concluded that the natural result of the use of the word was to 'confuse, mislead, and deceive purchasers thereof and the public into the belief that cotton thread is genuine silk,' [barring the business] from using the word 'cilk' in sales as well as advertising" (Fair 2014). By ruling on the side of consumer protection, as well as supporting honest competitors who did not seek to mislead the public by deceptive advertising, the FTC affirmed consumer protection in the face of the First Amendment's coverage of free speech. The US Congress supported the Federal Trade Commission by passing the Wheeler-Lea Act in 1938, formally amending the FTC's official mission to include outlawing unfair or deceptive practices, and thereby officially solidifying its role in consumer protection.

Radio, a popular means of entertainment and news since the 1920s, was a medium where people could hear products being described, usually in glowing terms. Following the end of the Second World War in 1945, radio was followed by television, where viewers had the added dimension of being able to see attractive images of products on the screen. Television opened previously unheard-of opportunities to advertise consumer items. It was the union of sight and sound in the modern age of advertising that brought commercial speech to the attention of the courts as well as the authority of regulatory agencies under federal law.

After fighting two world wars and undergoing the economic disaster of the Great Depression, the postwar years saw a greater spotlight being shined on the burgeoning field of advertising and its methods of persuading consumers. In 1946, a former ad copywriter named Frederick Wakeman wrote *The Hucksters*, a book that later became a movie. It sparked a public outcry with its exposé of the sometimes-unsavory techniques used by the operatives of the advertising industry and their clients.

Until the rise of television in the 1950s, the primary means of communication among most Americans in the first half of the twentieth century was radio as a source of entertainment and news. Radio programs had sponsors who promoted their products to consumers. As seen in *The Hucksters*, content was often dictated by those sponsors and the advertising agencies who wrote what on-air personalities would say. Consumers often took such celebrities to heart, believing that they sincerely used and liked the products they promoted. Unless the claims were obviously suspect, they were generally covered by the right to free speech. Consumers believed that what they heard was truthful. When television burst on the scene as a powerful medium of mass communication, advertisements took on an even greater degree of believability. On early TV, products were often praised by sincere-sounding personalities who were beloved by audiences.

In 1957, two events caught the attention of consumers as well as those who wondered how stringently advertising should be covered by the First Amendment right to free speech. The first was the release that year of a movie called *A Face in the Crowd*, based on a book written by Budd Schulberg. In the fictional storyline, a loveable on-air personality and pitchman for consumer products is unknowingly caught on an open microphone being broadcast nationwide saying such things as "I could make 'em eat dogfood and think it was steak!" (Schulberg 1957, 142). Some consumers began to wonder what was truth and what was fiction. The second event in 1957 was the publication of a book titled *The Hidden Persuaders* by journalist Vance Packard. It hit home for many people with its accusation of manipulation by the advertising industry, also taking aim at average consumers by warning of a "growing docility in responding to their manipulation" (Packard 1970, 4).

Another issue coming to light in the postwar era was the role of advertising in promoting the pharmaceutical industry. In some cases, ads touted certain prescription drugs as expensive new products, even though they were existing drugs with a new name and a higher price tag. This practice caught the attention of a congressional committee led by US Senator Estes Kefauver, who sponsored legislation to curtail such practices. At the same time, the committee noted that ads were also used to turn consumers away from other companies that sold lower-priced generic drugs when they became available. Protection under the First Amendment right to free speech was called into question, noting that the goal of ads by some pharmaceutical manufacturers was to undermine consumers' faith in generic products, replacing it with greater trust in brand-name versions. Although brand-name products were generally more expensive than generic versions of the same drug, "advertisers argued that they were worth the price due to the quality assurance that came with the brand" (Stole 2005, 6).

The 1965 Federal Cigarette Labeling and Advertising Act moved ad protection a bit farther away from being shielded by the First Amendment right to free speech. Following a report by the US surgeon general in 1964 that found cigarette smoking to be a health hazard, the legislation required that cigarette packages be labeled "*Caution: Cigarette Smoking May Be Hazardous to Your Health.*" The law was amended four years later to ban cigarette advertising on radio and television. Consumers of tobacco products had to depend on other means of promotion to find products they liked.

In the 1970s, however, the US Supreme Court ruled on several cases that recognized advertising as a type of speech that *did* deserve a certain degree of First Amendment protection. In *Bigelow v. Virginia* (1975), Justice Harry Blackmun declared that "the existence of commercial activity, in itself, is no justification for narrowing the protection of expression secured by the First

Amendment." In 1976, the Supreme Court ruled in favor of its support for the free flow of commercial information as long as it was accurate.

The stipulation of accuracy was put to the test in several cases involving scrutiny by the Federal Trade Commission. Those cases were eventually found *not* to be covered by the First Amendment right to free speech. In the 2000s, certain brands of over-the-counter diet pills enticed consumers by claiming the ability to "melt fat, eliminate cellulite and quickly lose massive amounts of weight without changing your diet or exercising" (Truth in Advertising 2012). Not only were the claims found to be untrue, but some of the pills could also be hazardous to health. Ads for the diet pills were found by the Supreme Court to not be protected as free speech, and the manufacturers were forced to pay millions of dollars to settle claims over false advertising. In 2015, the boundaries of free speech were again tested due to false claims that certain products aimed at seniors could curtail memory loss and dementia. The findings of a congressional committee on aging led to the FTC lodging charges against the manufacturer of the supplement.

With the rise of social media via the internet, some likened the online atmosphere to the Wild West in which anything goes. The FTC and the courts shared the responsibility of determining when certain claims regarding consumer goods were—and were not—protected as free speech. The 2009 Blogger Law curtailed the practice of posting fake blogs to attract consumer dollars by making untruthful claims about products. Under the new rules, bloggers had to disclose ties to the commercial entities they endorsed or face the risk of being fined. The law was enacted because it was not possible for the average consumer to determine which endorsements were truthful and which were a paid sales pitch, a breach that was not considered to be protected under the First Amendment.

With echoes from a century earlier when disgraced entertainer Fatty Arbuckle proved to be an unfortunate choice as a celebrity spokesperson, actions by the Federal Trade Commission in 2017 focused on celebrities who endorsed products by presenting themselves as social media "influencers." Those individuals received notifications from the FTC reminding them of the need to clearly reveal their connection to the businesses they endorse. That is, they are required to reveal that they are being paid to review the products they promote to consumers.

Advertisements aimed at certain consumer demographics, mainly children and adolescents, tend to receive greater scrutiny than mainstream "commercial speech," which is often protected under the First Amendment. The American Psychological Association (APA) classifies children as young people between infancy and adolescence. Adolescents, or teenagers, are generally classified as being roughly between the ages of twelve and twenty. The APA found that children and teens spend more than forty-four hours a week in front of computers, televisions, and game screens, which is more time than any other activity in their lives except sleeping. "Research has found strong associations between increases in advertising for non-nutritious foods and rates of childhood obesity" (American Psychological Association n.d.). The APA states that most children under six years of age are not able to tell the difference between entertainment and content that is an advertisement. Similarly, most older children do not fully understand the persuasive powers of advertising. While young children may not yet be able to make their own consumer purchases, they can persuade their parents to buy certain products.

Some areas of the food and beverage industry have promoted claims that they are self-regulating as regards marketing to children. However, critics of this methodology have not noticed significant changes, such as improvement in marketing healthier food in place of the non-healthy variety. The APA states that, generally, three out of every four foods advertised to children are unhealthy enough to contribute to obesity, adding that about half of all the advertising time on children's TV shows consists of ads for food products. "These ads are almost completely dominated by unhealthy food products. Children are rarely exposed to public service announcements or advertising for healthier foods" (American Psychological Association n.d.). Citing the national level of obesity as a health issue, some question why the government does not regulate advertisements for "junk food." Manufacturers and media sources that run these ads often state that the right to free speech under the First Amendment does not allow government agencies to regulate such advertising to children. However, "the First Amendment forbids some kinds of advertising regulation, but the government [does have] leeway to restrict advertising to children, especially younger children" (Change Lab Solutions 2013).

In recent years, the Supreme Court has generally ruled that freedom of speech includes advertising, protecting what the Court refers to as "commercial speech" unless it can be proven to be deceptive. For example, the Supreme Court struck down a Massachusetts ban on tobacco ads within 1,000 feet of schools. Without restricting the free speech of advertisers, the government may deliver its own public service announcements that warn against the health dangers of consuming an excess amount of certain foods or beverages. However, "the government would be hard pressed to defend a measure requiring soft-drink retailers to post signs saying 'Don't drink soda'" (Change Lab Solutions 2013).

There is no one-size-fits-all answer to whether advertising is covered by the First Amendment right to free speech, even in the name of consumer protection. When left to the judicial system, the interpretation of the First Amendment depends on the outlook of the deciding judges, including those of the US Supreme Court, who are appointed by the political party in power at the time. Some interpret "commercial speech" loosely, intervening only when the advertisement is obviously deceptive, misleading, and hazardous to the health of consumers and their families.

Further Reading

American Psychological Association. n.d. "The Impact of Food Advertising on Childhood Obesity." Accessed September 10, 2024. https://www.apa.org/topics/obesity/food-advertising-children.

Change Lab Solutions. 2013. "First Amendment FAQs." Accessed November 27, 2024. https://www.changelabsolutions.org/sites/default/files/FirstAmendmentFAQs_FINAL_201204.pdf.

Fair, Lesley. 2014. "FTC Milestones: Shared Beginnings in the Circle Cilk Case." Bureau of Consumer Protection. Accessed November 27, 2024. https://www.ftc.gov/enforcement/competition-matters/2014/11/ftc-milestones-shared-beginnings-circle-cilk-case.

Imperium Romanum. 2023. "Advertising in Ancient Rome." Accessed November 27, 2024. https://imperiumromanum.pl/en/article/advertising-in-ancient-rome/.

Packard, Vance. 1970. *The Hidden Persuaders* [40th printing]. New York: Pocket Books, 4.

Reynolds, Eileen. 2015. "We the Protestors: How America's Founders Forged the Freedom of (Ugly, Vitriolic) Speech." New York University. Accessed November 27, 2024. https://www.nyu.edu/about/news-publications/news/2016/june/stephen-solomon-on-revolutionary-dissent.html.

Richards, Jef. 2022. *A History of Advertising: The First 300,000 Years*. Lanham, MD: Rowman and Littlefield, 26, 27.

Schulberg, Budd. 1957. *A Face in the Crowd*. New York: Bantam Books, 142.

Schultz, David. 2009. "Commercial Speech." Free Speech Center, Middle Tennessee State University. Accessed November 27, 2024. https://www.mtsu.edu/first-amendment/article/900/commercial-speech.

Stole, Inger. 2005. *Advertising on Trial: Consumer Activism and Corporate Public Relations in the 1930s*. Urbana: University of Illinois Press, 6.

Truth in Advertising. 2012. "A Brief History of Deceptive Advertising." Accessed November 27, 2024. https://truthinadvertising.org/articles/timeline/.

Q11: Do consumer rights and protections cover the alleged "pink tax"?

Answer: The "pink tax" is not an actual tax in the sense of government tariffs like sales or property taxes. The phrase refers to the perception that women pay more than men do for similar—or even the same—products and services. Although there is opposition to the belief that such gender-based pricing discrimination exists, some studies have concluded that the pink tax does occur in the form of increased costs for women in certain situations. Critics claim that even if such an upcharge does exist, under the concept of *caveat emptor*, it is up to the buyer to beware, to do their research and choose products accordingly. Some statutes addressing the pink tax exist on the local level, but although bills have been introduced in the US Congress, there are no federal consumer protection laws regarding the pink tax at this time.

The Facts: According to writer Emily Crockett, who specializes in politics and gender, "Women pay a hidden tax on almost everything. It may not be a real tax levied by the government, but it has a real impact on women's pocketbooks" (Crockett 2016). Crockett is referring to a practice commonly known as the "pink tax," as pink is the color traditionally associated with girls, as blue is related with boys. As opposed to taxes collected by federal, state, or local governments to fund public services, the pink tax refers to companies making a higher profit by charging more for versions of their products aimed at women than those aimed at men. These might include such items as shampoo, deodorants, and razors as well as services such as dry-cleaning.

Critics of the pink tax theory claim that female consumers have the option not to buy the item if they feel there is price discrimination, and that women also have the right to purchase less expensive men's products if they wish. The counterargument is that many female consumers do not know that a so-called pink tax exists on the product they are purchasing. This not only costs them more money at the point of purchase than similar products marketed to men but also results in a long-term loss of thousands of dollars to their net wealth over the years. A few state and municipal governments have passed consumer protection laws to neutralize alleged gender-based price discrimination by enacting regulations to prohibit the practice, although the federal government has not.

The term "pink tax" came into popular usage in 1995, during the process of ratifying a California consumer protection law called the Gender Tax Repeal

Act. It was state legislation that sought to prohibit price discrimination on goods and services based on the gender of the consumer. In 2016, the pink tax gained widespread attention via social media sources that went viral. At that time, a CBS news program conducted an experiment in New York City. In the investigative piece, a female television producer and her male counterpart requested dry-cleaning services at several stores around Manhattan for a similar cotton shirt. When each visited the dry-cleaning establishments separately, they found that the female was often charged more than the male, and sometimes twice as much or even more.

The CBS report included the fact that an upcharge for women "dates back to at least the mid-1800s when women's hats and gloves were taxed higher" (CBS News 2016). One dry-cleaner stated to reporters that the reason his firm charged more for women was due to the fact this his pressing machines were designed for men's shirts and it was difficult to make women's garments fit into the machinery. The CBS report also cited a 2016 study by the New York City Department of Consumer Affairs that showed women paying more than men for virtually the same product. The study "compared nearly 800 items with clear male and female versions, and on average, the women's versions of a product cost seven percent more than the ones for men" (CBS News 2016).

The discrepancies are said to run from childhood to the opposite end of the age spectrum. Crockett asks, "Why on earth would a pink scooter cost twice as much as a red one? Are men's and women's adult diapers really so different that men should be able to get 25 percent more of them for the same price?" (Crockett 2016). She notes that the New York Department of Consumer Affairs study found that the pink tax constituted on average 13 percent for women's personal care products, 8 percent for women's clothing, 4 percent for girls' clothing, 7 percent for toys andaccessories aimed at girls, and 8 percent for home health care and senior products for women. As policy journalist Libby Nelson wrote, "The differences the Department of Consumer Affairs found were pervasive—and infuriating" (Nelson 2015). Other reports concurred, finding that items from baby shoes, deodorant, fragrances, razors, shampoo, and conditioners to walking canes and women's clothing are all more expensive for females.

These pricing differences add up over time. Writer Lane Gillespie, who covers financial issues, stated that in California during the single year of 2020, female consumers paid "an average of about $2,381 more, for the same goods and services, than men per year" (Gillespie 2023). Using that figure, over the course of sixty years, a woman's pink tax adds up to more than $142,000. Adjusting for less earning power, disabled, elderly, and minority women are especially impacted, particularly those on a fixed income such as Social Security. Gillespie notes that products such as adult diapers, canes, compression socks, and digestive health products are more costly when marketed to woman than to men.

The extent of the pink tax issue is debated by some sources who question the need for consumer protection laws to counteract it. "A 2021 national study by researchers from the University of Chicago, Booth; Northwestern University, Kellogg; and Cornerstone Research found that women's products were only more expensive than men's in one of six retail categories examined. The study's researchers questioned the need for legislative action against the pink tax" (Gillespie 2023). The federal government become somewhat involved in the matter of the alleged pink tax when, in 2018, "the US Government Accountability Office (GAO) examined prices for 10 categories of personal care products geared to women and men. Ultimately, GAO couldn't definitively conclude there was a pink tax—or that there wasn't" (Cole 2024). Nevertheless, several states and municipalities have initiated consumer protection laws based on the determination that gender-based price discrimination exists and is prevalent enough that it needs to be addressed: California (two laws passed, one in 1995 and another in 2023), Miami-Dade County, Florida (1997), New York City (1998), and New York State (2020).

In California, the law requires that men and women be charged the same price for a service if it takes the same cost, skill, and time to provide. The law covers services such as car repairs, clothing alterations, dry-cleaning, and haircuts, not individual products. Miami-Dade County's gender price discrimination ordinance covers both goods and services, with the Miami-Dade County Consumer Services Department in charge of enforcing the local law. While it does not allow straightforward price discrimination based on the gender of the consumer, it also takes into consideration such factors as the cost, time, and level of difficulty involved in providing goods or services. Those who have complaints can report them to the Miami-Dade Consumer Services Department, and may ultimately sue the alleged offender.

The New York State law bans manufacturers, retailers, or other businesses from charging different prices for goods that are "substantially similar," but are marketed for different genders. This 2020 state law joined a New York City ordinance that was enacted in 1998 in which the city's Department of Consumer Affairs was empowered to levy fines on firms such as dry-cleaners or hair salons that based prices solely on gender. "Specifically, the law prohibits the display of discriminatory pricing, meaning you shouldn't see a sign that says 'women's haircut $45, men's haircut $25' when you walk into a New York

City hairdresser" (Fontinelle 2023). Consumers can report complaints about suspected gender-based pricing on New York's "311" Customer Service Center to access governmental resources.

US Representative Jackie Speier, the former California legislator who sponsored that state's gender-based pricing act in 1995, introduced a similar proposal at the federal level in 2016. The purpose was to prohibit gender-based pricing in all fifty states. It incorporated the commonly used label of "pink tax" into its title, with the federal proposal officially being called the Pink Tax Repeal Act, followed by the subhead: "Prohibition on Gender-Based Pricing of Consumer Products and Services." It proposed that violators be subject to the Federal Trade Commission Act, within the classification of unfair or deceptive practices. Under the proposed legislation, clear violations of gender-based pricing would have come under the scrutiny of the Federal Trade Commission based on its consumer protection mandate. It was referred to the House Energy and Commerce subcommittee on Consumer Protection and Commerce, where it remained. Congress did not pass the bill in 2016 nor when it was reintroduced in 2021. In March of 2024, US Representative Norma Torres sponsored a new Pink Tax Repeal bill, once again seeking to prohibit different pricing of similar consumer products and services if they are based on the gender of the purchaser. The bill was again referred to committee where it remains as of this writing.

In 2016, soon after the CBS news report about upcharges for women was released, a neighborhood drugstore in New York City posted signs announcing that "all female customers could shop tax free, while all male customers were subject to a 7% man tax" (Cole 2024). The response was immediate, "creating backlash far beyond the intended purpose, [with] the small pharmacy being bombarded with emails and phone calls" (Gullo 2016). The signs came down after just one day. The business owner said that she did not really charge men more, but merely wanted to bring attention to the issue of gender-based pricing.

Some suggest that women can combat the pink tax through such tactics as buying clothes that do not need to be dry-cleaned, choosing products that are targeted at men or that are gender-neutral, figuring cost-per-ounce compared to comparable men's products, purchasing gender-neutral toys for girls, and contacting their local consumer protection agency if they see evidence of the pink tax. However, many—if not most—women and girls do not realize that products aimed at female consumers can be more expensive. If consumers are willing to pay more (even if unwittingly) for products marketed to women, there is little incentive for businesses to alter their approach.

Further Reading

CBS News. 2016. "CBS News Goes Undercover to Reveal Gender Price Discrimination." Accessed November 27, 2024. https://www.cbsnews.com/news/price-discrimination-gender-gap-cbs-news-undercover-dry-cleaners/.

Cole, Gail. 2024. "What Is the Pink Tax?" *Avalara*. Accessed November 27, 2024. https://www.avalara.com/blog/en/north-america/2023/05/what-is-the-pink-tax-and-will-it-have-an-impact-in-2023.html.

Crockett, Emily. 2016. "Women's Products Cost More. Here's How to Avoid the 'Pink Tax.'" *Vox*. Accessed November 27, 2024. https://www.vox.com/2016/3/1/11139280/avoid-pink-tax-women.

Fontinelle, Amy. 2023. "What Is the Pink Tax? Impact on Women, Regulation, and Laws." *Investopedia*. Accessed November 27, 2024. https://www.investopedia.com/pink-tax-5095458.

Gillespie, Lane. 2023. "The Pink Tax: Latest Updates and Statistics." Bankrate.com. Accessed November 27, 2024. https://www.bankrate.com/personal-finance/pink-tax-how-women-pay-more/#what-is.

Gullo, Joe. 2016. "NY Store Gets Backlash after Advertising 'Man Tax.'" ABC News10. Accessed November 27, 2024. https://www.news10.com/news/ny-store-gets-backlash-after-advertising-man-tax/.

Morgan Lewis Lawflash. 2002. "California 'Pink Tax' Law Prohibits Gender-Based Pricing of Consumer Products." Accessed November 27, 2024. https://www.morganlewis.com/pubs/2022/11/retail-dyk-california-pink-tax-law-prohibits-gender-based-pricing-of-consumer-products.

Nelson, Libby. 2015. "The Hidden Tax Women Pay on Just About Everything," *Vox*. Accessed November 27, 2024. https://www.vox.com/2015/12/23/10657762/women-products-cost-more.

Straka, Eric, Angela Smedley, and Kevin Simpson. 2022. "Will New 'Pink Tax' Legislation Green Light Class Actions Alleging Gender-Based Pricing Discrimination?" Winston.com. Accessed November 27, 2024. https://www.winston.com/en/blogs-and-podcasts/class-action-insider/will-new-pink-tax-legislation-green-light-class-actions-alleging-gender-based-pricing-discrimination.

US Government Accountability Office. 2018a. "Consumer Protection: Gender-Related Price Differences for Goods and Services." Accessed November 27, 2024. https://www.gao.gov/products/gao-18-500.

US Government Accountability Office. 2018b. "Is There a Pink Tax?" Accessed November 27, 2024. https://www.gao.gov/blog/2018/09/20/is-there-a-pink-tax.

4

Consumer Rights and Protections for Food and Beverages

In its most basic terms, food is the fuel that humans need to survive. Along with air and water, food is an absolute necessity in our lives. The nutrients in what we eat are vital to human health, but the quality and quantity of the food we ingest also has the potential to undermine our health.

Around 10,000 years ago, humans discovered the ability to grow their own crops instead of having to wander as nomads in search of edible plants to gather. Around the same time, instead of trying to hunt wild beasts as sources of meat, they found they could domesticate animals such as sheep, goats, and cattle to serve as food sources. In order to protect themselves along with their crops and animals, they banded together in settlements, often near sources of water. These became the prototypes for the cities and towns of modern civilization.

In addition to being utilized for food themselves, the waste from domesticated animals was found to be effective at enriching the soil to fertilize the fields where crops were planted. Their manure contains nitrogen, phosphorus, and other nutrients that plants need to grow. There was a downside to this symbiotic relationship, however. If contaminated water was used to irrigate the fields or if tainted meat was derived from infected animals carrying diseases like trichinosis, the food that humans ate could be dangerous. Through the centuries, illness and death have often been attributed to such causes as the wrath of angry deities or to the evils of witchcraft. The possibility of unsafe food was generally not considered as a factor until relatively recently in history, when scientific methods led to advancements in knowledge.

In the United States during the late nineteenth and early twentieth centuries, three events converged that would pave the way toward greater safety through consumer protections for the nation's food supply: first, a meat scandal during the Spanish American War of 1898; second, the 1906 publication of Upton Sinclair's book *The Jungle*; and finally, public outcry that resulted in the passage of America's Pure Food and Drug Act of 1906. Before those events took place, the first real challenge to the established American business practice of *caveat emptor* came from an unlikely source: fertilizer. Advances in developing alternative types of soil enrichment eventually decreased traditional reliance on manure and other animal by-products to replenish the growing fields. However, with increased reliance on fertilizers produced outside of the farm, consumers soon encountered adulteration in these products and demanded government oversight to protect their investments.

Q12: What part did fertilizer play in the development of consumer rights and protections?

Answer: With the growth of the Industrial Revolution and the population shift between small family farms to urban centers in the 1800s, the American food supply experienced a potential for catastrophe. Too much farming in the same place every growing season, with repeated plantings of a single crop, resulted in soil depletion. Over thousands of years of human history, the traditional solution to maintaining farmland had been adding animal-based waste to the soil in order to replenish its nutrients. However, by the mid-1800s, sources of fertilizer from domesticated animals were not enough. A highly potent source of fertilizer from outside the farm was found in guano, or seabird droppings, but as guano supplies ran low, suppliers began to adulterate the product by diluting it with other materials to stretch supply. The advent of chemical fertilizers was a scientific breakthrough for agriculture, but the quality of available products varied and consumers could not be sure of what was in them. This prompted public demands for government regulation along with a greater reluctance to accept the traditional rule of *caveat emptor*. It also led to the achievements of a scientist named Harvey Washington Wiley, who is considered the father of the kind of consumer protections for America's food supply that we depend on today.

The Facts: The road to consumer rights and protections in America could be said to have begun with bird droppings. In the mid-1800s, the need grew for more intensive large-scale agriculture, moving beyond the relatively simple requirements of individual farm families. Because of the rapid urbanization of America due to the Industrial Revolution, the nation's demographic patterns were shifting from rural areas to cities as people relocated in search of jobs. The number of farms was decreasing, but at the same time, the need for food in urban centers dramatically increased. Many farmers expanded their acreage to meet the rising demand. In addition, especially in America's southern states, huge plantations tended to harvest the same cash crop such as cotton or tobacco year after year, which steadily depleted the soil. Traditional methods of fertilization with domestic animal waste that had sustained small family farms for centuries were no longer enough.

As soil depletion resulting from intensive farming practices and urbanization put immense pressure on the nation's farmland, a miracle seemed to appear on the horizon at exactly the right time. In the early nineteenth century, American seafarers encountered something that looked like snow-capped mountains towering over waters in the Pacific Ocean and Caribbean Sea. What appeared to be mountain peaks were actually thousands of years of compressed seabird droppings, a substance that became known as guano. For untold millennia, deposits of seabird guano steadily built up on small islands where it rarely rained. Century after century of baking in the sun made the tall mountains of guano hard as rock. Local indigenous people described the substance as an exceptionally potent form of fertilizer; tests found it to have "a remarkably high nitrogen content that promoted plant growth" (Johnston 2017). When the news of this remarkable fertilizing substance became known throughout Europe and the United States, a rush was on to profit from the "guano islands."

Across America, both small farmers and owners of huge plantations created a tremendous demand for guano. However, as the material was located on small, remote islands, it was difficult to find, dig up, and transport. Prices rose to the point that in 1850, mining guano and keeping its prices reasonable became the leading topic of the State of the Union address by US President Millard Fillmore, who said that guano was so desirable "to the agricultural interest of the United States" that the government would "employ all the means properly in its power" to obtain it "at a reasonable price" (Fillmore 1850).

By that time, some fertilizer manufacturers were seeking to stretch their products—and profits—by cutting their guano-based fertilizing material with inert additives such as sawdust. As the guano was mined out, steadily becoming even more of a rarity, the increase in adulterated fertilizers became a critical problem. Crops began to fail because unsuspecting farmers bought fertilizing products containing ineffective additives that did nothing to replenish the soil. America relied on agriculture. Growing cities depended on farmers to provide food for urban masses. Effective fertilizer was vital for crops to flourish, and the average farmer did not have extra money to waste on products that did not work. If fertilizer had been adulterated with useless additives, the problem was not usually apparent until several months into the growing season, by which time it was too late for the farmer to try again with a different fertilizing agent. As supplies of guano ran out and newly developed chemical fertilizers became available, buyers experienced the same types of problems, as they could not be sure of the quality or type of ingredients in these manufactured products.

Many farmers in the mid-nineteenth century were becoming disenchanted by the concept of *caveat emptor*. Caution on the part of the buyer was not sufficient to protect farmers' livelihoods. Protests regarding the bogus commercial fertilizers that plagued American farmers were among the first calls for consumer rights and protections, challenging the prevailing ethos against government involvement in commerce. The outcry over fake products flooding the marketplace led several states to implement testing and inspection laws for commercial fertilizers. However, even with testing and inspection, some manufacturers "produced high-quality fertilizers to gain endorsements ... but then adulterated [their] products in subsequent seasons to pad profit margins" (Balleisen 2017, 115).

Despite the fraud committed by these fertilizer manufacturers, some Americans, including many in government positions, continued to promote *caveat emptor*. One supporter of unregulated free enterprise was the secretary of Maine's Board of Agriculture, whose solution to the problem of farmers paying for ineffectual fertilizer was instructing them to seek out "honest manufacturers and dealers" (Balleisen 2017, 116–17). The burden was placed on consumers to "shop around" rather than having the government enact laws regulating private enterprise. Fertilizer manufacturers "opposed new regulations as an unjust imposition on their commercial liberty" (Balleisen 2017, 117).

One of the states that implemented consumer protection laws mandating the inspection of fertilizers in the late 1800s was Indiana. A chemist at that state's Purdue University, Harvey Washington Wiley was known for publicly condemning the practice of adulterating fertilizers. In 1881, Wiley was appointed state chemist by the Indiana State Board of Health to analyze agricultural products so that the state government could regulate the manufacture and sale of commercial fertilizers in its jurisdiction.

In 1883, Wiley relocated to Washington, DC, to serve as chief chemist at the US Department of Agriculture (USDA). From his experience in the agricultural state of Indiana, Wiley brought a practical knowledge of the challenges faced by farmers, including their role as consumers who could find themselves being duped by paying for worthless fertilizing products. At the same time, Wiley felt that adulterated foods had become a related problem for American consumers and began running tests at the USDA on suspected impure foods. However, he was ordered by his department head "to concentrate only on science that could directly benefit farmers [by] making more effective fertilizers and pesticides" (Blum 2018, 40). Wiley's budget was cut by two-thirds because his supervisor questioned whether there was really a need to test for adulterants in food. Wiley persisted despite opposition from his superiors, analyzing various common grocery items in his basement lab at the USDA—at times, barely keeping his job. He was ordered to stop releasing his findings about unsafe food to the news media as well as through his speaking engagements, with his boss stating that "the Agriculture Department's mission did not include educating the public" (Blum 2018, 41).

Wiley kept up his work, and his efforts were bolstered by the 1906 publication of Upton Sinclair's *The Jungle*, a book that underscored his claims about unsafe food. The book generated a public demand throughout the nation for food safety regulations at the federal level. Many observers believe that had it not been for Wiley's work, which had started with testing fertilizers, the Pure Food and Drug bill of 1906, often called "Wiley's Law," probably would not have passed. But the bill did pass, eventually leading to others by setting a precedent. The path toward weakening the grasp of *caveat emptor* and strengthening consumer protections in America, particularly regarding food, had begun in a seemingly improbable place: fertilizer.

Further Reading

Balleisen, Edward. 2017. *Fraud: An American History from Barnum to Madoff.* Princeton, NJ: Princeton University Press, 115, 116, 117.

Blum, Deborah. 2018. *The Poison Squad: One Chemist's Single-Minded Crusade for Food Safety at the Turn of the Twentieth Century.* New York: Penguin, 40, 41.

Institute of Agriculture and Natural Resources. 2015. "Fertilizer Moves from Bones to Chemistry: A Historical Overview of Fertilizer Use." University of Nebraska-Lincoln Cropwatch. Accessed November 27, 2024. https://cropwatch.unl.edu/fertilizer-history-p2.

Fillmore, Millard. 1850. "December 2, 1850: First Annual Message." University of Virginia Miller Center. Accessed November 27, 2024. https://millercenter.org/the-presidency/presidential-speeches/december-2-1850-first-annual-message.

Johnston, Paul F. 2017. "The Smithsonian and the 19th Century Guano Trade." *Smithsonian.* Accessed November 27, 2024. https://americanhistory.si.edu/blog/smithsonian-and-guano.

Richardson-Price, Alex. 2016. "The Soil Depletion Crisis." *History Today*. Accessed November 27, 2024. https://www.historytoday.com/archive/history-matters/soil-depletion-crisis.

Science History Institute. n.d. "Harvey Washington Wiley." Accessed September 10, 2024. https://sciencehistory.org/education/scientific-biographies/harvey-washington-wiley/.

Q13: How were the "Margarine Wars" and "Pure Ketchup Campaign" significant in consumer protections for food?

Answer: The concept of *caveat emptor* was prevalent in the American marketplace through the nineteenth century, even pertaining to the nation's food supply. However, two commodities began to loosen the grip of the entrenched view that the buyer needed to beware and the government had no place interfering with private enterprise. Dairy-related products came under scrutiny when a new item called "oleomargarine" was introduced as a low-cost alternative to butter around 1870. Enraged dairy producers clamored for government intervention to put a stop to the new substance that was undercutting their market. Soon after, beginning in 1876, food processor Henry Heinz became an outspoken advocate of food safety, promoting the purity of his brand of ketchup. Both the "Margarine Wars" and the "Pure Ketchup Campaign" were early skirmishes in moving the nation toward the kind of consumer protections for food that we take for granted today.

The Facts: In the latter part of the 1800s, around the time when adulterated fertilizer was swaying support by farmers toward government regulation, two other consumer items initiated responses from those who hoped to counteract *caveat emptor* by encouraging greater government intervention in the marketplace: margarine and ketchup.

In 1869, Emperor Napoleon III of France was facing a problem that was also becoming more evident in the United States. With more French citizens moving to the city, generating the necessity to feed large numbers, butter had become both expensive and scarce. The emperor created a contest, offering a prize for the best alternative to butter. The result in that nation of food lovers was a combination of oils and water that came to be called "oleomargarine." "Oleo" referred to oil, and because the original substance was white in color, the name "margarine" was loosely derived from a Greek word for "pearl."

After its arrival in America during the 1870s, oleomargarine quickly became a success among consumers in the United States, much to the horror of American dairy farmers. "In the decade after margarine arrived . . . 37 margarine companies sprang up to make the stuff. The dairy lobby wasn't about to let butter get put out to pasture, though" (Eschner 2017). Recognizing the threat to their industry, butter producers were swift in their response, initiating what came to be called the "Margarine Wars." Seeking government regulations on oleomargarine, a marketing campaign by the dairy industry attempted to convince both politicians and the public that the substance was trying to impersonate butter in the marketplace. Not only that, they claimed, margarine was unhealthy. "Pro-butter political cartoonists pictured factories dropping everything from stray cats to soap, paint, arsenic, and rubber boots into the margarine mix [and] dubious scientific reports hinted that margarine caused cancer, or possibly led to insanity" (Eschner 2017).

Dairy lobbyists gained ground on the state level in 1877 when New York and Maryland passed laws regulating the manufacture and sale of oleomargarine. Wisconsin followed in 1881. By the mid-1880s, there were seventeen states that regulated the production of margarine, with some banning its manufacture and sale outright. That number would grow until some states gradually relaxed the margarine ban over time, although Wisconsin did not repeal its prohibition on margarine until 1967.

Even with many state governments approving restrictions, thereby interfering with private enterprise on the state level, margarine was still seen as a threat to butter manufacturers in other states, and therefore to butter production as a whole. Dairy lobbyists pushed for federal legislation so that the danger to their industry could be curbed across the nation, not just in individual states. The 1886 Oleomargarine Act was a federal law imposing restrictive tariffs as well as levying special taxes and annual license fees on producers of margarine. As a result, consumers would have to pay a higher price for what began as a low-cost alternative. The 1886 federal law remained in place until 1950, when it was repealed after surveys showed that American consumers favored abolishing the margarine tax.

Although the 1886 Oleomargarine Act protected an industry rather than consumers, its passing set a precedent for federal government involvement in the marketplace that would have long-term effects on consumer rights and protections for food in America. In addition, powerful supporters of unrestricted capitalism who traditionally maintained that the government had no place interfering with private enterprise began to see the value in government protections for a particular industry—in this case, dairy—against new competitors. Their own businesses might benefit from government protection someday.

Another legacy of the Margarine Wars was increased attention to coloring in food. Amid anti-margarine sentiment, some states enacted laws that required makers of oleomargarine to add pink coloring to the product, which was white in its pure form. The resulting pink color was somewhat off-putting, causing margarine manufacturers to stringently object. The mandate for pink margarine eventually faded, but it did inspire the federal government to review color standards for food. For example, in the 1970s, Red Dye No. 2 was said by Soviet scientists to cause cancer. The coloring was used in popular American food products such as Jell-O, Kool-Aid, and M&M candies. The federal government banned Red Dye No. 2 in 1976 after more than twenty years of debate. Government oversight in the color of food extended to fruits and vegetables, which the USDA continues to categorize into grades with color being an important criterion.

In 1876, a century before the Red Dye controversy, food manufacturer Henry J. Heinz (1844–1919) was producing a bright red tomato-based condiment called ketchup, a product that he considered to be a "blessed relief for mother and other women in the household" because it saved them from the labor-intensive process of making it themselves (Lukas and Overfelt 2003). Ketchup was not a new product. During the 1500s, international traders found it being used to enhance the flavor of food in China. To them, the Chinese word for the condiment sounded like "catsup" or "ketchup." It was a brownish fermented fish brine with no tomatoes in sight. After being brought to the United States, some ketchup recipes called for ingredients such as mushrooms, nuts, or shallots. The result usually ended up looking like lumpy soy sauce instead of what we now know as ketchup. When manufacturers started to bottle these early versions, consumers discovered that the brown liquid they had bought would spoil quickly.

In Pittsburgh, Pennsylvania, Henry Heinz started earning money as a young man in 1860 by selling grated horseradish based on his mother's recipe. He noticed that most other producers sold prepared horseradish in dark jars because "the dealers had adulterated it to so great an extent by adding turnip and wood fibers as filler" (Lukas and Overfelt 2003). To set his pure horseradish apart, Heinz bottled his in clear glass so consumers could see what they were buying.

Heinz noticed brisk sales of prepared brown ketchup, which sold well because it was so labor-intensive to make at home. Setting out to market the product himself, his H. J. Heinz Company, founded in 1869, went to work. Heinz staffers developed what Henry considered to be a product that was superior to the thin, lumpy, muddy brown substance being sold on the open market. He added a thick tomato base, which added stability to his product. Starting in 1876, he sold bright red "Heinz Ketchup" in clear bottles. This was not only to spotlight his product's cheery color but also, as he had done with his horseradish, to provide consumers with visual evidence of its purity.

In the face of malicious hostility by rivals, the Heinz company "helped standardize bottle and can sterilization, insisted that workers abide by strict rules of cleanliness, and even pushed for sanitary food processing legislation" (Bentley 2018). Going a step further, Henry Heinz opened his factory to public tours, the first known food processor to do so. "The tours were an immediate hit and by 1900 were attracting 20,000 visitors annually" (Lukas and Overfelt 2003). In addition, "Heinz welcomed government regulators into his factories and fought to make them come, all the while hoping that 'regulation would make the industry respectable and trusted'" (Slivka 2008).

Competitors claimed that Heinz ketchup was too expensive for average consumers, predicting that the new tomato ketchup would fail. They were wrong. Sales of Heinz ketchup skyrocketed, which Henry Heinz felt was a confirmation of his belief that American consumers would pay a little more for food that was safe and of good quality. Over time, other food processors followed Heinz's lead, with his tomato ketchup eventually becoming the industry standard. "Ketchup's appeal is in part because it embodies principles that Americans prize including consistency, value, and cleanliness" (Bentley 2018).

In the late 1800s and early 1900s, consumers were becoming more cognizant of issues involving food purity and safety. Henry Heinz was anxious to differentiate his company from unscrupulous producers who added unknown fillers and preservatives to their products. He was one of the first food producers to publicly support proposed laws on government involvement with food safety. Heinz even sent his son Howard to Washington "to get President Theodore Roosevelt behind the movement" (Lukas and Overfelt 2003).

None of Heinz's efforts were popular with his business rivals and other industrialists, especially those who resisted any government interference with private enterprise. They began circulating rumors that Heinz was using a secret—and possibly deadly—chemical agent as a preservative. "His competitors even spread rumors that the company was in favor of Prohibition [of liquor], which led to boycotts of Heinz products" (Slivka 2008). But Heinz survived the smear campaign, living to see his tomato ketchup become the gold standard. "In 1909, Heinz's sales were $6.13 million. By 1914 they'd almost doubled, to $12 million. By the time H.J. Heinz died in 1919 at the age of 75, the company's revenue exceeded $20 million and it employed more than 6,500 people" (Lukas and Overfelt 2003).

Throughout his life, Henry Heinz consistently fought for consumer protections. Despite strong opposition from other companies, he publicly supported the 1906 Pure Food and Drug Act. "He was risking his own business and his own position in the trade, because he knew in the long run it would be for the good of the food business and its best chance of survival" (Slivka 2008). Harvey Washington Wiley, the father of the 1906 Pure Food and Drug Act, recognized those efforts, writing to Heinz, "I feel I should have lost the fight if I had not had [your] assistance" (Slivka 2008). Ketchup and margarine paved the way for the consumer protections for food that we have today.

Further Reading

Bentley, Amy. 2018. "How Ketchup Revolutionized How Food Is Grown, Processed and Regulated." *Smithsonian*. Accessed November 27, 2024. https://www.smithsonianmag.com/innovation/how-ketchup-revolutionized-how-food-is-grown-processed-regulated-180969230/.

Eschner, Kat. 2017. "The 1870s Dairy Lobby Turned Margarine Pink So People Would Buy Butter." *Smithsonian*. Accessed November 27, 2024. https://www.smithsonianmag.com/smart-news/1870s-dairy-lobby-turned-margarine-pink-so-people-would-buy-butter-180963328/.

Hisano, Ai. 2020. "How the Government Came to Decide the Color of Your Food." *Smithsonian*. Accessed November 27, 2024. https://www.smithsonianmag.com/innovation/how-government-came-to-decide-color-your-food-180973962/.

Lukas, Paul, and Maggie Overfelt. 2003. "H.J. Heinz: At a Time When Prepared Food Was a Shady Business, Heinz's Transparent Jars, Factory Tours, and Focus on Food Safety Made His Store-Bought Condiments King." CNN. Accessed November 27, 2024. https://money.cnn.com/magazines/fsb/fsb_archive/2003/04/01/341007/.

Science History Institute. 2017. "Butter vs. Margarine: One of America's Most Bizarre Food Battles." Accessed November 27, 2024. https://chemheritage.org/stories/distillations-pod/butter-vs-margarine/.

Slivka, Anne. 2008. "H.J. Heinz: Concerned Citizen or Clever Capitalist?" The Ellis School. Accessed November 27, 2024. https://www.theellisschool.org/list-detail?pk=29093.

Q14: How did the "Poison Squad" advance consumer rights and protections?

Answer: By the end of the nineteenth century, there was growing interest in the safety of America's food supply. Prior to that time, food products—as well as almost all other consumer items—were marketed under the aegis of *caveat emptor*, leaving it up to the buyer to beware when making a purchase. For the most part, official regulations did not offer protections because those in power maintained that the government had no business interfering with private enterprise. However, by the late nineteenth and early twentieth centuries, newspaper stories were bringing abuses by the food industry to the attention of average consumers, and a few individuals were publicly fighting for food safety. While those individuals were somewhat known locally, it took a scientific experiment focusing on toxic food additives to gain the kind of traction that was needed to challenge *caveat emptor*. Dubbed the "Poison Squad" by the press, the project's colorful nickname generated national attention on greater consumer protections to defend Americans from dangers in the food they ate.

The Facts: In the late nineteenth and early twentieth centuries, several individuals called for consumer protections for food, although their influence was limited. One of the first people to assert concerns about food safety was chemist John Newell Hurty (1852–1925). In 1884, Hurty became a professor of pharmacy at Indiana's Purdue University. The previous year, his old friend Harvey Washington Wiley, another Purdue faculty member, had left the university after being chosen to direct the Bureau of Chemistry at the US Department of Agriculture (USDA) in Washington. Hurty, like Wiley, developed a strong interest in public health. Named Indiana's chief health officer in 1896, Hurty was determined to reduce his state's disease rates.

Especially angered about practices in marketing milk, he was appalled by the contamination of the food product and the unsanitary processes involved in the dairy industry. Hurty's tests determined that milk, a necessity for children, was generally either swarming with bacteria or preserved with toxic chemicals. He claimed that dirty milk was responsible for such common diseases as dysentery and typhoid, which resulted from a lack of sanitation. Hurty convinced the Indiana legislature to pass a food safety law in 1899. It was not until the next century that the federal government challenged private enterprise by passing the first national pure food act.

With an interest in public health, Alice Lakey (1857–1935) of Cranford, New Jersey, became chair of her town's Improvement Association. In the early 1900s, recognizing a link between better sanitary practices and good health, Lakey arranged public education programs for the town. For one such occasion, she contacted the US Department of Agriculture requesting a guest speaker to lecture about impure food. In 1903, Harvey Washington Wiley, chief of the

USDA's Bureau of Chemistry, came to Cranford to speak. Inspired by his work toward seeking a national food safety law after dozens of proposals had failed, Alice Lakey began speaking at women's clubs around the country on the topic.

Women did not yet have the right to vote, but in 1904, Lakey persuaded the New Jersey Federation of Women's Clubs to petition Congress to enact a pure food and drug bill. She also convinced the National Consumers League (NCL) to support the cause of pure food. When the NCL decided to probe conditions in food processing plants in 1905, they appointed Lakey to head the investigation committee. That year, Lakey personally met with President Theodore Roosevelt to urge his support for a pure food bill. Roosevelt said he would do so if enough signed letters were sent to Congress. Lakey then "influenced over one million women to write letters supporting the bill" (Redman 2007, 139). After the Pure Food and Drug Act was passed in 1906, Lakey continued to work for improved food safety. For her efforts, "Lakey was the first woman to be listed in *Who's Who*," an annual publication that is a biographical listing of notable people (Redman 2007, 139).

Another individual who gained fame during the late 1800s and early 1900s became the first of America's superstar chefs. As head of the Boston Cooking School, Fannie Merritt Farmer (1857–1915) believed in what she considered to be a scientific approach to cooking. Under her leadership, the school taught not only how to cook, but also emphasized the critical roles of nutrition and sanitation for good health. In 1896, she first published *The Fannie Farmer Cookbook*. It was aimed at average homemakers and domestic servants instead of professional chefs, instructing Americans on the basics of health, nutrition, and food safety. Her recipes were easily duplicated, giving homemakers control over the food they prepared and helping to improve the family's physical health.

Farmer specifically stated in her cookbook that following the principles of food science would lead to reduction in disease. In an age before home refrigeration, she showed ways to preserve foods without the kind of harmful chemicals that were routinely being added to commercially processed food products. She was a charismatic public speaker who gained fame by addressing women's clubs across the country. Farmer was one of the first women to lecture at Harvard Medical School, where she stressed the special importance of providing healthy food for chronic invalids and sick people. She also joined the call for federal regulations to ensure pure food for the consumers of the nation. "Farmer was the first prominent figure to advocate scientific cookery. Her cookbook remains in print to this day" (Eschner 2017).

With individuals such as Hurty, Lakey, and Farmer emerging into the spotlight, a new emphasis on the importance of food safety was taking hold in the country. All three figures were prominent in a limited way. However, their fame did not approach that of one person they all championed, a man whose name became synonymous with America's first pure food act that endeavored to protect the nation's consumers: Harvey Washington Wiley (1844–1930).

Wiley spent his early years in Indiana as a chemist who began his career analyzing ineffective additives in fertilizers. He also began to investigate food and drugs, believing that they contained harmful substances that were being sold to unsuspecting consumers. After Wiley was recruited to head the Bureau of Chemistry at the US Department of Agriculture as chief chemist in 1883, he issued report after report about harmful additives in food, most of which were ignored by his politically appointed superiors.

Rapid industrialization and urbanization meant that food had to travel farther from its source to reach city dwellers. In that era, before widespread refrigeration, food spoiled quickly. Manufacturers added "chemical preservatives into food to keep it fresh as it traveled from the farm into rapidly growing American cities. Milk no longer went rancid! Meat no longer spoiled!" (Twilley and Graber 2018). These preservatives increased profits for manufacturers, as they could sell products that were past their prime and would otherwise have to be discarded. Today's notion of a "Sell By" date was a nonexistent concept.

Like his friend, fellow Indianan John Hurty, Wiley was appalled at what was being added to preserve milk, including formaldehyde, a routine additive borrowed from the embalming process performed by undertakers. Mealtime in the average American home at the time often contained other common additives, including chalk, copper sulfate, methyl alcohol, plaster of Paris, prussic acid, salicylic acid, sodium benzoate, and/or sulfuric acid. "And almost everything contained borax, a buffering agent used in many cleaning products, including the laundry detergent booster called '20 Mule Team Borax'" (Watson 2023). Because there were no labeling requirements, the foods purchased by consumers did not list ingredients. Wiley attempted to gain support for his efforts toward pure food by speaking about additives on the lecture circuit, even reciting a poem he wrote in 1899 titled *I Wonder What's in It*. Wiley invited listeners to envision an imaginary American dinner at which the meal looks delicious, but

> We cannot help asking, "What's in it?
> Oh, maybe this bread contains alum or chalk
> Or sawdust chopped up very fine

Or gypsum in powder about which they talk,
Terra alba just out of the mine." (Blum 2018b, xi)

The poem contains a virtual checklist of adulterations that were present in food products at the time of its writing, along with "germs, each armed with a hook / to grapple with liver and spleen" (Blum 2018b, xi).

Wiley risked his job by going over the heads of his supervisors when he submitted a pure food law proposal to the US Congress in 1899. In the face of influence by lobbyists from food processors along with congressmen who opposed any type of government regulations, the bill was buried. Dozens of subsequent pure food proposals met the same fate, even those that were seriously watered down. Wiley pushed for proper food labeling, to let consumers know that the product they were buying contained substances like borax. When he went a step further, publicly asserting that certain common chemical additives in food should be banned, the food industry rose up to protest. Wiley accused lobbyists of trying to kill congressional legislation. The result was that "bills were banned, blocked, tabled. Congress slashed Wiley's budgets. His name was slurred in industry propaganda" (Watson 2023). Still, Wiley carried on.

Wiley might have continued to labor in relative obscurity had it not been for his passion about the need for food safety to protect American consumers and his particularly inventive mind. He decided to launch a study that he called the Hygienic Table Trials, which would later become known popularly by the much catchier name, the "Poison Squad." In 1902, Wiley requested $5,000 from the USDA (about $175,000 in today's money) to begin his food testing. He wanted to study the effects of various preservatives that were routinely being added to foods sold to American consumers. Wiley began his study by selecting a dozen healthy young male volunteers, all government workers, who were paid $5 a month (about $154 today) to consume three meals a day containing various commonplace food additives. "All were graduates of the civil service exam, all were screened for 'high moral character'" (Fessenden 2015). They were sworn to secrecy, pledging to provide one year of service on the project, promising to eat only food that was prepared in the USDA lab as part of the experiment. Wiley hung a sign outside the kitchen that read "NONE BUT THE BRAVE CAN EAT THE FARE" (Watson 2023).

The volunteers understood the dangers in the work they were undertaking and agreed to waive their right to sue the government "for damages—including death—that might result from their participation in the program" (Fessenden 2015). There were rumors that some deaths had occurred, but this was not proven. That is not to say that the young men remained as healthy as they had been when they went in. The first tests by Wiley's group concerned the use of borax as an additive, commonly used to preserve milk and added to meat that was starting to decompose. "Borax caused headaches, stomach aches, vomiting. ... [The] strapping young men [were] sickened, nauseated, 'losing flesh'" (Watson 2023). In tests of other substances, the young men experienced problems "including irritation, nausea, headache, vomiting and weight loss" (Blum 2018b, 183). Meanwhile, American consumers were eating food with the same additives. As the volunteer participants in Wiley's group were all males, it is hard to say what effect the same quantity of additives in adulterated food was having on women and children with smaller bodies, as well as on older people or invalids with less resiliency.

Eventually word leaked about the experiment and the toxic effects of food additives on healthy human bodies. A Washington, DC, newspaper reporter thought that the name "Hygienic Table Trials" was rather lackluster and dubbed the experiment the "Poison Squad," which caught on. Fannie Farmer may have been a household name in many homes due to her cookbook, but a catchy name like the Poison Squad swept the nation like wildfire, becoming the focus of newspaper articles and cartoons. The study's young volunteers "became celebrities with their own theme song, *The Song of The Poison Squad* by S.W. Gillilan, which included the upbeat lyrics: 'On Prussic acid we break our fast; we lunch on a morphine stew'" (Edwards 2015). The publicity brought attention to the fact that the public were ingesting food with the same additives that sickened the Poison Squad.

After the study was over, the Poison Squad volunteers apparently regained their strength on a steady diet of healthy food. As one author wrote, "No one knows what happened to them, but we thank them for their service. In the new century, the worst of the additives that Americans had once devoured found other uses. Borax became a laundry agent, copper sulfate a pesticide. Formaldehyde returned to labs" (Watson 2023). The Poison Squad advanced the cause of consumer protections in the food we eat, safeguards we often take for granted today. While the young volunteers went back to lives of anonymity, Harvey Washington Wiley did not. Bolstered by the strength of publicity surrounding the Poison Squad trials, he kept battling waves of political and industrial opposition. After decades of fighting for consumer protections in the American food supply, he ultimately emerged victorious. Even though his name is largely forgotten today, when the landmark 1906 Food and Drug Act was finally passed, it was widely known as "Wiley's Law."

Some observers feel that it may not be prudent to consign Wiley and the Poison Squad to being relics of a long-forgotten age. "In theory, Wiley's success should ensure that all preservatives added to our food today are safe. But in reality, a legislative update in 1958 created a loophole that means that, today, we have no idea exactly how many additives are in our food or how safe they are" (Twilley and Graber 2018).

Further Reading

Blum, Deborah. 2018a. "The 19th-Century Fight Against Bacteria-Ridden Milk Preserved with Embalming Fluid." *Smithsonian.* Accessed November 27, 2024. https://www.smithsonianmag.com/science-nature/19th-century-fight-bacteria-ridden-milk-embalming-fluid-180970473/.

Blum, Deborah. 2018b. *The Poison Squad: One Chemist's Single-Minded Crusade for Food Safety at the Turn of the Twentieth Century.* New York: Penguin, xi, 31, 183.

Edwards, Phil. 2015. "None But the Brave: The 1902 Poison Squad That Tested the Chemicals Put in Our Food—by Eating Them." *Vox.* Accessed November 27, 2024. https://www.vox.com/2015/1/8/7507855/weird-food-heroes.

Eschner, Kat. 2017. "Fannie Farmer Was the Original Rachael Ray." *Smithsonian.* Accessed November 27, 2024. https://www.smithsonianmag.com/smart-news/fannie-farmer-was-original-rachael-ray-180964564/.

Fessenden, Maris. 2015. "Early Food Safety Workers Tested Poisons by Eating Them." *Smithsonian.* Accessed November 27, 2024. https://www.smithsonianmag.com/smart-news/early-food-safety-workers-us-tested-poisons-eating-them-180953864/.

"The Poison Squad: The American People Had No Idea What They Were Eating." 2020. *American Experience.* Accessed November 27, 2024. https://www.pbs.org/wgbh/americanexperience/films/poison-squad/.

Redman, Nina. 2007. *Food Safety: A Reference Handbook—Second Edition.* Santa Barbara, CA: ABC-CLIO, 139.

Twilley, Nicola, and Cynthia Graber. 2018. "The 'Poison Squad' That Shook America's Faith in Preservatives." *The Atlantic.* Accessed November 27, 2024. https://www.theatlantic.com/science/archive/2018/08/the-poison-squad-that-shook-americas-faith-in-preservatives/568753/.

Watson, Bruce. 2023. "Saved by the Poison Squad." *American Heritage.* Accessed November 27, 2024. https://www.americanheritage.com/saved-poison-squad.

Q15: What impact did Upton Sinclair's *The Jungle* have on consumer rights and protections?

Answer: In 1906, a novel titled *The Jungle* by American author Upton Sinclair (1878–1968) was published. The book would ultimately lead to a watershed event for consumer protection in the United States, the landmark Pure Food and Drug Act of 1906. Sinclair stated that his intention in writing *The Jungle* was to depict the suffering of destitute laborers who were working in Chicago's meatpacking industry. However, in the process, he exposed not only the exploitation of people for profit, but also the filthy, inhumane conditions at meatpacking plants that sent tainted products to the marketplace for sale to unsuspecting consumers. The American public was already outraged by abuses in the meatpacking industry that took place during the Spanish American War in 1898. US President Theodore Roosevelt (1858–1919) had first-hand knowledge of what came to be called the "embalmed beef" scandal, using his clout to drive approval of food safety laws. For the first time, the federal government claimed the power to truly regulate private enterprise in order to protect American consumers from the worst abuses of *caveat emptor*.

The Facts: On March 26, 1899, the *New York Times* ran a lengthy, eye-catching headline: "Roosevelt on Army Beef; Testifies That the Canned Roast Stuff Sickened His Men. Would Sooner Eat His Hat. It Was Slimy and Nasty—A Disgrace to the Country—'Embalmed Beef on Transport'" ("Roosevelt on Army Beef" 1899). According to science writer Deborah Blum (2020), there were accusations that tainted meat supplies had killed more soldiers in the Spanish American War than those who were shot by the enemy. Serving in Cuba during the war, soldiers ranking from officers to enlisted men, including Theodore Roosevelt and his Rough Riders, accused the Army of feeding them meat that was rotting or decayed and packed with the preservative formaldehyde, a chemical used by undertakers to embalm human corpses.

The federal government held hearings amid a public uproar. They found that the "embalmed beef" had been sold by companies who packed their products with chemicals "to mask the stench of the rotten meat. Troops who consumed the meat fell ill, becoming unfit for combat, and some died" (Rouse n.d.). Although the US Secretary of War resigned amid overwhelming evidence, the hearings concluded that the beef served to soldiers was no worse than what was being sold in American grocery stores. This fact may have been seen by some as a classic example of good news/bad news. In any case, no charges were brought against the military.

A former supervisor at a leading meatpacking plant signed an affidavit "stating that the company's common practice was to pack and sell 'carrion'" (Rouse n.d.). *Merriam-Webster* dictionary defines "carrion" as dead, putrefying flesh such as roadkill. However, because there were no federal laws regarding food safety, the meatpackers could not be prosecuted. In the face of public outrage, the packing companies stated they would monitor themselves.

Since the late 1800s, Harvey Washington Wiley at the US Department of Agriculture had been proposing food safety bills to protect American consumers. Still, "Congress remained reluctant to alienate the food and chemical industries, which provided legislators with thousands of dollars every year" (Blum 2020). But feeding rotten meat to American fighting men, harming them while they were trying to win a war for the United States, had angered the public. It was still on the minds of many people in 1906 when the meatpacking industry again found itself in the middle of an uproar.

Attention became focused on what was called the Beef Trust, a group consisting of about a half-dozen large meatpacking companies, with their packing plants near the massive Chicago stockyards. From time to time, there were articles by journalists at a few small publications describing exploited workers, filthy packing plants, inhumane conditions, and tactics by the Beef Trust to avoid inspection. But the publications were not generally the kind of mainstream media that would be guaranteed to catch the attention of the majority of the public.

That changed in 1906 after Upton Sinclair finally found a company willing to publish his shocking book, *The Jungle*. The 26-year-old Sinclair had done his research by living in a Chicago settlement house among workers "who smuggled him into meatpacking plants so he could view conditions firsthand" (Diedrick n.d.) When submitting his manuscript for the novel, Sinclair found that publishers were unwilling to accept it. One found the book to be "gloom and horror unrelieved" (Blum 2020). Among other issues, there was a demand to "cut Sinclair's overt comparisons of worker life to an existence in a wild forest with 'the strong devouring the weak'—the source of his title" (Blum 2020). One potential publisher, albeit a reluctant one, launched a secret, independent investigation, finding it hard to believe that Sinclair's allegations were even remotely true. The investigators, including the publisher's attorney, "returned disgusted and horrified by what they'd seen" (Blum 2020). Reassured that everything in Sinclair's book was true, and then some, advance copies were sent to the Associated Press and United Press for nationwide coverage, along with copies for magazines and newspapers in every major American city. After *The Jungle* was published by Doubleday on February 26, 1906, the book became a bombshell. Even those who did not buy one of the 150,000 copies that sold in the first year knew about it from the press or by word of mouth. It even "attracted the attention of prominent figures around the world, such as Winston Churchill, who praised Sinclair for making the 'great Beef Trust stink in the nostrils of the world' " (Greenspan 2022).

At the time, tuberculosis, which was highly contagious for both humans and animals, was one of America's leading causes of death. Sinclair's book "described diseased cattle arriving by railroad in Chicago to be butchered and sold to American housewives … Tuberculosis germs thrived in the moist, stinking air of the processing plants and spread from animal to animal, worker to worker" (Blum 2020). In addition, the book "related that the packers routinely put out poisoned bread to keep the rat population down, and 'then the rats, bread and meat would go into the hoppers together' " (Blum 2020). Many people were particularly disturbed by descriptions of the rendering rooms where there were open vats of acid set into the floor to help break down the carcasses. Workers occasionally fell in and were eaten alive by the acid. As Sinclair wrote, they might "be overlooked for days till all but the bones of them had gone out into the world as … Durham's Pure Leaf Lard" (Sinclair 2001). Severed fingers from workers on the cutting line were ground up with the rest of the meat that was shipped across America.

Sinclair's publisher sent an autographed copy of the book to President Theodore Roosevelt, who ordered that the claims in *The Jungle* be investigated by the US Department of Agriculture. The USDA "fact-checkers" reported back that the book was mostly exaggerations, if not out-and-out lies. Roosevelt secretly instructed other investigators—outside the USDA—to take a look because he "distrusted its close ties to the meatpacking industry" (Greenspan 2022). Among other things, Roosevelt's secret investigators found that during the processing, meat was "gathering dirt, splinters, floor filth, and the expectorations of tuberculous and other diseased workers" (Greenspan 2022). As employees were not granted restroom breaks, laborers were observed urinating alongside the meat, with their excrement joining the animal manure that ended up in the food products on American dinner tables.

President Roosevelt ordered two more private investigations of conditions in the plants., which were found to be as bad as Sinclair had depicted in *The Jungle*, if not worse. Roosevelt invited the author to come to Washington, where they found that they both backed federal food safety laws. The president referred to the Beef Trust by stating, "Mr. Sinclair, I bear no love for those gentlemen, for I ate the meat they canned for the army in Cuba" (Klein 2023).

But there were also economic factors that inclined a seasoned politician like Roosevelt to act. In addition to sales of meat dropping within the United States after *The Jungle* was published, "Germany and France banned American meat products, and British imports of American canned meat ceased" (Klein 2023). The European refusal to import American meat helped the president to pressure Congress to stop stalling on food safety legislation. Roosevelt preempted opposition to federal regulations from the Beef Trust by hinting that he would release the complete reports of their repugnant business practices if they did not comply.

After years of delay, the legislation moved through Congress with remarkable speed. "On June 30, 1906, Roosevelt signed the first comprehensive federal food safety laws in American history" (Klein 2023). The Meat Inspection Act set sanitary standards for meat processing and also prohibited companies from adulterating or mislabeling their products. Among the provisions of the second piece of legislation, the Pure Food and Drug Act of 1906, the US Food and Drug Administration (FDA) was created, allowing for federal inspections of food processing plants. These two important acts paved the way for all future legislation aimed at protecting consumers. However, resistance from the food industry continued and "manufacturers were able to persuade the government to water down some of the regulatory requirements in 1906" (Blum 2020).

Sinclair found that his efforts had not gone exactly as he had planned. "Hoping to arouse sympathy for the workers, he said he had 'aimed at the public's heart and by accident I hit in in the stomach'" (Arthur 2006, 83). Even if Sinclair missed his target, he succeeded in making history, as his book resulted in the passage of revolutionary consumer protection legislation. "Since its publication in 1906, *The Jungle* has never been out of print. It remains one of the seminal books in American history, a novel that changed the country" (Klein 2023).

Sinclair went on to write almost 100 books, including *Oil!* (1926), which was the basis for the 2007 Academy Award-winning film *There Will Be Blood*, and his Pulitzer Prize-winning book *Dragon's Teeth* (1943), describing the rise of Nazi Germany. He was known throughout America, continuing to lecture well into his eighties. On October 19, 1963, at age eighty-five, Sinclair spoke to an audience of 3,000 students at Indiana University on a topic called "Changing America—and What Will Happen If You Try." Speaking to students who were about the same age as he was when he wrote *The Jungle*, Sinclair's speech "was appealing for a generation of college students whose idealism had been aroused by the election as president of the energetic young John F. Kennedy. Simply put, it was that one man, fired by the zeal to end injustice, could do it" (Arthur 2006, xi). Sinclair had done just that in 1906. He died in 1968 at the age of ninety, but his efforts live on through his contributions to America's consumer protections for food, enforced by the Food and Drug Administration, which was created in great part due to his revolutionary book.

Further Reading

Arthur, Anthony. 2006. *Radical Innocent: Upton Sinclair*. New York: Random House, xi, 83.

Blum, Deborah. 2020. "Gloom and Horror Unrelieved." *American Experience*. Accessed November 27, 2024. https://www.pbs.org/wgbh/americanexperience/features/poison-squad-gloom-horror-unrelieved/.

"Correspondence between Theodore Roosevelt and Upton Sinclair (1906): Letter 1." 2007. *W. W. Norton & Company Studyspace*. Accessed November 27, 2024. https://wwnorton.com/college/history/foner2/contents/ch18/documents05.asp.

Diedrick, James. n.d. "The Jungle." *Encyclopedia of Chicago*. Accessed September 10, 2024. http://www.encyclopedia.chicagohistory.org/pages/679.html.

Greenspan, Jesse. 2022. "7 Things You May Not Know about 'The Jungle.'" *The History Channel*. Accessed November 27, 2024. https://www.history.com/news/7-things-you-may-not-know-about-the-jungle.

Klein, Christopher. 2023. "How Upton Sinclair's 'The Jungle' Led to US Food Safety Reforms." *The History Channel*. Accessed November 27, 2024. https://www.history.com/news/upton-sinclair-the-jungle-us-food-safety-reforms.

Olsson, Karen. 2006. "Welcome to The Jungle." *Slate*. Accessed November 27, 2024. https://slate.com/culture/2006/07/upton-sinclair-s-the-jungle.html.

"Roosevelt on Army Beef." 1899. *New York Times*. Accessed November 27, 2024. https://www.nytimes.com/1899/03/26/archives/roosevelt-on-army-beef-testifies-that-the-canned-roast-stuff.html.

Rouse, Kristen. n.d. "Meat Inspection Act of 1906." *Britannica*. Accessed September 10, 2024. https://www.britannica.com/topic/Meat-Inspection-Act.

Sinclair, Upton. 2001. *The Jungle*. Unabridged edition. Mineola, NY: Dover Publications.

Q16: Do consumer rights and protections cover beverages?

Answer: In the same manner as the nation's food supply, the beverages consumed by Americans were unregulated until abuses became widely known. This awareness led to growing demands for government intervention into private enterprise for the safety of the American people, especially its most vulnerable: babies and children. Milk was one of the commodities that began to come under scrutiny, followed by a public outcry for greater consumer protection. Important advocates include little-known individuals from the 1800s such as John Newell Hurty as well as widely known figures from contemporary times including Ralph Nader and former New York City mayor Michael Bloomberg. Through the years, there have been various attempts to apply consumer protections through government regulation over the beverages we drink. Some have been more successful than others.

The Facts: Some Americans in the late nineteenth century were starting to believe that the government had a duty to protect the citizens of the nation, not only through its military strength but by regulating unsafe products and unscrupulous business practices that harmed the American people. While much public attention was turned to the "embalmed beef" scandal of 1898, there had been some earlier outrage associated with a life-giving source of nourishment for babies: milk. Under the traditional rule of *caveat emptor*, it was the buyers' responsibility to beware and to make their own choices about what to buy. Babies did not have that opportunity, and parents were often unaware of what was in the milk they fed their children. By the latter half of the 1800s, many food items were made in factories by distant manufacturers. Products were processed in unknown conditions and with unknowable effects. Just before the Civil War (1861–5), a watershed moment in consumer protections came in 1858 when a New York publication, *Frank Leslie's Illustrated Newspaper*, spurred a public demand for government regulation of milk. It was due to a dreadful reason: what was called "swill milk."

The report on swill milk in New York dairy operations appalled many people, especially parents whose babies had died for unknown causes. Swill, a by-product left over from the fermentation process in making whiskey, was fed to milk cows because it was so cheap. Readers learned about diseased, malnourished cows that were permanently tethered, existing in nightmarish conditions. The animals were fed swill from distilleries, often collapsing where they were tied because the weakened bones in their legs could not support them. Reporters found "fly-ridden, maggot-infested milk factories where the animals stood in their own waste, subsisting on warm swill which contained sugar and alcohol but little nutrition. Over the cow's short, miserable life, its teeth tend to rot before the animal stopped giving milk and was sent to slaughter—or dropped dead in the stall" (Blum 2018a, 23). Their milk, already thin and often contaminated, was diluted with water and colored with chalk before being sold to mothers to feed their babies. "Pediatricians linked swill milk to a list of childhood symptoms of ill health ... [such as] frequent retchings and occasional vomitage, irregular bowels with tendency to diarrhea" (Blum 2018a, 23). Illness, misery, and death ensued. Subsequent to the report in *Frank Leslie's Illustrated Newspaper*, there was a public outcry that compelled the state legislature of New York to pass the "Swill Milk Bill" to curtail the worst offenses. However, for many, especially grieving parents, it was too little too late. In addition, the law had no real long-term effect on food safety, since it only pertained to New York.

Two old friends from Indiana became known for their dedication to stemming the glut of unsafe food that was being sold to American consumers. One, Harvey Washington Wiley, gained national fame for his "Poison Squad" experiments at the US Department of Agriculture as well as his role in the eventual passage of the Pure Food and Drug Act of 1906, often called "Wiley's Law." The other was Indiana's chief public health officer, John Newell Hurty, who may have been less well known than Wiley but also had a role in saving innumerable lives, particularly the most vulnerable ones.

When Hurty took over as Indiana's chief public health officer in 1896, his department found "sticks, hairs, insects, blood, and pus in milk." They also "tracked such a steady diet of manure in dairy products that it estimated that the citizens of Indianapolis consumed more than 2,000 pounds of manure in a given year" (Blum 2018a). Hurty did not hesitate to state that the deaths of many children could be linked to what he termed filthy milk. Indiana passed a state Pure Food Law in 1899 but provided no money for enforcement or testing. Hurty also railed against adulteration of milk by dairymen to increase their profits. Across the nation, dairy farmers "thinned milk with water ... and colored the resulting bluish-gray liquid with dyes, chalk, or plaster dust" (Blum 2018a).

Meanwhile, in the nation's capital, Harvey Washington Wiley was coming to the same conclusions as his friend Hurty. Under Wiley, the US Agriculture Department's first detailed examination of food products was published in 1887. Studying milk, it "found a routinely thinned product, dirty and whitened with chalk" (Blum 2018b, 24). Milk not only had bacteria swimming in it but also in at least one sample, "worms wriggling at the bottom of the bottle" (Blum 2018b, 24), which investigators found had been introduced when a local dairyman thinned the milk with stagnant water.

The dairy industry responded to the reports of bacteria by adding formaldehyde to milk, ostensibly to combat bacterial growth but also to salvage milk that had gone sour, allowing the aged product to be sold for a longer period of time. Formaldehyde "had been directly linked to deaths—notably of children drinking what came to be called embalmed milk—without any move by producers to discontinue the preservative's use. The preservative's usefulness in salvaging bad milk— otherwise unsaleable—was too valuable to lose. American corporations successfully and repeatedly blocked efforts to pass even modest food safety regulations" (Blum 2018b). In 1900, the *Indianapolis News* reported the deaths of three babies from formaldehyde poisoning, and in 1901 Hurty "referenced the deaths of more than 400 children due to a combination of formaldehyde, dirt, and bacteria in milk" (Blum 2018a). When a reporter asked Hurty if formaldehyde was really bad for infants, Hurty replied, "I guess it's all right if you want to embalm the baby" (Blum 2018a, 63).

Several years later, the efforts of people such as Hurty and Wiley eventually led to the passage of the Pure Food and Drug Act of 1906. Its provisions included the creation of the federal Food and Drug Administration (FDA) to protect the nation's consumers, even the littlest ones. Today, the FDA is responsible for regulating the safety of milk that is sold through interstate commerce, although individual states control the sale of dairy products within their jurisdictions.

Another group of beverages, soft drinks, have also been scrutinized over the years. Although current debates focus on the sugar content in soda and its detrimental health effects, in the past, soft drink manufacturers were criticized mainly for the claims they made regarding the health *benefits* of their products. Food historian Libby O'Connell notes that the late 1800s produced a flood of sparkling beverages with brand names we recognize today, some entering the market with questionable advertising. One promised to purify the blood; another claimed to aid digestion; others assured consumers that their soda would fight headaches, exhaustion, and impotence as well as addiction to opium and morphine. "Once government regulation required some semblance of truth in advertising ... the companies quickly dropped their boasting" (O'Connell 2015).

In 2012, a proposal in New York City sought to restrict the sale of soft drinks larger than 16 ounces. The ordinance was meant to protect consumers by banning "super-size" sugary drinks to help curb obesity. The plan was supported by Mayor Michael Bloomberg, who was widely mocked and condemned as a result. Opponents to the soda ban called him "Nanny Bloomberg," and he was portrayed in cartoons wearing a frumpy woman's dress.

When the New York City Board of Health approved the measure, lawsuits were filed to overturn the ban. Within months, the state's Supreme Court found that "the board of health had overstepped the authority it was granted to fulfill its mission: protecting against and preventing diseases" (Godoy and Aubrey 2013). A representative of the American Beverage Association (ABA), the soft drink industry's trade group, said that the court's ruling provided "a sigh of relief to New Yorkers and thousands of small businesses in New York City that would have been harmed by this arbitrary and unpopular ban. … With this ruling behind us, we look forward to collaborating with city leaders on solutions that will have a meaningful and lasting impact on the people of New York City" (Godoy and Aubrey 2013). The soda ban went down the drain, but the mayor carried the "Nanny Bloomberg" label for a long time.

Although the fizz went out of the proposed New York City soda ban, it had an interesting side effect a thousand miles away. Legislation in Mississippi that was dubbed the "Anti-Bloomberg Bill" prevented towns and counties in Mississippi from regulating portion sizes. Through its enactment, the Mississippi law was essentially a ban on bans. A state representative who was also a restaurant owner said, "We believe there's enough regulation" (Yan 2013).

Critics of sugary soft drinks have pushed for health warnings to be added to soda product labels in the same way that they are used for alcoholic beverages, on which appear cautionary warnings regarding drinking and driving and the risks of drinking when pregnant. In 2015, San Francisco passed a law requiring the following label to appear on advertisements for sugary drinks: "WARNING: Drinking beverages with added sugar(s) contributes to obesity, diabetes, and tooth decay. This is a message from the City and County of San Francisco." However, the US Court of Appeals ruled the law to be unconstitutional by infringing on soda companies' right to commercial speech under the First Amendment. Some jurisdictions have attempted to tax soft drinks, in much the same way as there is a levy on tobacco products. According to the American Beverage Association, "more than 40 discriminatory taxes on our products have been proposed and rejected. The fact is taxes won't make people healthier, just poorer" (American Beverage Association n.d.).

The US Food and Drug Administration maintains a level of federal oversight regarding soft drinks to ensure that they are safe, sanitary, and honestly labeled. The FDA also established "Current Good Manufacturing Practices" for carbonated soft drinks, describing "the basic steps manufacturers and distributors must follow to make sure carbonated soft drinks are safe" (US Food and Drug Administration 2018). The FDA looks at additives such as food coloring to determine if they are safe for human consumption. It oversees the nutrition facts panel on carbonated soft drinks, which typically includes elements such as per-serving size for calories, carbohydrates, fat, protein, sodium, and sugar along with the name and address of the manufacturer or distributor. Diet carbonated soft drinks must also state whether they contain phenylalanine, which can cause health issues for individuals whose body is unable to process it. The agency also monitors the level of benzene in soft drinks. While benzene is meant to inhibit the growth of bacteria, it can be a carcinogen in large amounts. According to the FDA, soft drink samples are regularly tested to determine that benzene levels do not pose a safety concern for consumers.

Indeed, debates over soda and its proposed regulation are fueled partly by America's intense love for these beverages. Charles Passy, a writer for *Marketwatch* states, "Our love of soda goes beyond the taste. To drink ... almost any of our revered soda brands is to drink our history and popular culture. America has been defined by soda in the same way France defined its empire on wine, Germany on beer, and Britain on tea" (Passy 2015).

American consumers also purchase a significant quantity of alcoholic beverages, including beer, wine, distilled spirits, or some combination, all of which have been subject to various regulations over the nation's history, some in the name of protecting consumers and others to protect the beverage industry. For example, the federal Bottled-in-Bond Act of 1897 came about due to issues involving the quality of American bourbon in the unregulated marketplace of the late 1800s. Disgruntled drinkers felt that the quality of bourbon was inconsistent, and a growing negative reputation for the product as a whole meant that top-shelf bourbon distilleries were losing sales. With the support of the US Secretary of the Treasury, a group of distillers lobbied for tax incentives for those manufacturers who ensured that their product met certain requirements. These conditions included being produced at one single distillery and aged for at least four years in a "bonded warehouse" controlled by US Treasury agents. The bourbon could not contain added coloring or flavoring and could not be blended with other spirits. Products that met the requirements were entitled to promote themselves as "Bottled in Bond." The federal government essentially became the guarantor of a distilled spirit's authenticity. Consumers were reassured, and manufacturers benefited both from increased sales and tax breaks. Along with the 1886 Oleomargarine Act (see Question 13), the Bottled-in-Bond Act of 1897 marked the incursion of the federal government into private enterprise and proved to be pivotal in establishing a precedent for governmental involvement in food and beverage regulation.

Protections for consumers in other areas of the alcohol industry proved more elusive. In order to lengthen shelf life and increase profits before their product ran the risk of becoming unsellable, some nineteenth-century bottlers of beer used salicylic acid as a preservative. Scientists discovered that salicylic acid caused gastric bleeding as well as kidney damage when taken in large amounts, such as the cumulative effect of having several drinks daily. Often the chemical was used to preserve inexpensive products that were consumed by low-income customers and those who were alcoholics. Salicylic acid was banned in France as a preservative in wine and was prohibited in Germany for both wine and beer. "The Germans, however, did permit breweries to use the chemical in beers made for export to the United States. After all, American authorities had shown no interest in regulating its use" (Blum 2018b, 33).

During Prohibition and the ban on the manufacture and sale of alcoholic beverages in the United States, which lasted from 1920 to 1933, some bootleggers recognized the opportunity to produce low-grade beverages for people who could not do without alcohol. Bootlegged concoctions were often adulterated by adding "wood alcohol, isopropyl alcohol, and other toxic compounds, turning reports of paralysis and death into a newspaper staple. … The phrase 'blind drunk' derives from the capacity of wood alcohol to attack the optic nerve and destroy retinal cells" (Okrent 2011, 221). One newspaper headline in the *New York World* of January 1, 1927, reported that there were "4 new rum deaths, 20 more to Bellevue [Hospital], 76 die here in year" (Okrent 2011, 221). Outside New York City, it is unknown how many people died or were injured in low-income communities and rural areas where such casualties might not have been reported to authorities. Not only were there no protections against such adulterated products during Prohibition, but accusations arose that the American government was poisoning its own people. Federal regulations increased the amount of methanol, a poisonous substance, required in industrial alcohols to dissuade people from using these products to make illegal liquor. " 'It gives a greater warning to the drinker that he is getting hold of something that he should leave alone,' a government chemist told the *New York Times* at the time. But people didn't stop drinking. Thirsty for any booze they could get, many Americans risked drinking the super-poisoned alcohol—and thousands died as a result" (Lopez 2014).

Today, one of the main areas of concern for regulators is misleading advertisements for alcohol, in which the federal government can invoke its power to monitor private enterprise. The Department of the Treasury, through the Tobacco Tax and Trade Bureau and under the Federal Alcohol Administration Act, is tasked with regulating the marketing and advertising of alcoholic beverages and products in the United States. Factors such as promulgating false, misleading, or untrue statements are prohibited as are claims that distilled spirits are "bonded" or otherwise made under government supervision. In addition, the Federal Trade Commission (FTC) has intervened in certain alcohol-related consumer protections. These include a breathalyzer application for smartphones that was hugely successful on the television program *Shark Tank*, on which entrepreneurs compete for funding for their product ideas. According to the FTC, "deceptive claims about the accuracy of the devices' readings left consumers floundering" (Fair 2017). Some states also have consumer protections regulating alcohol, many of which surround underage drinking. The alcoholic beverage industry also has some self-imposed guidelines, attempting to stay in the good graces of both the government and the consumers they serve.

As popular as milk, soft drinks, and alcoholic products are, there is one beverage that can claim every human as a consumer: the water we drink. There are those who feel strongly that clean water should take a prominent place in the pantheon of consumer protections. While a person can arguably survive for a few weeks without food, the scientific consensus is that an average human can survive only two to four days without water.

From its earliest days, America's fresh water in lakes, rivers, and groundwater became polluted by being used as a toxic waste dump, trash heap, or toilet. Water used in the White House was no exception. In the mid-1800s, two US presidents—William Henry Harrison and Zachary Taylor—died in office from causes that are often attributed to cholera, which is carried by water or on foods that have been washed in contaminated water. After becoming critically ill in 1862, Abraham Lincoln's twelve-year-old son Willie died and Lincoln's other son, nine-year-old Tad was severely weakened, dying at age eighteen. Various causes were attributed at the time, but modern scientists propose that many health problems for presidential families who lived at the White House were caused by its water supply, which came from the contaminated Potomac River. Soldiers camped upstream in Washington, DC, often utilized the river as a place to dump garbage, use as a latrine, and toss carcasses of dead animals such as army mules.

In 1948, the Federal Water Pollution Control Act was passed. According to the Environmental Protection Agency (EPA), it was the first major law in the United States to address water pollution, which can cause cholera, diarrhea, dysentery, hepatitis A, polio, and typhoid. Until then, untold numbers of people died or were weakened for the rest of their lives. The EPA cites growing public concern about water pollution as leading to the passage of the Clean Water Act of 1972. In addition, with consumer activist Ralph Nader instrumental in its passage, the Safe Drinking Water Act of 1974 was approved by Congress, with amendments added in 1986 and 1996. The EPA has the power to set standards for drinking water quality and to monitor states, local authorities, and water suppliers who are responsible for implementing and enforcing those standards. The EPA's current drinking water regulations are especially concerned with substances such as arsenic, lead, and microbials.

According to the EPA, there are approximately 156,000 public water systems in the United States, with the vast majority of Americans getting their tap water from one of those systems. Although federal, state, and local entities are tasked with working together to protect the nation's drinking water, headline-making incidents do occur, one of the most significant began in 2014 when the drinking water of Flint, Michigan, was found to be contaminated with lead and bacteria, exposing about 100,000 people to tainted water. The Centers for Disease Control found that over half the residents in Flint reported more health problems than usual subsequent to consuming the contaminated water. Effects of lead poisoning can include anemia, brain damage, hearing loss, kidney damage, problems in the immune system, and toxicity to the reproductive organs. Children are especially vulnerable even to low levels of exposure to lead, with consequences including abnormally stunted growth, behavioral problems, learning disabilities, inability to concentrate, lowered IQ, and interference with thought processes that can last a lifetime. Although the city of Flint changed its water supply source in 2015, class action lawsuits were filed based on claims that more than 45,000 Flint residents, especially children, were injured by consuming lead in drinking water. In 2024, a class-action settlement included payment of $1,500 for each child.

Activists continue to demand stricter consumer protections for the water that Americans drink, while those who oppose further regulations think that current restrictions are enough. Regulations regarding water safety are often added or rolled back with changes in political administrations. For example, in 2023 Congress overturned the Biden administration's protections for thousands of small streams, wetlands, and other waterways, "advancing long-held Republican arguments that the regulations are an environmental overreach and burden to business ... [and that overturning them] eases regulatory burdens for small businesses, manufacturers, farmers and 'everyday Americans'" (PBS NewsHour 2023).

While changing administrations bring changes in consumer protections for beverages, government regulation of beverages has certainly increased since the country's early days. These regulations have sometimes benefitted consumers and sometimes benefitted businesses. As the United States has moved away from its buyer-beware beginnings, opposition to government involvement in beverage regulation has often included claims of infringement on personal freedom for individuals and/or reducing profits for producers.

Further Reading

Alcohol.org. 2022. "Rules & Regulations About Marketing Alcohol." Accessed November 27, 2024. https://alcohol.org/laws/marketing-to-the-public/.

American Beverage Association. n.d. "Protecting Consume Choice." Accessed September 20, 2024. https://www.americanbeverage.org/initiatives-advocacy/protecting-consumer-choice-freedom/.

AP News. 2024. "Firm Announces $25M Settlement Over Role in Flint, Michigan, Lead-Tainted Water Crisis." Accessed November 27, 2024. https://apnews.com/article/flint-water-settlement-engineers-lead-children-374879027660211f2a1d6c83a0071c24.

Blum, Deborah. 2018a. "The 19th-Century Fight Against Bacteria-Ridden Milk Preserved with Embalming Fluid." *Smithsonian.* Accessed November 27, 2024. https://www.smithsonianmag.com/science-nature/19th-century-fight-bacteria-ridden-milk-embalming-fluid-180970473/.

Blum, Deborah. 2018b. *The Poison Squad: One Chemist's Single-Minded Crusade for Food Safety at the Turn of the Twentieth Century.* New York: Penguin, 3–288.

Centers for Disease Control and Prevention. 2020. "Flint Water Crisis." Accessed November 27, 2024. https://www.cdc.gov/casper/php/publications-links/flint-water-crisis.html?CDC_AAref_Val=https://www.cdc.gov/nceh/casper/pdf-html/flint_water_crisis_pdf.html

Centers for Disease Control and Prevention. 2024. "Drinking Water Facts and Stats." Accessed November 27, 2024. https://www.cdc.gov/drinking-water/data-research/facts-stats/?CDC_AAref_Val=https://www.cdc.gov/healthywater/drinking/public/index.html.

Fair, Lesley. 2017. "FTC Challenges Claims for Smartphone Breathalyzer Pitched on 'Shark Tank.'" Federal Trade Commission. Accessed November 27, 2024. https://www.ftc.gov/business-guidance/blog/2017/01/ftc-challenges-claims-smartphone-breathalyzer-pitched-shark-tank.

Federal Trade Commission. n.d. "Alcohol." Accessed September 20, 2024. https://www.ftc.gov/business-guidance/industry/alcohol.

Godoy, Maria, and Allison Aubrey. 2013. "Judge Overturns New York City Ban on Big Sugary Sodas." NPR. Accessed November 27, 2024. https://www.npr.org/sections/thesalt/2013/03/11/174037195/judge-overturns-new-york-city-ban-on-big-sugary-sodas.

Harrison, Rachel. 2020. "Can the Government Stick Warning Labels on Soda Bottles?" New York University. Accessed November 27, 2024. https://www.nyu.edu/about/news-publications/news/2020/april/warning-labels-on-soda.html.

Lopez, German. 2014. "The US Government Once Poisoned Alcohol to Get People to Stop Drinking." *Vox.* Accessed November 27, 2024. https://www.vox.com/2014/8/8/5975605/alcohol-prohibition-poison.

O'Connell, Libby. 2015. *The American Plate: A Culinary History in 100 Bites*. Reprint edition, Naperville, IL: Sourcebooks, 237.

Okrent, Daniel. 2011. *Last Call: The Rise and Fall of Prohibition*. New York: Scribner, 221.

Passy, Charles. 2015. "In Defense of Soda." Marketwatch. Accessed November 27, 2024. https://www.marketwatch.com/story/in-defense-of-soda-2014-07-23.

PBS NewsHour. 2023. "House GOP Votes to Overturn Biden Administration Water Protections." Accessed November 27, 2024. https://www.pbs.org/newshour/politics/house-gop-votes-to-overturn-biden-administration-water-protections.

US Environmental Protection Agency. 2023a. "Background on Drinking Water Standards in the Safe Drinking Water Act (SDWA)." Accessed November 27, 2024. https://www.epa.gov/sdwa/background-drinking-water-standards-safe-drinking-water-act-sdwa.

US Environmental Protection Agency. 2023b. "Regulatory and Guidance Information by Topic: Water." Accessed November 27, 2024. https://www.epa.gov/regulatory-information-topic/regulatory-and-guidance-information-topic-water.

US Food and Drug Administration. 2018. "Carbonated Soft Drinks: What You Should Know." Accessed November 27, 2024. https://www.fda.gov/food/buy-store-serve-safe-food/carbonated-soft-drinks-what-you-should-know.

Yan, Holly. 2013. "No Soda Ban Here: Mississippi Passes 'Anti-Bloomberg' Bill." CNN. Accessed November 27, 2024. https://www.cnn.com/2013/03/21/us/mississippi-anti-bloomberg-bill/index.html.

Q17: Have consumer rights and protections for food replaced the principle of *caveat emptor* ("buyer beware")?

Answer: Yes, but gradually. Beginning in the mid-1800s, abuses involving such staples as milk and meat led to a public outcry for regulations to protect the nation's consumers regardless of the traditional operating principle in the American marketplace of *caveat emptor*. Untold numbers of people died over the years due to abuses by some food processors, which gradually came to light in the growing news media of the late nineteenth century. Arguments by opponents of consumer protections focused on the belief that the government had no place interfering with private enterprise in America's capitalist economy. They also maintained that government intervention would be an assault on people's personal freedom, specifically the right to choose whatever product they wanted. Another argument was the potential for reducing profits to manufacturers, which opponents felt ran contrary to the free enterprise system. Slowly, against entrenched interests, governmental entities began enacting legislation that would eventually protect consumers in many fields. The measures that weakened the grip of *caveat emptor* began with the food industry.

The Facts: Two of the earliest interventions by the American government into the realm of *caveat emptor* concerned the safety of pharmaceuticals. The first took place in 1813 when President James Madison signed legislation called the Act to Encourage Vaccination. It established a national source of smallpox vaccine, even providing free postage to anywhere in the country to help counteract the dreaded disease. Thirty-five years later, during the Mexican War in 1848, there were reports that American soldiers were dying from ineffective drugs administered to treat their wounds and illnesses. Confident that the bogus medicines did not come from upstanding US firms but from foreign countries, the federal government was granted the power to inspect drugs coming into the United States via the Drug Importation Act of 1848. Those two pieces of legislation in 1813 and 1848 helped safeguard people's physical health. Government protections for food in the United States took a while longer.

In the year 1202, amid grumblings among the peasantry about the contents of food in his kingdom, England's King John proclaimed the first English food law. The Assize of Bread, as it was called, prohibited the adulteration of bread with ingredients like ground peas and beans. It would take more than 700 years for the government of the United States to become similarly involved with food-related consumer protections. In 1880, chemist Peter Collier from the US Department of Agriculture (USDA) recommended the passage of a national food safety law following his investigations into adulterated food products. The bill was defeated in Congress. During the next twenty-five years, more than one hundred such bills were introduced in Congress, but none were passed. Bolstered by big business, *caveat emptor* was still the rule of the marketplace.

The tide began to turn in 1883, when Harvey Washington Wiley joined the USDA. He defied his politically appointed superiors by widely publicizing his studies of dangerous food additives, most memorably with his group of testers called the "Poison Squad." Still, Congress was unmoved until the embalmed beef scandal during the Spanish American War of 1898 caused a national uproar over formaldehyde-laden rotten beef being fed to American soldiers. After investigations, lawmakers were satisfied when meatpackers vowed to regulate themselves. Opponents of government interference upheld *caveat emptor* rather than permit intervention in the food industry.

Adding to increasing efforts calling for food safety by Harvey Washington Wiley, a shocking book called *The Jungle* by Upton Sinclair was published in 1906, revealing filthy conditions in the factories that sold impure meat to American consumers. Still, growing public opinion in favor of consumer safety did not sway many elected officials. Congressional opposition to pure food legislation came chiefly from three sources: (1) lawmakers who objected on what they claimed to be constitutional grounds and concerns with the federal government extending its power; (2) congressmen who underrated the problem of impure food; and finally, (3) politicians who were concerned with how a pure food law might affect their supporters and contributors, and therefore, their political careers. "Many of the congressmen feared to oppose the powerful business interests … [on whom they] depended for re-election" (Regier n.d.).

However, by 1906, lawmakers were getting the message that voters were outraged by abuses in the food industry. Meat sales slowed within the country in response to Sinclair's book, and some European nations stopped importing meat from the United States. These events helped a powerful, progressive President Theodore Roosevelt to pressure on Congress. In addition, the American Medical Association (AMA) brought its power to bear in favor of a pure food and drug act. While the organization was more interested in bogus medicines, the two issues—pure food *and* drugs—were linked together in the proposed law. The AMA was therefore prepared "to rally all 135,000 physicians in the country. … To get the bill passed, the doctors would, if need be, contact every patient, county by county" (Blum 2018, 133).

When the Pure Food and Drug Act was enacted on June 30, 1906, it became the first such piece of legislation to be passed by the US Congress. The Meat Inspection Act was passed the same day, overriding meatpackers' vows to police themselves. For the first time, the federal government was empowered to take precedence over *caveat emptor* in order to protect American consumers from abuses by some in the food industry.

Some food manufacturers and their political supporters felt that the 1906 law was too stringent. Conversely, there were critics who felt that the law was too weak. For example, the 1906 law only prohibited *interstate* commerce in adulterated food, thus excluding products that did not cross state lines. The law failed to set standards for harmful ingredients, and "did not name a single toxic compound to be regulated" (Blum 2018, 158). The Pure Food and Drug Act of 1906 also included a clause that no dealers would be prosecuted, even if there were deaths or injuries resulting from the products they sold, knowingly or otherwise. Enforcement of the law was difficult, and in the words of journalist David Graham Phillips, it had been weakened to the point where it was "a gift to the food processors and the chemical manufacturers" (Blum 2018, 158). Still, the

1906 law was the first real incursion by the federal government into regulating private enterprise for the safety of the American people. In addition, it included a major stipulation, one that would carry long-term ramifications: the creation of what became the Food and Drug Administration (FDA) as a federal agency with the power to protect consumers.

Some food products found themselves on a different path toward government regulation. Fertilizer regulations, established in response to product adulteration that threatened the nation's food supply in the late 1800s, opened the door for further regulation after complaints arose from European markets about the inconsistency of American grain, which could vary enormously from one producer to the next. This lack of consistent quality damaged faith in American products, cutting into the nation's grain sales abroad. Subsequently, politicians from states that produced grain pushed for federal oversight, and the United States Grain Standards Act was passed in 1916.

Throughout the jazzy decade of the Roaring Twenties, there was a general attitude in the United States of "anything goes." But with the economic disaster known as the Great Depression of the 1930s, the American people got angry. They sought greater help from their government, including consumer protections, and received quite a few under President Franklin Delano Roosevelt. His administration launched programs and regulations that are collectively referred to as the "New Deal."

Major milestones in government regulatory powers occurred with increasing frequency during this time, resulting in a more significant decline of *caveat emptor* than in the past. Under the New Deal, the federal Food, Drug, and Cosmetic Act of 1938 was passed by Congress, containing provisions such as authorizing factory inspections for manufacturers of food products, pharmaceuticals, and beauty aids. It also added the remedy of court injunctions and prosecutions for malfeasance. Under the Wheeler-Lea Act of 1938, the Federal Trade Commission (FTC) was given the authority to oversee advertising associated with products regulated by FDA to ensure ads were not deceptive. In 1939, the first food standards were issued by the FDA, pertaining to canned tomatoes, tomato paste, and tomato purée.

In the years following the Second World War, during the late 1940s and beyond, many more consumer protections were implemented. There was greater latitude to counteract *caveat emptor* when consumer safety was involved. Amid the newfound prosperity of the postwar years and the cornucopia of new food items being steadily rolled out into the marketplace, Americans demanded more consumer safety in what they bought to feed their families. Many had fought the war for the American way of life; some now expected their government to fight for them in return.

The postwar years saw a historic rise in literacy that allowed average citizens to learn more about abuses than ever before. Along with the juggernaut of television, there were consumer groups such as Consumers Union and publications such as *Consumer Reports* that were able to get their message out about product safety. With access to advocacy groups, average citizens could band together to fight against wealthy vested interests. Advertisers and manufacturers who misled consumers were less likely to be tolerated. With this new mindset, Americans made their concerns known to elected officials. More than ever before, consumers had the power to respond if they felt they were being ignored.

The Food Additives Amendment was enacted in 1958, requiring manufacturers to establish the safety of what they were adding to food. The Delaney Proviso, a 1958 amendment to the Food, Drug, and Cosmetic Act of 1938, prohibited the FDA from granting approval for any food additive shown to induce cancer in humans or animals. It was put to the test a year later when the US cranberry crop was recalled three weeks before Thanksgiving of 1959. The FDA tested for aminotriazole, a weed-killer found to cause cancer in laboratory animals. Berries that passed the investigation were allowed to label themselves as having passed FDA inspection, "the only such endorsement ever allowed by FDA on a food product" (US Food and Drug Administration 2023).

In a message to Congress, President John F. Kennedy introduced the Consumer Bill of Rights in 1962. Its provisions included the right to safety by being protected against products that are hazardous to health or life. Along with the right to safety, it included the right to be informed, the right to choose, and the right to be heard.

In 1966, the Fair Packaging and Labeling Act required all consumer products sold via interstate commerce to be honestly and informatively labeled and for the FDA to enforce the law for foods, drugs, and cosmetics. The FDA began overseeing sanitation programs for milk, shellfish, and food service in 1969 to prevent the potential for food poisoning. The agency also issued food processing regulations in 1973 for canned goods.

After many preservatives and other unsafe substances in food were barred by consumer protection laws, there was a significant drop in stomach cancer among Americans, a usually fatal illness linked to highly processed and preservative-laden foods. The American Cancer Society tracked cancer rates over several decades, starting in the 1930s. The year when the Pure Food and Drug law of 1938 was enacted, the rate of stomach cancer in the United States was 24.6 percent. By the 1990s, after significant consumer protections in the food industry had gone into effect, the rate had dropped to 2.9 percent (Wingo et al. 2003).

The government intervened in the baby formula industry in 1980 with the Infant Formula Act, which established FDA controls over that food segment. In 1982, packing regulations were issued by the FDA for a number of products, including a requirement for all nonprescription drugs sold in the United States to be packaged in tamper-resistant containers. Going further, the federal Anti-Tampering Act of 1983 made it a crime to tamper with packaged consumer products, including food items.

In the early 2000s, labeling requirements on food products were extended to listing caloric content, food allergies, and trans fats. By this time, some felt that *caveat emptor* in relation to the food supply had been dealt a death blow by regulation—or overregulation, depending on viewpoint. However, in 2008, Americans were becoming ill at alarming rates after eating a trusted food staple, one that children and low-income people often depend on: peanut butter. Nine deaths and up to 22,000 severe illnesses in almost all states across the nation were linked to a salmonella outbreak from a line of peanut butter made by the Peanut Corporation of America. "The company used factories that were deliberately unregistered to avoid government attention. Many of the jars and containers, produced in notably unsanitary conditions, contained the pathogenic bacteria salmonella" (Blum 2018, 288). The peanut butter was a low-cost brand that tended to be used in schools and nursing homes, exposing children and the elderly to the bacteria.

In a highly publicized trial, American consumers were outraged when e-mails came to light from a Peanut Corporation of America executive who also served on the US Department of Agriculture's Peanut Standards Board. After salmonella was detected in the products, employees were directed to "turn them loose"—to release the contaminated peanut butter into the marketplace (NBC News 2015). In another e-mail, the executive expressed concern that a delay for further testing would be "costing us huge $$$$$" (NBC News 2015). For his role in the deadly salmonella outbreak, he was sentenced to twenty-eight years in prison, "the stiffest punishment ever handed out to a producer in a foodborne illness case" (NBC News 2015).

In 2011, President Barack Obama signed the Food Safety Modernization Act (FSMA) into law. It was a sweeping update to the FDA's protective mandate, increasing the agency's power of enforcement and directing the FDA to build partnerships with state and local authorities. However, rollbacks during the Trump administration diminished some of its provisions.

Traditionally, arguments against consumer protections for food products have involved the need to protect profits. However, industries with good standards may benefit financially from consumer protection laws. For example, two of the strongest supporters of pure food laws were manufacturers Henry Heinz and Oscar Mayer, both of whom welcomed federal inspectors into their plants. Their corporate income was not jeopardized, with both companies continuing well into the twenty-first century as two of the most recognizable, respected, and profitable brands in the food industry.

According to Pulitzer Prize-winning science writer Deborah Blum, "the story of consumer protection in the United States is often the story of a country playing defense, an account of government regulators waking up, time and time again, to yet another public health crisis" (Blum 2018, 287). However, in at least one instance, there was an exemplary instance of food processors and governmental entities working together to solve a problem. In 1919 and 1920, a number of deadly botulism cases struck consumers throughout the country, killing almost twenty people in several states and leaving others violently ill. The problem was traced to canned black olives. Subsequently, processors from the canning and olive industries came together to fund a Botulism Commission. They set a goal of coming up with specific strategies to safely process canned olives in order to prevent such a crisis from happening again. The Botulism Commission led to strict regulations and a statewide inspection service that was funded by the industries themselves but overseen by the California State Board of Health.

Not only was the strategy of government and industry working together successful in the canned olive industry, but within a few years, many of its standardized practices expanded to other canned food products such as sardines, tuna, and many vegetables. By working together to solve the botulism problem, "an industry threatened with destruction instead came back with a set of practices that not only revolutionized canned food, but the entire relationship between science, government, and the food industry in America today" (Zeide 2018). Their efforts strengthened consumer protections and confidence in food products by legitimately policing themselves for the good of consumers rather than simply letting the buyer beware.

Further Reading

Balleisen, Edward. 2017. *Fraud: An American History from Barnum to Madoff.* Princeton, NJ: Princeton University Press, 121.

Blum, Deborah. 2018. *The Poison Squad: One Chemist's Single-Minded Crusade for Food Safety at the Turn of the Twentieth Century*. New York: Penguin, 158, 287, 288.

Horowitz, Roger. 2005. *Putting Meat on the American Table: Taste, Technology, Transformation*. Baltimore, MD: Johns Hopkins University Press, 1.

NBC News. 2015. "Ex-Peanut Exec Gets 28 Years in Prison for Deadly Salmonella Outbreak." Accessed November 27, 2024. https://www.nbcnews.com/news/us-news/former-peanut-exec-gets-28-years-prison-outbreak-n431241.

Regier, C. C. n.d. "The Struggle for Federal Food and Drugs Legislation." *Law and Contemporary Problems*. Accessed September 10, 2024. https://scholarship.law.duke.edu/cgi/viewcontent.cgi?article=1686&context=lcp.

US Food and Drug Administration. 2023. "Milestones in U.S. Food and Drug Law." Accessed November 27, 2024. https://www.fda.gov/about-fda/fda-history/milestones-us-food-and-drug-law.

Wingo, Phyllis A., Cheryll J. Cardinez, Sarah H. Landis, Robert T. Greenlee, Lynn A. G. Ries, Robert N. Anderson, and Michael J. Thun. 2003. "Long-term Trends in Cancer Mortality in the United States, 1930–1998." *American Cancer Society Journals*. Accessed November 27, 2024. https://acsjournals.onlinelibrary.wiley.com/doi/10.1002/cncr.11380.

Zeide, Anna. 2018. "The Botulism Outbreak That Gave Rise to America's Food Safety System." *Smithsonian*. Accessed November 27, 2024. https://www.smithsonianmag.com/history/botulism-outbreak-gave-rise-americas-food-safety-system-180969868/.

5

Consumer Rights and Protections for Cosmetics, Pharmaceuticals, and Healthcare

With the passage of the Pure Food and Drug Law of 1906, a dent was made in the dominance of *caveat emptor* in the marketplace for the first time in American history. However, the 1906 law did not cover some consumer products, such as cosmetics, unless it could be proven that they were mislabeled. That was because cosmetics were not considered either food or drugs and were therefore unregulated. There was also a gray area surrounding over-the-counter remedies such as patent medicines.

Perhaps with the enactment of the 1906 law, some consumers felt a false sense of confidence that the government would protect them from harm. That proved not to be the case with certain products, even those that were advertised as being safe. People who used dangerous cosmetics could find themselves permanently maimed, disfigured, or in some extreme situations, dead. Cosmetics remained essentially unregulated until the late 1930s, after several tragedies occurred. One of the most effective ways the US Food and Drug Administration (FDA) brought dangerous products to the public's attention was a starkly illustrated display first shown at the 1933 World's Fair. Seen by millions of people, the exhibit came to be known as the *American Chamber of Horrors*. Consumer outrage led to the eventual passage of the federal Food, Drug, and Cosmetic Act of 1938, the first such piece of consumer-related legislation in America since 1906. That law increased the authority of the FDA to protect consumers by expanding its scope into the cosmetics industry. In the twenty-first century, the Modernization of Cosmetics Regulation Act of 2022 (MoCRA) further increased the FDA's role regarding cosmetics.

Over-the-counter (OTC) drugs, or medicinal products that can be sold directly to consumers without a prescription, were also generally unregulated during the late nineteenth and early twentieth centuries. The lack of oversight led to what many considered a wide-open market for patent medicines, often called "snake oil." Today, over-the counter medications in a booming consumer industry offering products to treat conditions from allergies to urinary pain have to meet certain FDA criteria. The FDA determines what substances require a prescription in order for the product to be dispensed to consumers. The agency is tasked with implementing the 1987 Prescription Drug Marketing Act (PDMA) to regulate the effectiveness and safety of prescription drugs sold to American consumers. The New Drug Application (NDA) process, enacted in 2022, formally allocates authority to the FDA to oversee the approval procedure for new drugs to be marketed in the United States.

There are also guidelines that establish consumer rights and protections regarding people's medical care. Some of the areas covered include provisions for consumer choice, offering understandable information about healthcare providers, and avenues for consumers to register complaints if they feel that have been deceived or overcharged.

As with many areas of proposed consumer rights and protections, there are opposing voices regarding the field of cosmetics, pharmaceuticals, and healthcare. Opponents fear that an atmosphere of overregulation would result in stifling free enterprise as well as discouraging innovation.

Q18: Are cosmetics covered by consumer rights and protections?

Answer: Until 1938, cosmetics were not regulated unless it could be proven that they were mislabeled. The effects on many unsuspecting American consumers could be disastrous, with results including disfigurement, illness, and death. Many people seem to have presumed that under the Food and Drug Law of 1906, products being sold in the marketplace could not harm them. But cosmetics were not considered food or drugs. They remained unregulated until a public outcry in the 1930s triggered a response that strengthened the role of the federal Food and Drug Administration (FDA) in protecting the nation's consumers via the Food, Drug, and Cosmetic Act of 1938. In the twenty-first century, the Modernization of Cosmetics Regulation Act of 2022 (MoCRA) expanded the FDA's regulatory powers.

The Facts: According to the *Merriam-Webster* dictionary, "cosmetics" are defined as a wide array of products relating to how a person looks. Cosmetics are generally things that are used for the sake of enhancing appearance as well as to correct perceived defects, especially of the face—in short, to make a person more attractive. While cosmetic products have traditionally been aimed at female consumers, contemporary manufacturers have expanded the field. The prevailing wisdom is that because every person—a man as well as a woman—wants to be visually appealing, it is more acceptable nowadays for men to pay attention to such things. Cosmetics marketed to males are often called "men's grooming products." A random internet search reveals items promoted especially for males to include men's shampoo, conditioner, hair styling gel, skin care items, blemish concealer, skin cleanser, eye cream, facial toner, lip balm, hand lotion, moisturizer, shower gel, and sunscreen. The well-groomed twenty-first-century male might also utilize enhanced shaving products, splash on aftershave lotion, apply antiperspirant/deodorant, and dab on a touch of manly cologne.

However, throughout the centuries, cosmetics have traditionally been the domain of women. In the past, many, if not most, were made at home, a task that was not easy. The formidable Martha Washington (1731–1802), America's original First Lady, had instructions for making what she called "the finest lip salve in the world, [resulting in] a tinted lip balm containing … a sheer reddish coloring from the alkanet root" (Carter 2021, 4). According to beauty writer Ilise Carter, other ingredients in Mrs. Washington's recipe included balsam of Peru, best hog's lard, spermaceti (a waxy substance harvested from the head of a whale), virgin wax, and "six new raisins of the sun, dried small" (Carter 2021, 3).

Apart from the expense and difficulty in purchasing store-bought cosmetics, there was an additional reason for home brew. Throughout America's colonial days and beyond, there were admonitions against women using cosmetics at all. The arguments against makeup fell into several major categories. The first were moral objections in the sense that makeup was "deceptive, un-American, unnatural, [and] blasphemous" (Carter 2021, 6). According to this line of thinking, potential suitors could possibly be fooled by the true level of attractiveness of their intended. The second group of arguments centered on the belief that everyone knew it was makeup that was responsible for the attempt at a natural glow, not one's own youthful radiance, so the wearer only looked duplicitous and foolish. Another point of contention was that only actresses and women of ill-repute (often synonymous) wore makeup, so no decent woman should do it. Finally, there were claims that makeup was bad for the skin and that cosmetics of all varieties were dangerous. For many years, that argument had some validity.

Some of the ingredients in early cosmetics were indeed cause for alarm. "Lead, arsenic, and ethanol (then known as 'spirit of wine') were chief among them, but without oversight and industry standards, there's no telling what other caustic ingredients made their way into pots and boxes of color cosmetics and skin care" (Carter 2021, 6). A woman who was harmed often came up against a "blame the victim" mentality. If she suffered injuries from cosmetics that were hazardous, it was presumably her own fault, for being indecent and vain enough to use them in the first place. Her accusers might cite the Biblical book of *Ecclesiastes*, which contains admonitions against vanity.

Regulation and consumer protections were therefore not considered necessary on moral and religious grounds as well as on beliefs about the foolishness of female vanity. What those social arbiters did not consider was the fact that women *had* to look good for men. They were essentially chattel for their fathers and then for husbands, with the approximate legal status of a piece of furniture, a bit less than a cow. They had to attract and hold a man for protection since women alone were an aberration. There were few professions open to women, no financial security, no credit. Women had to be as appealing as possible, in any way they could, to attract and keep a man. If they needed to resort to cosmetics, it was a price they were willing to pay. What they did not know was that the price could be the loss of their life.

When the Pure Food and Drug Act of 1906 became law, it prohibited the sale of adulterated food and drugs as they pertained to interstate commerce. It laid the foundation for what became the federal Food and Drug Administration (FDA), which would emerge as America's primary consumer protection agency. However, cosmetics were not a priority. That would change in 1938 with the passage of a stronger consumer protection law, but until that time, consumers were unknowingly purchasing products that could have tragic effects. If ingredients in many cosmetics had been listed on the label, they would have read like the script of a horror movie.

For example, there was arsenic. For centuries, the predominant beauty ideal for women to achieve in order to be admired by men was pale white skin, a living symbol of the upper class, whose privileged status in society enabled them to stay comfortably indoors and never work outside in the sun. Arsenic did the trick by destroying red blood cells, which leads to pale skin but could also lead to death. Arsenic was present in powders and soaps, and arsenic wafers were advertised as safe and harmless. When eaten, the arsenic wafers not only lightened a woman's complexion but also gave her a bright-eyed look, which was the effect of the substance interfering with cellular respiration. Arsenic could also cause baldness, a disastrous problem for a woman trying to attract a man. If she stopped taking an arsenic-laced product abruptly, her skin would become mottled with lesions along with alternating dark and light patches, so women tended to keep using these products.

Belladonna, translated from Italian as "beautiful lady," is a plant that is also known as Deadly Nightshade. It was used in eye drops to dilate women's pupils, giving them a wide-eyed look that was prized. Belladonna also caused sensitivity to light as well as visual distortion and could ultimately cause death. There were other ways to make women's eyes more attractive to men, such as one found in a newspaper article from 1899 that outlined the process for eyelash extensions. First, a standard needle was threaded with a long hair, generally taken from the head of the client. Then the eye, "in order that the process may be as painless as possible, [is] rubbed with a solution of cocaine" (Wischhover 2013). The desired look was achieved by weaving a needle in and out of the eyelid, then trimming the looped hair.

Like arsenic-laced products, facial makeup containing lead and mercury also helped produce desirably pale skin. Abdominal pain, desiccated skin, and gray hair were side effects from lead-based products as the consumer was slowly being poisoned. Mercury in cosmetics can cause birth defects, depression, fatigue, kidney ailments, liver problems, and tremors before long-term use leads to death.

Along with those lethal cocktails, the early twentieth century saw what were considered to be ultra-modern advances in female beauty through the "miracle" of radiation. After radium was discovered in 1898, manufacturers were quick to market radium-infused skin creams, claiming invigorating radioactive properties for unsuspecting consumers. An ad from 1915 stated, "If placed on the face where the skin has become wrinkled or tired, the radio-active forces immediately take effect on the nerves and tissues. A continuous steady current of energy flows into the skin, and before long the wrinkles have disappeared" (Wischhover 2013). For convenience while resting overnight, radioactive chin straps were also available for the woman who hoped to lose her wrinkles. Unfortunately, she could also lose her life.

The modern phenomenon of X-rays, discovered in 1895, opened the door for a new approach to an embarrassing problem for women: unwanted body hair. It was an especially big hit in the 1920s. Practitioners promoted the benefits of X-ray depilation for areas such as the upper lip, although the process could take several hours of exposure to radiation. Although X-rays were marketed as perfectly safe, the result could be baldness, disfigurement, thickening of the skin, ulcerations, and cancer. Eventually the problem of such radiation exposure came to light, but X-ray hair removal was not officially taken off the market until

1946, a year after the end of the Second World War. The horrendous effects on survivors of the atomic bomb in 1945 may have been an indication that radiation was not a beauty treatment.

Product lines that contained lethal ingredients were purchased by consumers who had no idea what they were buying. Many presumed that after the passage of the Pure Food and Drug Act of 1906, government regulations ensured their safety. They were wrong. American consumers continued to be injured by dangerous products in the unregulated marketplace. The 1930s took a special toll. Perhaps it was the economic deprivations of the Great Depression that motivated women to try looking better in dark times. Many were forced to attempt finding a job if their husband or father became unemployed. More than ever, such women had to look their best to impress the males who did the hiring.

In 1930, a product called Koremlu was advertised as a safe, permanent hair-removal cream. It was primarily applied to unsightly growth on women's upper lips, but the problems it caused manifested themselves everywhere on the body. Unknown to consumers, one of Koremlu's active ingredients was thallium acetate, an extremely toxic substance used as rat poison. Women bought Koremlu in good faith, presuming it was harmless because it was freely advertised and sold as being safe. Women went permanently bald and experienced paralysis and damage to the eyes. After two years on the market and untold numbers of Koremlu victims, the *Journal of the American Medical Association* (*JAMA*) came to the rescue in 1932. *JAMA* published articles about the effects of the popular product, describing it as "a viciously dangerous depilatory" (Eschner 2017). Because Koremlu was not classified as a drug, the Food and Drug Administration could not step in because it did not have the power to regulate cosmetics. After lawsuits were filed, using *JAMA* as a reference, the manufacturer declared bankruptcy.

One year later, in 1933, a mascara called Lash Lure promised to give women permanently alluring eyelashes. Instead, it left many permanently blind. A chemical in Lash Lure known as p-Phenylenediamine "caused horrific blisters, abscesses and ulcers on the face, eyelids and eyes of Lash Lure users, and it led to blindness for some. In one case, the ulcers were so severe that a woman developed a bacterial infection and died" (Eschner 2017).

Gouraud's Oriental Cream, a skin cream that advertised itself as a magic beautifier, was neither magic nor beautifying. At least one woman "developed dark rings around her eyes and neck, followed by bluish black gums and loose teeth" (Eschner 2017). These were the results of mercury poisoning. An ad from 1907 states that the Gouraud compound removed pimples, rash, freckles, skin diseases, and "every blemish on beauty. … [it] is so harmless we taste it to be sure it is properly made" ("Dr. T. Felix Gouraud's Oriental Cream" 1907). The alleged tasting process apparently did not detect calomel, which is a mercury compound also called mercurous chloride, a chemical that can be used as a fungicide.

Advocates of *caveat emptor* believed that consumers had the right to buy or not to buy any product that was on the market. Consumers in a free-market economy, they felt, were the ones who had responsibility of researching a product and determining if they needed to beware. In addition, many of those who opposed regulation felt that the Pure Food and Drug Act of 1906 was more than enough government interference into private enterprise.

Many consumers may not have realized that cosmetics were not covered by the 1906 law. The only authority the FDA had was determining if misleading claims on labels were unlawful. No such authority existed over untrue claims that were made in advertising, which many felt were protected by the First Amendment. Still, many people believed their government would protect them if there was any wrongdoing. Some staff at the FDA felt that consumers needed more protection than what was allocated under the law. In 1933, an FDA display called the *American Chamber of Horrors* spotlighted the need for further regulation by showcasing products the agency did not have the power to oversee (see Question 20 for more information). The ensuing public outcry ultimately led to the passage of the Food, Drug, and Cosmetic Act of 1938, expanding the consumer protections of the 1906 act to cover cosmetics.

While cosmetics currently do not need FDA approval before they go on the market, the FDA does have the power to regulate color additives that are put in them. The Modernization of Cosmetics Regulation Act of 2022 (MoCRA) expanded the FDA's authority to regulate cosmetics beyond the 1938 law. For the first time, the FDA was given the authority to order a mandatory recall of a harmful product if the manufacturer will not do so voluntarily. This step is taken in cases where there is a reasonable probability that a cosmetic is adulterated or misbranded and that the use of the product will cause serious health problems or death for consumers.

Further Reading

Carter, Ilise. 2021. *The Red Menace: How Lipstick Changed the Face of American History*. Lanham, MD: Prometheus Books, 3, 4, 6.

"Dr. T. Felix Gouraud's Oriental Cream." 1907. University of Washington Libraries. Accessed September 10, 2024. https://digitalcollections.lib.washington.edu/digital/collection/advert/id/491/.

Eschner, Kat. 2017. "Three Horrifying Pre-FDA Cosmetics: From Mercury-loaded Face Cream to Mascara That Left You Blind." *Smithsonian*. Accessed November 27, 2024. https://www.smithsonianmag.com/smart-news/three-horrifying-pre-fda-cosmetics-180963775/.

US Food and Drug Administration. 2018. "80 Years of the Federal Food, Drug, and Cosmetic Act." Accessed November 27, 2024. https://www.fda.gov/about-fda/fda-history-exhibits/80-years-federal-food-drug-and-cosmetic-act.

Wischhover, Cheryl. 2013. "The Most Dangerous Beauty Through the Ages." *New York Magazine*. Accessed November 27, 2024. https://www.thecut.com/2013/12/most-dangerous-beauty-through-the-ages.html.

Q19: Do consumer rights and protections safeguard over-the-counter products?

Answer: Over-the-counter (OTC) medications can be sold directly to consumers without a prescription. OTC products treat a variety of conditions ranging from allergies and colds to insomnia and motion sickness. To protect consumers, OTC medications have to meet certain criteria set by the Food and Drug Administration (FDA). According to the FDA, OTC drugs must meet the same effectiveness, quality, and safety standards as prescription drugs. That was not always the case throughout the history of America. Particularly in the nineteenth and early twentieth centuries, patent medicines and "snake oil" potions were sold to consumers freely, generating enormous profits to their purveyors as well as often being ineffective and occasionally lethal for the consumer.

The Facts: Most estimates indicate that today's OTC drug industry in the United States generates about $50 billion annually. Currently, some of the most popular OTC products include those addressing a wide range of conditions including allergies, colds, congestion, constipation, coughing and sneezing, diarrhea, dry eyes, insomnia, and motion sickness. There are OTC antacids, diuretics, eye drops, fever reducers, nasal sprays, and pain relievers, as well as aids for those hoping to lose weight.

Makers of OTC products in the United States are represented by the Consumer Healthcare Products Association (CHPA), a trade association for what is termed the personal healthcare industry. According to CHPA, an OTC medicine is a nonprescription product that the FDA has found to be safe and effective based on the instructions and warnings on the label. The organization adds that the

FDA "requires a wider margin of safety for OTC medicines than for prescription drugs" (Consumer Healthcare Products Association 2023).

OTC products that are sold directly to consumers today do have some FDA oversight, but that was not always the case. In the past, the OTC drug industry was considered by some to be a virtual Wild West due to the unregulated glut of patent medicines and "snake oil." According to the *Merriam-Webster* dictionary, patent medicines are nonprescription medicinal preparations whose formulas are typically said to have been granted a patent by the government due to alleged proprietary ingredients that must be kept secret from potential competitors. The contents of such potions were often incompletely or inaccurately disclosed, with results of unproven effectiveness and questionable safety.

In the United States, the 1800s and early 1900s were a kind of golden age of patent medicines. In fact, they lent their name to a popular form of entertainment called "medicine shows." In a time with few entertainment options, especially for rural areas, these touring performances traveled from town to town, drawing a crowd through magic acts, musical numbers, and exotic dancers. Shows were generally run by men who dubbed themselves "doctors" as they peddled their own patent medicines. The products were advertised as liniments, tonics, magic elixirs, miracle cures, and so on, claiming to do everything from smoothing wrinkles to curing cancer, from restoring sexual prowess to prolonging life.

The purveyors of patent medicines were strong supporters of the unregulated free enterprise system as well as the concept of *caveat emptor*. Their position was that the buyer had the chance to be wary of whatever they considered buying. Around the time of the Civil War, patent medicines were an enormous industry, "eventually generating hundreds of millions of dollars in revenue by selling 'cure all' products at a buck a bottle. By the 1860s, potion proprietors were the nation's largest advertisers" (Danna 2015, 1). Adjusting for inflation, what cost "a buck" ($1) in 1860 would be more than $33 in 2022, no small investment for a cash-poor farmer.

Probably the most successful early OTC cure-all product carved its own niche in the American vocabulary: "snake oil." Originally a liniment made from the oil of a Chinese water snake, it was believed to help the muscle aches of Asian railroad workers who brought it with them to the United States from China. Some entrepreneurial types took notice, but since "there were no Chinese water snakes handy in the American West, many healers began using rattlesnakes to make their own versions of snake oil" (Gandhi 2013). An eye-catching demonstration at medicine shows was slitting open a live rattler, ostensibly to extract the oil. However, the snake oil being sold to unsuspecting consumers usually did not contain any rattlesnake oil, which would have been ineffective at best since it came from a different species than Chinese water snakes. In at least one brand that was sold widely in the late 1800s, the alleged snake oil substance in the bottles sold to consumers consisted of "a fatty oil believed to be beef fat, red pepper and turpentine" (Gandhi 2013). When the Pure Food and Drug Act of 1906 took effect, federal officials started clamping down on snake oil. After one well-publicized investigation in 1917, the phrase "snake oil" embedded itself into current usage as an expression indicative of fraud or deception.

Perhaps the most recognizable patent medicine of the late nineteenth and early twentieth centuries enjoyed a high degree of consumer loyalty. Marketed between 1873 and 1906 as Lydia Pinkham's Vegetable Compound, it was promoted as a product to help ease "women's complaints." Doctors at the time were virtually all males, having little knowledge of the female body. Without personal experience with pregnancy, childbirth, menstruation, or menopause, their diagnosis for women patients was often that the "complaint" was all in their heads. As one of the few ways to find relief, many women kept a bottle of Lydia Pinkham's on hand at all times.

Far from being a fictional advertising symbol, the real-life Lydia Estes Pinkham lived from 1819 to 1883. The product bearing her name featured a portrait of the grandmotherly looking Pinkham. She was presented as someone who understood the discomforts faced by other women to the point that "advertisements for Lydia Pinkham's Vegetable Compound made Pinkham the most recognizable woman in late nineteenth century US" (Horwitz 2017). Her over-the-counter vegetable compound was said to be based on a mixture of wild roots and herbs. However, it "turned out to be 20.6 percent ethanol" (Blum 2018, 105–6), also known as ethyl alcohol and grain alcohol. Lydia was not alone. Alcohol was a primary ingredient in many patent medicines of the era, whether or not it was listed on the label. The Pinkham family "ostensibly fell on the side of temperance movements, most of which demonized consumption [of alcohol]. But when it came to health matters, the family would join others … who saw value in liquor for 'medicinal purposes' " (Danna 2015, 6).

Other products sold to consumers included Daffy's Elixir and Hamlin's Wizard Oil, general purpose cure-alls. Another, A.B.C. Liniment, which was sold for pain relief, had at least some degree of truth in advertising, as it was named for its three primary ingredients: aconite (also known as wolfsbane), belladonna, and chloroform. Hadacol was a product marketed as a vitamin supplement. Its slogan was "Get That Wonderful Hadacol Feeling" ("And Now You Know" 2018).

That feel-good feeling may have come from the 12 percent alcohol it contained, which helped make it popular in 'dry' counties, especially in the South, where liquor was banned. At the other end of the feel-good spectrum was Mrs. Moffat's Shoo-Fly Powders for Drunkenness, an alleged remedy for intoxication that was also said to act as a knock-out drug.

The burgeoning news media covered sometimes-gruesome stories about injuries and deaths caused by unregulated patent medicines being sold to consumers. In the early 1900s, the USDA Bureau of Chemistry under Harvey Washington Wiley became involved, adding patent medicine "cure-alls" to the products they examined. The scientists found that many of these products were basically flavored alcohol. As the Bureau of Chemistry investigated OTC panaceas, opponents of regulation cited the consumer's freedom to choose. A group claiming to represent makers of patent medicines labeled the Bureau of Chemistry studies as an attack on personal freedom. "Its officers warned publicly that if their products were subject to regulation, government control of people's lives would know no limits" (Blum 2018, 106).

Traditionally, the defense of *caveat emptor* was grounded on the freedom of consumers to choose whatever they wished to buy. However, that did not include a portion of the population who had no opportunity to decide what product to purchase, or to voice an opinion on its effects: infants and children. One example of an unregulated over-the-counter product aimed at children was called Mrs. Winslow's Soothing Syrup, which was advertised as a patent medicine to calm crying babies. It was put on the market in 1849 and was recommended for when a child started teething, whether the infant was crying or not. The syrup was highly addictive, as its ingredients were morphine and alcohol. There were also other "soothing syrups" on the market for children that were "laced with morphine, heroin, and chloral hydrate, among other sedatives" (Blum 2018, 219). It is unknown how many children became addicted to those substances for life, starting at an early age. Nor is it known what remedy there was for their addiction and/or attempted withdrawal, or what effect there was on their mental and physical growth.

Bureau of Chemistry staff believed that the use of narcotics in over-the-counter medications posed an enormous public health risk to children. However, they also believed that the politically appointed head of the USDA was hiding this information from consumers. Even after being labelled as a "baby killer" by the American Medical Association in 1884, Mrs. Winslow's Soothing Syrup, which had been sold to consumers since before the Civil War, was not removed from the market until the 1930s.

Amid the adversity of the Depression era in the 1930s, there were other unregulated products that joined the over-the-counter marketplace, occasionally turning lethal. In 1937, more than one hundred people died, many of them children, after being poisoned by a cough syrup sweetened with a solvent found in antifreeze. Under the Food and Drug Act of 1906, there was no provision for the manufacturer to test this OTC product for safety. Despite the resulting deaths, "the only charge possible under the law was mislabeling; the syrup had been labeled an 'elixir' despite the fact that it did not contain alcohol" (Blum 2018, 285). The public was outraged over the cough syrup tragedy and the lack of consequences to the manufacturer responsible for the deaths. News of the tragedy came on the heels of a well-known graphic display created by the FDA in 1933 called *American Chamber of Horrors*, which illustrated the limits of the FDA's reach and was still fresh in the minds of many American consumers (see Question 20 for more information).

Although nothing could bring back the dead children or others who had perished, the American political atmosphere began shifting away from solid support of *caveat emptor.* The Food, Drug, and Cosmetic Act of 1938 was passed to replace its 1906 predecessor. For the first time, consumers began to have the kind of protections against harmful cosmetics and OTC drugs that we enjoy today.

Further Reading

Billingsley, Alyssa. 2023. "11 Common Medications You Can Get Over the Counter." *GoodRx Health.* Accessed November 27, 2024. https://www.goodrx.com/drugs/otc/common-over-the-counter-medications.

Blum, Deborah. 2018. *The Poison Squad: One Chemist's Single-Minded Crusade for Food Safety at the Turn of the Twentieth Century.* New York: Penguin, 105, 106, 219, 285.

Clarke, Pat. 2016. "How FDA Strives to Ensure the Safety of OTC Products." U.S. Food and Drug Administration. Accessed November 27, 2024. https://www.fda.gov/drugs/special-features/how-fda-strives-ensure-safety-otc-products.

Consumer Healthcare Products Association. 2023. "Regulation of OTC Medicine." Accessed November 27, 2024. https://www.chpa.org/public-policy-regulatory/regulation/regulation-otc-medicines.

Danna, Sammy. 2015. *Lydia Pinkham: The Face That Launched a Thousand Ads.* Lanham, MD: Rowman & Littlefield, 1, 6.

Gandhi, Lakshmi. 2013. "A History of 'Snake Oil Salesmen.'" National Public Radio. Accessed November 27, 2024. https://www.npr.org/sections/codeswitch/2013/08/26/215761377/a-history-of-snake-oil-salesmen.

Horwitz, Rainey. 2017. "Lydia Pinkham's Vegetable Compound (1873–1906)." Arizona State University. Accessed November 27, 2024. https://embryo.asu.edu/pages/lydia-pinkhams-vegetable-compound-1873-1906.

Louviere, Mike. 2018. "And Now You Know: Hadacol, the Feel Good Elixir." *Orange Leader*. Accessed November 27, 2024. https://www.orangeleader.com/2018/09/22/hadacol-the-feel-good-elixir/.

Q20: What role did the *American Chamber of Horrors* play in modern consumer protections?

Answer: In the 1930s, an exhibit that became known as the *American Chamber of Horrors* was an eye-catching display that was later adapted as a book. Presented by the Food and Drug Administration (FDA) at the 1933 World's Fair, the display explicitly illustrated the harmful effects of some unregulated cosmetics and over-the-counter (OTC) products that were being sold to unsuspecting consumers. The resulting public outcry was instrumental in bringing about the passage of the Food, Drug, and Cosmetic Act of 1938, the first federal consumer protection law to have been passed since 1906. Overcoming years of industry resistance, the 1938 statute marked the first time in the nation's history that cosmetics and OTC products were subject to government regulation. The 1938 law, spurred in great part by information from the *American Chamber of Horrors*, formed the basis for many of the consumer rights and protections that are often taken for granted today.

The Facts: American consumers gained an ally in Ruth deForest Lamb (1896–1978). In 1933, she became the first Chief Educational Officer at the FDA. Abuses in cosmetics and OTC drugs were generating criticisms of the government for not protecting consumers. Lamb, however, understood the limitations of the 1906 Pure Food and Drug Law. She stated that tragedies happened "not because Government officials are incompetent or callous, but because they have no real power to prevent them" (US Food and Drug Administration 2018b).

Believing there was a need for further regulation beyond the Pure Food and Drug Act of 1906, Lamb developed an innovative way of proving her point, using a methodology that was based on her background. In the 1920s, she had been one of the first women to earn a living in the growing field of advertising. Moving to the FDA in 1933, she used her advertising skills to help make average Americans aware of the dangers in certain products. This awareness, she felt, would not only safeguard them from specific products but might also motivate them to demand that their elected officials do something to protect them.

The Chicago World's Fair of 1933, also called the "Century of Progress International Exposition," was projected to be a huge event with tens of thousands of people expected to attend. Crowds exceeded expectations, as *millions* of fairgoers passed through the gates. With fellow FDA staffers, Ruth Lamb created an exhibit of some of the worst one hundred unregulated products on the market across the country. The FDA had no legal authority to ban products such as Lash Lure, a type of mascara that was causing blindness and even death for its users. On the principle that "a picture is worth a thousand words," Ruth Lamb displayed Lash Lure and other products in before-and-after photos, showing the damage they had done to people, usually women.

Other products in the display included the lethal depilatory Koremlu, which contained toxic thallium acetate as its active ingredient, and weight-loss drugs containing the chemical dinitrophenol, found to have side effects such as cataracts and fatal blood disorders. A product called Othine was promoted to lighten skin and remove brown spots (also called age spots or liver spots) on the face or hands from exposure to the sun. Because its active ingredient was mercury, Othine caused bone deterioration, loss of teeth, and damage to blood cells, "resulting in an inability to fight off infection and often times [causing] death" (Poches 2019). Because these items were classified as cosmetic products, they were "beyond the reach of the law" (Poches 2019).

After the World's Fair closed, the exhibit traveled to Washington, DC. When First Lady Eleanor Roosevelt attended, she was appalled at the injuries suffered by Americans as a result of products that were being legally and openly sold to consumers. Noting her horrified response, reporters covering the First Lady dubbed the display a "chamber of horrors." After seeing the display, many American consumers in the 1930s realized they were facing a quagmire of misleading labels as well as constant newspaper, magazine, and radio advertisements that were full of fraudulent claims. Based on the *Chamber of Horrors* display, many consumers made their displeasure known to their elected officials. First Lady Eleanor Roosevelt pitched in by mobilizing women's clubs.

The *Chamber of Horrors* display had reached millions of attendees at the 1933 World's Fair, but Ruth deForest Lamb was not done. She took a leave of absence from the FDA to write a book called *American Chamber of Horrors: The Truth about Food and Drugs*, published in 1936. In it, she documented "tactics employed by many industries, advertisers, trade associations, and lawyers to thwart enactment of effective regulation" (US Food and Drug Administration 2018a). Lamb also spurred consumers not to see themselves as powerless victims but rather as being in a position to exercise the power of the vote over elected officials. There was strength in numbers, even among American women, who had only recently earned the right to vote. Lamb dedicated her book to the many women's organizations sponsoring the proposed new law.

The *Chamber of Horrors* had illustrated the dangers of an unregulated system, but despite intensified lobbying by consumer groups, Congress was slow to act, as some in office were afraid to anger businesses that could influence their chances of reelection. A "furious counteroffensive by the affected industries slowed the legislative push produced by the *Chamber of Horrors*, [but] eventually new federal legislation was secured" (Bartholomew 2017, 10). President Franklin Roosevelt signed the Food, Drug and Cosmetic Act of 1938 into law. For the first time, the FDA was given the authority to oversee the cosmetics industry. After the law's enactment, Lash Lure, the toxic mascara, was the first product forced to be removed from store shelves.

Along with beauty aids, other unregulated products in the marketplace suddenly found themselves in the spotlight. The early twentieth century saw the popularity of products containing radium, a radioactive substance discovered in 1898. Radium became known as exciting and modern. It was so popular that it seemed to be everywhere, credited with all sorts of thrilling attributes. Bath salts containing radium were promoted to ease conditions such as arthritis, insomnia, nervous disorders, and rheumatism as well as general lethargy. There was a radium hand cleaner guaranteed not to irritate the skin. Radium suppositories were indicated as an enhancement to sexual performance.

Arguably the most memorable radium case involved a product named Radithor that had been manufactured since 1918. It was aimed at men as a radium-infused energy drink to restore vigor and alleviate impotence, complete with a catchy advertising slogan: "A Cure for the Living Dead." The product was endorsed by a popular celebrity named Eben Byers (1880–1932), a famed athlete and wealthy socialite who proclaimed that Radithor was a miracle cure-all. Apparently, it wasn't. When Byers died in 1932, the *Wall Street Journal* ran an article titled, "The Radium Water Worked Fine Until His Jaw Came Off" (Prisco 2020). At his autopsy, it was discovered that Byers's body was chock full of cancerous tumors and abscesses in his brain. He had holes in his skull and bones that were so brittle they easily snapped. Byers was exhumed for study in 1965, more than three decades after his death. His body was found to still be "highly radioactive and dangerous" (Seaver 2022). Reburied in a lead-lined coffin, "radiation will likely continue to affect his remains for centuries" (Seaver 2022).

For decades after the passage of the Food, Drug, and Cosmetic Act of 1938, if a safety issue with a product were to arise, the FDA could not force manufacturers to remove the product from store shelves; any recall would have to be voluntary. If the manufacturer refused to recall the product, the FDA could issue an advisory informing consumers about health concerns with the product. Between 2004 and 2016, "on average, 396 cosmetic-related individual health problems, or 'adverse events' were submitted per year to the FDA … though in 2016, the agency received 1,591 reports, a 300-percent increase" (Isaacs-Thomas 2019). Under the 1938 law, cosmetic products could be FDA-*regulated* but are not FDA-*approved*. "The law does not require cosmetic products and ingredients, other than color additives, to have FDA approval before they go on the market" (US Food and Drug Administration 2022). Manufacturers did not need to register cosmetic products with the FDA or to list the ingredients before putting them on the market. However, when the Fair Packaging and Labeling Act (FPLA) took effect in 1967, the FDA was empowered to work with the Federal Trade Commission regarding cosmetics on the market via interstate commerce. The two agencies could look at issues such as whether the label states the identity of the product, the net quantity of the product's content, and the name and place of business of the manufacturer or distributor.

The Modernization of Cosmetics Regulation Act of 2022 (MoCRA) was passed to become "the first update to federal cosmetics regulation in over eighty years … greatly expanding the regulatory oversight granted to the US Food and Drug Administration (FDA) to oversee the cosmetics industry" (Brock 2023). Under MoCRA, facilities that produce cosmetics are now required to register with the FDA. Manufacturers must include contact information, note certain allergens on product labels, and keep adequate safety records. The law also "grants the FDA mandatory recall authority and access to records relating to cosmetic products that represent a health threat to consumers" (Brock 2023). Some lawmakers have expressed the opinion that manufacturers need to be careful so that people are not harmed but also so as not to invite overregulation for "an industry that has generally posed relatively minimal risk to human health" (Isaacs-Thomas 2019).

Further Reading

Bartholomew, Mark. 2017. *Adcreeep: The Case Against Modern Marketing*. Stanford, CA: Stanford University Press, 10, 11.

Brock, Lexi. 2023. "The Ugly Truth: Cosmetic Regulation & Consumer Protection in 2023." *Wake Forest Law Review*. Accessed November 27, 2024. https://www.wake

forestlawreview.com/2023/02/the-ugly-truth-cosmetic-regulation-consumer-protection-in-2023/.

Isaacs-Thomas, Bella. 2019. "Why Your Cosmetics Don't Have to Be Tested for Safety." *PBS NewsHour*. Accessed November 27, 2024. https://www.pbs.org/newshour/health/why-your-cosmetics-dont-have-to-be-tested-for-safety.

Lamb, Ruth D. 1936. *American Chamber of Horrors: The Truth about Food and Drugs*. New York: Farrar & Rinehart.

Poches, Olivia. 2019. "The American Chamber of Horrors." University of Wisconsin–Madison. Accessed November 27, 2024. https://gobigread.wisc.edu/2019/05/the-american-chamber-of-horrors.

Prisco, Jacopo. 2020. "When Beauty Products Were Radioactive." CNN. Accessed November 27, 2024. https://www.cnn.com/style/article/when-beauty-products-were-radioactive/index.html.

Seaver, Carl. 2022. "The Strange Story of Eben Byers, Who Drank Radium Until His Jaw Fell Off." *History Defined*. Accessed November 27, 2024. https://www.historydefined.net/eben-byers/.

US Food and Drug Administration. 2018a. "The American Chamber of Horrors." Accessed November 27, 2024. https://www.fda.gov/about-fda/histories-product-regulation/american-chamber-horrors.

US Food and Drug Administration. 2018b. "80 Years of the Federal Food, Drug, and Cosmetic Act." Accessed November 27, 2024. https://www.fda.gov/about-fda/fda-history-exhibits/80-years-federal-food-drug-and-cosmetic-act.

US Food and Drug Administration. 2018c. "The 1938 Food, Drug, and Cosmetic Act." Accessed November 27, 2024. https://www.fda.gov/about-fda/histories-product-regulation/1938-food-drug-and-cosmetic-act.

US Food and Drug Administration. 2018d. "Ruth deForest Lamb: FDA's First Chief Educational Officer." Accessed November 27, 2024. https://www.fda.gov/about-fda/fda-history-exhibits/ruth-deforest-lamb-fdas-first-chief-educational-officer.

US Food and Drug Administration. 2022. "FDA Authority Over Cosmetics: How Cosmetics Are Not FDA-Approved, but Are FDA-Regulated." Accessed November 27, 2024. https://www.fda.gov/cosmetics/cosmetics-laws-regulations/fda-authority-over-cosmetics-how-cosmetics-are-not-fda-approved-are-fda-regulated.

Q21: Are there consumer rights and protections for prescription drugs?

Answer: Yes, particularly since the use of prescription drugs in the United States has grown through advances in pharmaceutical science that sharply increased beginning in the 1960s. In contrast to over-the-counter (OTC) drugs that can be sold directly to consumers, prescription drugs require an order from an authorized medical professional to be dispensed. The differentiation is determined by the US Food and Drug Administration (FDA), usually because a prescription drug requires medical expertise beyond what average consumers could provide for themselves. Prescription drugs must include specific directions and labeling information if the FDA finds that certain pharmaceuticals can be addictive, could contribute to drug abuse, have the potential to do harm, or may be toxic in some circumstances. In addition to more new pharmaceutical products being marketed in recent years, the increased use of prescription drugs has also reflected the growth of direct-to-consumer advertising in mass media.

The Facts: According to Texas Tech University, "the world's oldest known prescriptions were recorded on a clay tablet in Mesopotamia (modern-day Iraq), ca. 2400 BC [with ingredients including] 'hair from the stomach of a cow'" (Texas Tech University 2023). In the United States, pharmacists could prepare and prescribe medicines into the 1950s. Then, the 1951 Durham-Humphrey Amendment to the federal Food, Drug and Cosmetic Act of 1938 modified their role. The amendment mandated that certain drugs must carry a statement declaring that federal law prohibits the distribution of the medication without a prescription. Henceforth, the pharmacist would need a doctor's order to dispense medications apart from those that were classified by the FDA as OTC drugs, which could be purchased directly by consumers.

In the 1950s, the array of new medications on the market was steadily increasing, building on research that was done during the Second World War. For example, mass production of penicillin during the wartime era led to that antibiotic becoming known as a "wonder drug" for its treatment of infections. It saved countless lives, especially among wounded soldiers. After the war, pharmaceutical labs developed additional types of antibiotics for average Americans, including streptomycin and tetracycline.

Amid the prosperity of postwar America, pharmaceutical research abounded. "A wave of government spending was spawned by two seminal influences: a comprehensive new federal science and technology policy and the anti-'Red' sentiment that dollars spent for science were dollars spent for democracy" (American Chemical Society 2000). With expanded research funded by the US government in an effort to stay ahead of the Russians during the Cold War, most American consumers embraced prescription medicines for themselves and their growing families. Parents trusted the prescription drugs they gave their children in the midst of the unprecedented postwar "Baby Boom." People had faith that their government, through the Food and Drug Administration (FDA), provided a high level of consumer protection that they could depend on.

People also had faith in science and its practitioners, who were often considered miracle workers. A prime example was "the heroic-scientist image of Jonas Salk [1914–1995], savior of children through the conquest of polio via vaccine" (American Chemical Society 2000). On April 26, 1954, Randy Kerr, a six-year-old second grader in Fairfax, Virginia, "was the first school child to be inoculated during the field trial" ("National Foundation for Infantile Paralysis" n.d.). Within a few years, thousands of American schoolchildren were provided with the Salk vaccine to protect them from the scourge of polio. Many parents considered it a miracle. Until that time, scores of American children were routinely killed or paralyzed for life every year by the terrifying disease. Salk, who tested the serum on his own family, chose not to patent the polio vaccine or seek any profits from it so that it could be distributed everywhere free of charge.

Many parents likely would have paid any price to spare their children from polio. Amid the free-spending consumerism that mushroomed during the postwar era, average Americans had enough money for prescription medication, which they considered a reasonable expenditure. At a time when prescription drugs became popular consumer items, perhaps none were more popular than the tranquilizers that were marketed in the postwar era. Approved by the FDA in 1955, one was meprobamate, a tranquilizer sold under the brand name of Miltown. This prescription drug became a familiar part of American life. Milton Berle, the most popular TV comedian of the time, was known to call himself "Miltown" Berle. Unbeknownst to many, the drug's popularity came with a downside, as meprobamate proved to be addictive.

Other products aimed at calming the stress of postwar Americans hit the marketplace during this era. In 1961, Librium was highly successful when it was mass-marketed as a treatment for tension. Valium, a similar type of anti-anxiety medication, was marketed in 1963 "and rapidly became the most prescribed drug in history" (American Chemical Society 2000). Coming of age in the postwar era, many young people observed the behavior of their parents who were eagerly consuming drugs such as tranquilizers. Setting the stage for the psychedelic 1960s and cocaine-drenched 1970s, Baby Boomers went on to develop their own drug culture involving a wide variety of pharmaceuticals.

However, before that happened, a tragic situation emerged that somewhat diminished consumers' faith and unquestioning acceptance of prescription drugs. It also underscored little-known efforts by the FDA and the heroism of its scientists. In the years following the Second World War, pharmaceutical companies were earning billions of dollars. "By 1960, drugs were the most profitable industry in the United States. Pills promising to ease every ache, pain and worry became a trusted part of daily life" (Vanderbes 2023, xv). In the early 1960s, pregnant women suffering from morning sickness were prescribed a new drug called thalidomide, which was marketed as being totally risk-free. However, "no one—not the chemists who patented it, the doctors who prescribed it, or the firms that sold it—knew how the drug worked inside the human body. The research had been shoddy, the safety claims imprudent" (Vanderbes 2023, xv).

Alarming reports were coming in from Europe, Canada, Japan, and other countries where the drug was sold. There were horrendous birth defects—babies born without arms and legs—for thousands of children whose mothers were prescribed the allegedly risk-free drug. In 1962, Dr. Frances Oldham Kelsey (1914–2015), an FDA medical officer, refused to approve thalidomide for sale in the United States. She recognized the danger in thalidomide by reading the scientific documentation. Kelsey came under tremendous corporate pressure to allow FDA approval but refused to do so, saving untold numbers of Americans from lifelong deformity. Despite her refusal, thalidomide was already being widely circulated across the United States because its manufacturer distributed the drug *prior to* FDA approval. "The FDA would eventually beg the Justice Department to bring criminal charges against the firm" (Vanderbes 2023, xvii). However, no indictments were filed. In the face of thalidomide victims across the United States, Congress was moved to pass the Kefauver-Harris Drug Amendments of 1962, "which ushered in a more cautious approach to the drug approval process … to require all drug manufacturers to evaluate the drug's safety in pregnancy" (Miller and Nicolas 2023).

Pregnancy was pervasive in the postwar years from 1946 to 1964. Most approximations of the number of Baby Boomers estimate that about 75 million Americans were born during that time. In 1960, a new prescription drug pertaining to reproduction was marketed for the first time in human history. "Perhaps no contribution of chemistry in the second half of the 20th century had a greater impact on social customs than the development of oral contraceptives" (American Chemical Society 2000). Known commonly as the birth control pill, or simply "The Pill," this prescription drug fueled the white-hot cauldron of the 1960s and 1970s in what came to be known as the sexual revolution.

At first, the Pill seemed like a godsend. When it was introduced, it was convenient and effective in most cases. There were early reports of women suffering such issues as nausea, depression, and weight gain, but many of the Pill's boosters considered those conditions a reasonable exchange for safe, effective birth control. However, about two years after the FDA granted its approval, more severe side effects were being reported, including fatal blood clots and strokes. About a dozen women died, although the manufacturer "maintained that there was no conclusive proof that the Pill caused those deaths, and the FDA assured doctors the drug was safe" ("The Side Effects of the Pill" 2023). As more women turned to the Pill, there continued to be reports of serious side effects. When women met with their doctor, "it was common for their complaints to be dismissed as exaggerated. In other cases their ailments were just considered the price that women had to pay in return for such an effective contraceptive. Neither the drug companies nor the FDA provided doctors with much information on potential side effects due to the Pill" ("The Side Effects of the Pill" 2023).

In the face of what some felt to be inadequate consumer protection for those who used the Pill, some women turned to other means of contraception. An intrauterine device (IUD) called the Dalkon Shield became popular in the early 1970s, but reports filtered back that it too was not without risks. There were cases of "IUD failure, infections and pregnancy. ... According to various reports, there were more than a dozen cases of women who died after miscarrying with a Dalkon IUD still inside them" (Sifferlin 2015). By 1974, reported effects of the device had reached the point that practitioners were ordered to stop prescribing the Dalkon Shield, which at that time was being used by more than three million women. In 1976, the Medical Device Regulation Law, an amendment to the federal Food, Drug, and Cosmetic Act of 1938, authorized the Food and Drug Administration to regulate medical devices that were intended to be marketed to consumers. The FDA would henceforth be required to regulate medical devices during their development, testing, production, and use. It was passed "after some 200,000 women reported injuries from ... the Dalkon Shield" (Blum 2018, 287). Facing lawsuits, the manufacturer of the Dalkon Shield filed for bankruptcy, although the company alerted women through an expensive media campaign that they should have the device removed.

A contemporary case of bankruptcy amid the potential for billions of dollars in lawsuits involved the pharmaceutical company Purdue Pharma. The company was found to have falsely marketed the opioid OxyContin as a nonaddictive painkiller. The Consumer Protection Branch of the US Department of Justice stated that "with more than 84,000 Americans dying annually from prescription drug and synthetic opioid overdoses ... [the agency is] committed to using every available tool to prevent overdose deaths and hold accountable those responsible for the opioid crisis" (US Department of Justice 2023). The Department of Justice cites reliance on the 1938 Food, Drug, and Cosmetic Act as well as partnerships with the FDA in efforts to protect consumers. The Consumer Protection Branch has pursued "both criminal and civil actions against wrongdoing entities and individuals up and down the prescription opioid supply chain" (US Department of Justice 2023). It has sought damages from corporate figures who knew opioids were highly addictive but continued to profit from the sale of the drug.

The array of prescription products on the market today can be both confusing and costly to the average consumer, a situation reminiscent of the era of *caveat emptor*, in which the buyer had to decide whether they could trust the pharmaceuticals they purchased. Americans spend significantly more per capita on prescription drugs than any other country. This is unlikely to decrease, because new drugs are continually being introduced and prices are rising. According to the Center for Medicare and Medicaid Services (CMS), prescription drug spending through the year 2025 is estimated to grow an average of 6.3 percent per year (Olson and Sheiner 2017). Some observers claim that the cost of prescription pharmaceuticals in America "has grown at an unsustainable annual rate … making prescription drugs the fastest-rising component of all health care expenditures" (Avorn 2005, 17).

Recent years have seen a substantial increase in direct-to-consumer advertising (DTCA) for prescription drugs in magazines, on television, via the internet, or through other media. At this time, prescription drug advertisements aimed directly at consumers are only permitted in two countries: New Zealand and the United States. In the United States, "the top advertised drugs are also the top selling drugs. This demonstrates that advertising clearly has an effect on the market" (Genereaux 2023). Classic rock music often appears in ads for medication targeting the aging Baby Boomer generation, perhaps making the products more attractive to consumers. Opponents of DTCA claim that consumers are more likely to suggest a highly advertised drug to their doctor rather than the other way around. When the doctor agrees to prescribe the "as-seen-on-TV" product, it may be more expensive than or not as effective/appropriate for the patient as an alternative medication. Advertisements can also result in unnecessary prescriptions and distort or simplify drug information, insufficiently conveying the risks while maximizing idealized portrayals of presumed benefits. On television, a rapid voice-over at the end of the ad (or small print in other media) lists a multitude of possible side effects that are often difficult for consumers to understand. Supporters of DTCA state that prohibiting such ads would not be in the best interest of consumers because it would limit patients' choices. They claim that DTCA motivates more people to see their physicians and that it promotes "meaningful discussions between doctors and patients about their health, otherwise unknown diagnoses, and available treatments. … Patients also may be more likely to discuss problems with their doctor that they previously did not feel comfortable discussing" (Genereaux 2023).

Direct-to-consumer advertising of prescription drugs "increased dramatically from $166 million in 1993 to $4.2 billion in 2005" (Donohue 2006). According to the Government Accountability Office (GAO), those numbers have continued to rise. "From 2016 through 2018, drug manufacturers spent about $18 billion—roughly $6 billion each year—to advertise over 500 drugs to consumers" (US Government Accountability Office 2021). The GAO states that "manufacturers concentrated the majority of their DTCA spending on about 40 drugs, about half of which FDA had approved for use from 2014 through 2017. Advertisements that appeared on television comprised the largest share of manufacturers' spending across the 3 years" (US Government Accountability Office 2021).

Some observers have noted what they have considered to be a disturbing trend in the FDA's oversight of consumer protection for prescription drugs. Dr. Jerry Avorn, chief of Harvard University's Division of Pharmacoepidemiology and Pharmacoeconomics, cited an FDA advisory committee in 1999 that reviewed clinical trials for several anti-inflammatory/painkiller drugs said to raise the risk of heart attacks or strokes, including one called Vioxx. "Ten of the thirty-two panel members had financial ties to the companies that made the drugs being evaluated … and were ten times more likely to vote in the drug's favor than were members without such ties" (Avorn 2005, xviii). Avorn claims that if the individuals with financial ties to the pharmaceutical companies had recused themselves from the vote, the drugs would not have been approved. Five years later, in 2004, amid evidence that Vioxx was playing a part in greater cardiovascular risk among its consumers, the medication was withdrawn from the market after billions of dollars' worth of the drug had been sold. Some critics pointed to the prevalence of aggressive DTCA in the medication's popularity. In 2008, after a three-year investigation concerning Vioxx advertisements by twenty-nine states and the District of Columbia, the drug maker agreed to pay a settlement of more than 50 million dollars. Avorn, while critical of some factors regarding the FDA's role in consumer protection of prescription drugs, states unequivocally that "medications are one of the finest achievements in all of science, and when used appropriately, the good they do far outweighs their harm. … Most doctors make sound prescribing decisions much of the time, and most drugs are both effective and reasonably safe" (Avorn 2005, 18).

When the FDA was given responsibility for consumer protection in the drug market beginning in 1906, there were relatively few prescription pharmaceuticals on the market, certainly much fewer than today. In the aftermath of the thalidomide tragedy, the 1962 Kefauver-Harris Amendments tasked the FDA with greater accountability to protect consumers of prescription products, requiring that drugs "be proved not only safe but also effective before being marketed" (Donohue 2006). In addition, the twenty-first-century scourge of both the Covid-19 pandemic and America's opioid epidemic have added to the agency's mandate. The agency regulates one trillion dollars' worth of products every year, attempting to ensure the safety and effectiveness of prescription drugs, biological products, and medical devices as well as animal drugs and feed while also overseeing cosmetics and OTC consumer products. It attempts to enforce "more than 200 laws that constitute one of the world's most comprehensive and effective networks of public health and consumer protections" (US Food and Drug Administration 2021).

Further Reading

American Chemical Society. 2000. "The Pharmaceutical Century: Ten Decades of Drug Discovery." Accessed November 27, 2024. https://farmamol.web.uah.es/The%20Pharmaceutical%20Century/Ch4.html.

Avorn, Jerry. 2005. *Powerful Medicines: The Benefits, Risks, and Costs of Prescription Drugs*. New York: Vintage, xviii, 17, 18.

Blum, Deborah. 2018. *The Poison Squad: One Chemist's Single-Minded Crusade for Food Safety at the Turn of the Twentieth Century*. New York: Penguin, 287.

Donohue, Julie. 2006. "A History of Drug Advertising: The Evolving Roles of Consumers and Consumer Protection." National Library of Medicine, National Institutes of Health. Accessed November 27, 2024. https://www.ncbi.nlm.nih.gov/pmc/articles/PMC2690298/.

Genereaux, Grace. 2023. "Addicted to Advertising: Should the U.S. Continue to Allow Direct-to-Consumer Drug Advertising?" *Wake Forest Law Review*. Accessed November 27, 2024. https://www.wakeforestlawreview.com/2023/02/addicted-to-advertising-should-the-u-s-continue-to-allow-direct-to-consumer-drug-advertising/.

Miller, Amanda, and Samar Nicolas. 2023. "Federal Regulation of Medication Dispensing." National Institutes of Health. Accessed November 27, 2024. https://www.ncbi.nlm.nih.gov/books/NBK582130/.

"National Foundation for Infantile Paralysis Poliomyelitis Vaccination Field Trial Record." n.d. Smithsonian. Accessed September 10, 2024. https://www.si.edu/object/national-foundation-infantile-paralysis-poliomyelitis-vaccination-field-trial-record%3Anmah_694741.

Olson, Peter, and Louise Sheiner. 2017. "The Hutchins Center Explains: Prescription Drug Spending." Brookings Institution. Accessed November 27, 2024. https://www.brookings.edu/articles/the-hutchins-center-explains-prescription-drug-spending/.

"The Side Effects of the Pill." 2023. *American Experience*. Accessed November 27, 2024. https://www.pbs.org/wgbh/americanexperience/features/pill-side-effects/.

Sifferlin, Alexandra. 2015. "Why People Were Scared of IUDs." Time. Accessed November 27, 2024. https://time.com/4106290/dalkon-shield-history/.

Texas Tech University. 2023. "The History of Pharmacy." Accessed November 27, 2024. https://www.ttuhsc.edu/pharmacy/museum/pharmacy.history.aspx.

US Department of Justice, Consumer Protection Branch. 2023. "Opioid Enforcement Effort." Accessed November 27, 2024. https://www.justice.gov/civil/consumer-protection-branch/opioid.

US Food and Drug Administration. 2017. "Prescription Drugs and Over-the-Counter (OTC) Drugs: Questions and Answers." Accessed November 27, 2024. https://www.fda.gov/drugs/frequently-asked-questions-popular-topics/prescription-drugs-and-over-counter-otc-drugs-questions-and-answers.

US Food and Drug Administration. 2021. "Laws Enforced by FDA." Accessed November 27, 2024. https://www.fda.gov/regulatory-information/laws-enforced-fda.

US Food and Drug Administration. 2022. "New Drug Application (NDA)." Accessed November 27, 2024. https://www.fda.gov/drugs/types-applications/new-drug-application-nda.

US Government Accountability Office. 2021. "Prescription Drugs: Medicare Spending on Drugs with Direct-to-Consumer Advertising." Accessed November 27, 2024. https://www.gao.gov/assets/gao-21-380.pdf.

Vanderbes, Jennifer. 2023. *Wonder Drug: The Secret History of Thalidomide in America and Its Hidden Victims*. New York: Random House, xv, xvii.

Q22: Is healthcare shielded from consumer rights and protections?

Answer: Medical care in general is not immune from certain kinds of consumer rights and protections. In recent years, with the rise of technology, there have been tremendous advances in America's healthcare field, as well as a greater emphasis on the rights and protections available to consumers of medical services. Many of today's life-saving procedures, such as open-heart surgery, often seem to be miraculous. However, with such remarkable advances, there have also come rising medical costs as well as issues concerning health insurance. Periodically, there have been calls for a major reorganization of America's healthcare system to provide more equitable services for all consumers of medical care regardless of socioeconomic status. These proposals have often led to arguments that such a restructuring would mean initiating a universal healthcare plan. Opponents of such a system have labelled it "socialized medicine," an arrangement that they feel would be detrimental to American consumers and the nation as a whole.

The Facts: In 1799, former president George Washington (1732–1799) felt unwell, suffering from a sore throat. After calling a trusted physician who utilized the conventional wisdom of the day, the doctor proceeded to remove the bad "humours," or fluids in the body that were thought to cause disease. Removing them was done by draining blood from the patient to let the bad humours out, a procedure that was common medical practice for hundreds of years. Unfortunately, in most cases, bloodletting hurt rather than healed the patient. About 40 percent of Washington's blood was drained from his body, and he died at age sixty-seven.

In Washington's era, there were few, if any, consumer rights and protections of any kind, particularly those pertaining to patients in America seeking medical care. It would take about two hundred years for that to happen. Prior to the latter part of the twentieth century, most consumers of medical care were bound by the rule of *caveat emptor*, even in matters of health. However, in the 1960s and 1970s, there were tremendous social changes in America, with great strides in all areas of consumer rights and protections, including healthcare.

In 1973, the Patient's Bill of Rights was introduced by the American Hospital Association (AHA). It was revised in 1992 and updated in 2003. Briefly, it is

a listing of what consumers of medical services should reasonably be able to expect such as information about their individual case, access to medical records, and type of treatment. Under the Patient's Bill of Rights, consumers of healthcare have the right to expect that they and their families will be kept informed about the status of their condition, will be treated fairly, and will have some control over medical decisions. The AHA encouraged each healthcare facility in the United States to adapt these rights to fit the needs of their particular community. "That's why there's not one single version of the Patient's Bill of Rights, but many versions" (Bazemore 2016a).

While the AHA's Patient's Bill of Rights was not legally binding, there are some consumer protections that are guaranteed by federal law, including the right of access to one's medical records as well as the right to keep those records private. In 2003, the AHA introduced a new conceptual model to promote the sense that healthcare is a partnership between the medical team and the patient/consumer. Replacing the original Patient's Bill of Rights, the Patient Care Partnership is meant to be available in a brochure distributed upon hospital admission, printed in several languages to inform consumers of medical care in simple terms what they may reasonably expect. These expectations include a clean and safe environment, high-quality care, involvement in their treatment, and protection of their privacy. Also generally included are sections on assistance when leaving the hospital as well as pointers for help with billing claims.

In June 2010, US President Barack Obama (1961–) announced a collaboration of the Department of Health and Human Services, Department of Labor, and Department of the Treasury on a Patient's Bill of Rights to help Americans with preexisting conditions, protect their choice of doctors, and end lifetime limits on the care that the patients/consumers may receive. According to the Centers for Medicare and Medicare Services, "These new protections create an important foundation of patients' rights in the private health insurance market that puts Americans in charge of their own health" (Centers for Medicare and Medicaid Services 2023). Congress passed the Patient Protection and Affordable Care Act (ACA) in 2010, establishing patient rights, including the right to buy insurance despite having preexisting health conditions in many circumstances without being denied coverage or facing additional charges. It instituted the right to many types of preventive care, to have some choice of a healthcare provider, maintain health insurance despite becoming sick, and the right to essential health benefits over the course of one's lifetime.

The American Medical Association (AMA) states that "physicians can best contribute to a mutually respectful alliance with patients by serving as their patients' advocates and by respecting patients' rights" (American Medical Association 2023). The AMA adopted a Code of Ethics, under which patients as consumers have the right:

(a) To courtesy, respect, dignity, and timely, responsive attention to his or her needs.

(b) To receive information from their physicians and to have opportunity to discuss the benefits, risks, and costs of appropriate treatment alternatives, including the risks, benefits and costs of forgoing treatment. Patients should be able to expect that their physicians will provide guidance about what they consider the optimal course of action for the patient based on the physician's objective professional judgment.

(c) To ask questions about their health status or recommended treatment when they do not fully understand what has been described and to have their questions answered.

(d) To make decisions about the care the physician recommends and to have those decisions respected. A patient who has decision-making capacity may accept or refuse any recommended medical intervention.
(e) To have the physician and other staff respect the patient's privacy and confidentiality.
(f) To obtain copies or summaries of their medical records.
(g) To obtain a second opinion.
(h) To be advised of any conflicts of interest their physician may have in respect to their care.
(i) To continuity of care. Patients should be able to expect that their physician will cooperate in coordinating medically indicated care with other health care professionals, and that the physician will not discontinue treating them when further treatment is medically indicated without giving them sufficient notice and reasonable assistance in making alternative arrangements for care. (American Medical Association 2023)

Many of the recent enhanced consumer rights and protections in the healthcare field have been aimed at helping give Americans a greater role in their own medical care. Part of empowering consumers regarding their own health is what is called *informed consent*. "According to the AMA, a patient can only make an informed choice about whether or not to receive a treatment if they have enough information about the treatment, its benefits, and side effects" (Bazemore 2016b). It is considered the duty of the doctor to provide appropriate information for the consumer to make intelligent decisions regarding their health. Informed consent is not to be taken lightly: "Failure to obtain informed consent is a crime—medical malpractice, specifically—and the doctor can be charged with negligence" (Bazemore 2016b). As a guideline, the AMA lists six basic items constituting informed consent: the diagnosis, the customary treatment or procedure, risks and benefits of the treatment, alternatives to the treatment, risks and benefits of alternatives, and risks and benefits of *not* having the treatment.

In recent years, along with an increased awareness and concern regarding mental illness have come more protections for consumers needing care for mental health issues. The Affordable Care Act expanded the right to benefits that were not previously insured, including mental health benefits. Historically, however, consumer protections concerning mental health and mental health treatment were almost nonexistent.

One area of particular concern for consumers regarding mental health was involuntary commitment. As opposed to voluntary hospitalization, it is now "most closely scrutinized under law because involuntary commitment unwillingly deprives a person of liberty" (Cochran and Caton 2016). Throughout much of our nation's history, however, women were frequently subjected to involuntary commitment to mental health facilities, at the time known as "insane asylums." Women could be committed for such alleged offenses as reading, seeking an education, having ambitions outside the home, fighting for the right to vote, standing up to abusive husbands, or going through the change of life. "A woman's menstrual cycle alone could see her committed" (Moore 2021). For centuries, the conventional wisdom held by doctors, who were virtually all male, was that "assertive, ambitious women were unnatural, and therefore sick. … [One man] found he could arrange his wife's committal simply 'by the request of the husband' and specifically 'without the evidence of insanity required in other cases'" (Moore 2021). Mary Todd Lincoln (1818–1881), widow of President Abraham Lincoln, was involuntarily committed to a mental hospital by her only surviving son due to her frequent bouts of depression and migraine headaches. With standard treatment procedures for "insane" women including everything from beatings to ice baths to genital mutilation, there were few protections for those involuntary consumers of mental health care.

It was not until the latter part of the twentieth century that Congress passed the Protection and Advocacy for Mentally Ill Individuals Act of 1986. The law "created a protection and advocacy system for persons with mental illnesses similar to the system already in place for persons with developmental disabilities" (Cochran and Caton 2016). In that way, consumers of mental health care could receive a higher degree of rights and protections.

Navigating the modern healthcare system can be a bewildering maze, particularly in a hospital setting. Many hospitals have established a liaison between patients/consumers and healthcare professionals through an official called an ombudsman. According to the *Merriam-Webster* dictionary, "ombudsman" is derived from a Swedish term for "representative." In America, an ombudsman is a person who investigates and helps settle complaints. Within a hospital setting, the services of the facility's ombudsman are generally free of charge. At one average institution, the Cleveland Clinic in Ohio, a hospital spokesperson stated that in one year, the facility's ombudsman department "handled over 22,000 cases … and when [patients] leave they are so pleased, they send thank-you notes" (Advisory Board 2023). Many advocates of the ombudsman system believe that patients as consumers may be too intimidated to bring their concerns directly to doctors or hospital administrators, but by serving as a middle ground, ombudsmen "hear more from patients than anyone in uniform ever will" (Advisory Board 2023).

Patients as consumers have the right to involve the hospital's ombudsman in matters concerning their care within the hospital setting but seldom beyond. Some healthcare consumers choose to hire a private patient advocate to help with such matters as navigating visits to doctors and monitoring at-home treatments. Hospital ombudsmen typically assist patient/consumers at no charge, but "hiring a private patient advocate can be expensive ... and neither Medicare nor private insurance will reimburse for the cost" (Advisory Board 2023).

Many healthcare systems established ombudsman programs amid the general atmosphere of the consumer rights movement that grew in strength during the 1960s and 1970s and included advances for patients' rights. That movement was underscored by two polarizing medical cases that focused public attention on private tragedies. Both involved the "right to die."

In 1975, Karen Ann Quinlan (1954–1985) fell into a coma at age twenty-one after an evening out with friends. She remained on a respirator for several months in what doctors called a persistent vegetative state, having sustained severe brain damage and lost nearly all cognitive functions. Quinlan's father asked physicians to turn off the respirator in order to end her suffering, but the doctors refused. The case went to the New Jersey Supreme Court in a ruling that became known as America's first "right to die" case. "Based on the right to privacy, the court ruled that 'no compelling interest of the state could compel Karen to endure the unendurable'" ("Top Ten Comas" n.d.). The patient/consumer was determined to have certain rights and protections even while in a vegetative state. Quinlan was taken off life support but made headlines again when she survived in a nursing home for ten more years.

Terry Schiavo (1963–2005) was also deemed to be in a persistent vegetative state after collapsing from heart failure in 1990 at age twenty-seven. She had been kept alive on a feeding tube for ten years when her husband petitioned to take her off life support. There were objections from "social conservatives, concerned the case would set a precedent for the right-to-die movement" ("Top Ten Comas" n.d.). Despite congressional intervention that sent her case into federal court, doctors unplugged her feeding tube. She died less than two weeks later.

Both cases directed a spotlight on issues involving consumer rights for patients. Besides the question of who has the right to decide a person's fate, some observers also asked whether the Quinlan and Schiavo cases would have been so contentious if the patients had not been in a financial position to obtain hospital services. This brought the issues of healthcare access and "universal healthcare" for all Americans to the forefront. Universal healthcare is a system of providing medical care and hospital stays for every patient/consumer regardless of socioeconomic status. The structure of such services is handled via government regulation of the healthcare industry and funded through subsidies derived from taxes. A number of countries around the world have adopted universal healthcare, including Australia, Canada, Germany, Italy, Japan, New Zealand, Portugal, Singapore, South Korea, Spain, Switzerland, and the United Kingdom.

The concept is not new. Norway adopted universal healthcare in 1912. US President Harry Truman (1884–1972) proposed a national healthcare plan in 1945. Truman's plan contained goals that included lowering the cost of individual medical care, addressing the lack of trained healthcare providers in low-income communities, increasing funds for medical education and research, and alleviating the burden of long-term care. Believing that healthcare for all citizens is a basic human right, Truman presented his plan to Congress. His proposed program was primarily to be funded through taxation in order to cover costs. However, "it was quickly shot down as people began to fear an increase in taxes. Some people even feared the program would be a 'Communist' act, giving too much control to the federal government" (Harry S. Truman Library and Museum n.d.). In the United States, proposals for universal healthcare are often accompanied by a negative association with Communism through the pejorative term "socialized medicine," invoking the specter of socialism. Arguments against Medicare and the Affordable Care Act often centered on objections to what were seen as socialist programs. In 1965, the Medicare Act was passed under US President Lyndon Johnson (1908–1973) to provide healthcare for American citizens aged sixty-five and older. At the bill-signing ceremony for the law, Johnson enrolled former president Harry Truman as the first beneficiary of the plan, presenting the 81-year-old Truman with the nation's first Medicare card, followed by one for Truman's wife Bess.

Consumer rights and protections are invoked by both sides of the debate over universal healthcare. Supporters claim it is the right of all American consumers to have equal access to quality care regardless of socioeconomic status. Apart from a goal of reducing the healthcare gap between the "haves" and "have nots," supporters of a universal healthcare system argue that the nation would be in a position to quickly address emerging diseases such as Covid-19 by having a system with a central directive to combat the pandemic, plus funding from the government to do so. Supporters also claim that a universal system would be poised to adopt preventive health initiatives, benefitting consumers by eliminating costly medical treatments before they are needed for such conditions as diabetes and obesity. Advocates state that any strains on the national economy would be mitigated by reducing the financial impact of an unhealthy, uninsured, low-income segment of the population, whose costs must be paid by other Americans. For example, "the uninsured diabetic population is responsible for 55% more emergency room visits each year than their insured diabetic counterparts" (Zieff et al. 2020). In addition, obesity rates are greater in lower socioeconomic populations. "The costs of obesity in the US, when limited to lost productivity alone, have been projected to equate to 66 billion dollars annually" (Zieff et al. 2020). Supporters of universal healthcare say those costs have to be ultimately absorbed by American consumers, leaving people with less discretionary income to spend.

Opponents of universal healthcare have a different interpretation, particularly regarding how such a system would impact average consumers. They note the high tax rates in those countries that maintain a universal healthcare system, depleting the discretionary income of the average consumer. For example, Sweden has a tax rate of 56.6 percent on income over $85,841; Belgians are taxed 50 percent on income over $45,037; and Ireland levies a 48 percent tax rate on income over $40,696 (Gilbert 2023). In the United States, there are currently seven tax brackets ranging from 10 percent to 37 percent, with the highest tax rate affecting incomes over $600,000 for single taxpayers.

Those who oppose universal healthcare also point out that the United States covers a huge geographical territory, ranging from densely populated urban sprawls to large swaths of sparsely occupied rural zones. The nation runs from Arctic tundra to tropics to deserts, all of which are home to inhabitants with different healthcare needs. Along with its vast geography, opponents observe that America is home to a diverse range of cultural, ethnic, political, racial, religious, and socioeconomic populations. Those demographics are usually not as widely varied in other countries, and all of those factors present different health needs and challenges across the United States. "Thus, critics of universal healthcare in the US argue that implementation would not be as feasible—organizationally or financially—as other developed nations" (Zieff et al. 2020).

In addition, opponents argue that initiating universal healthcare would require huge upfront costs that would affect consumers. These include adapting infrastructure to handle increased demand, which might predictably come from a previously uninsured and often unhealthy segment of the population. Implementing universal healthcare would also require massive administrative oversight at the federal, state, and local levels. Opponents believe doctor's offices, hospitals, out-patient clinics, and pharmacies would be overwhelmed, with additional staff needed to handle the increased number of patients. One way or another, all of those costs would have to be passed along to consumers. Shortages in medical staffing in the United States are already an issue in some areas. Opponents to universal healthcare argue that consumers would be hurt by long wait times and inferior care. According to research by the National Institutes of Health, in a 2017 study covering about a million procedures in Canada, the median waiting time for certain kinds of surgery was twenty to fifty-two weeks. "Similarly, average waiting time for elective hospital-based care in the United Kingdom is 46 days, while some patients wait over a year" (Zieff et al. 2020). These potential outcomes are often the central point of campaigns to discourage government intervention in the America healthcare system. An ad that appeared in Washington, DC, newspapers contained the message, "In America, you wait in line to see a movie. In government-run health care systems, you wait to see a doctor" (Potter 2009).

While issues such as tax increases and waiting time are major concerns for many opponents of universal healthcare, one of their most basic arguments is a time-tested one: that the government has no place interfering with private business. Governmental presence in medical care, they feel, would inevitably lead to the kind of inefficiency and disorganization that often follows bureaucratic involvement. Intrusion by the government, they argue, would also deter the incentive for medical innovation by entrepreneurs.

Many patients/consumers believe they are sufficiently covered by rights and protections in healthcare at the current time. Both the supporters of universal healthcare and its opponents seem to agree that it would be a radical shift for American consumers if such a system were to be implemented in the United States.

Further Reading

Advisory Board. 2023. "What Hospital Ombudsmen Really Do (And Why Some Patients Hire Their Own Advocates Instead)." Accessed November 27, 2024. https://www.advisory.com/daily-briefing/2019/10/03/patient-advocates.

American Medical Association. 2023. "Patient Rights." *AMA Code of Medical Ethics.* Accessed November 27, 2024. https://code-medical-ethics.ama-assn.org/ethics-opinions/patient-rights.

Bazemore, Nichole. 2016a. "Here's Everything You Need to Know about the Patient's Bill of Rights." *Forbes*. Accessed November 27, 2024. https://www.forbes.com/sites/amino/2016/03/21/heres-everything-you-need-to-know-about-the-patients-bill-of-rights/?sh=506b66d76d01.

Bazemore, Nichole. 2016b. "Not All Doctors Get Informed Consent—Here's Why It's Hurting Patients." *Forbes*. Accessed November 27, 2024. https://www.forbes.com/sites/amino/2016/03/28/not-all-doctors-get-informed-consent-heres-why-its-hurting-patients/?sh=46f42c0e496c.

Centers for Medicare and Medicaid Services. 2023. "Patient's Bill of Rights." Accessed November 27, 2024. https://www.cms.gov/marketplace/private-health-insurance/patient-bill-of-rights.

Cochran, Doug, revised by Rochelle Caton. 2016. "A Brief History of Patient Rights Nationally and at the South Carolina Department of Mental Health." South Carolina Department of Mental Health. Accessed November 27, 2024. https://scdmh.net/patients_families/patient-advocacy-2/3343-2/.

Donohue, Julie. 2006. "A History of Drug Advertising: The Evolving Roles of Consumers and Consumer Protection." National Library of Medicine, National Institutes of Health. Accessed November 27, 2024. https://www.ncbi.nlm.nih.gov/pmc/articles/PMC2690298/.

Gilbert, Nestor. 2023. "Top Ten Countries with Highest Tax Rates." *Finances Online*. Accessed November 27, 2024. https://financesonline.com/top-ten-countries-with-highest-tax-rates/.

Harry S. Truman Library and Museum. n.d. "The Challenge of National Healthcare." Accessed September 10, 2024. https://www.trumanlibrary.gov/education/presidential-inquiries/challenge-national-healthcare.

Moore, Kate. 2021. "Declared Insane for Speaking Up: The Dark American History of Silencing Women Through Psychiatry." *Time*. Accessed November 27, 2024. https://time.com/6074783/psychiatry-history-women-mental-health/.

National Institutes of Health. 2016. "Patient Rights." Accessed November 27, 2024. https://medlineplus.gov/patientrights.html.

Olejarczyk, Jacob, and Michael Young. 2022. "Patient Rights and Ethics." National Library of Medicine, National Center for Biotechnology Information. Accessed November 27, 2024. https://www.ncbi.nlm.nih.gov/books/NBK538279/

Potter, Wendell. 2009. "How Corporate PR Works to Kill Health Care Reform." Center for Media and Democracy. Accessed November 27, 2024. https://www.prwatch.org/node/8552.

"Top Ten Comas." n.d. *Time*. Accessed September 10, 2024. https://content.time.com/time/specials/packages/completelist/0,29569,1864940,00.html.

Zieff, G., Z. Kerr, J. Moore, and L. Stoner. 2020. "Universal Healthcare in the United States of America: A Healthy Debate." National Library of Medicine, National Institutes of Health. Accessed November 27, 2024. https://www.ncbi.nlm.nih.gov/pmc/articles/PMC7692272/.

6

Consumer Rights and Protections in Transportation

Consumer protection in the field of transportation is a relatively new development in the United States. For much of the country's history, the average American's traveling companion was *caveat emptor*, otherwise known as "buyer beware." In the nation's early days, roads that were often little more than rutted trails were the primary means of travel by wagon, horse, or foot when there was no body of water nearby to make the trip by boat. Hazards such as highwaymen and natural disasters made for many precarious journeys. On a stagecoach, consumer protection would have been an unknown concept. Arriving in one piece with their money and belongings intact was enough for many.

With the coming of the Industrial Revolution in the mid-1800s, improved transportation forged America's destiny. The expansion of railroads for long-distance travel and the growth of streetcars in cities during the late 1800s and early 1900s meant that people, goods, food products, and raw materials moved around the country with speed and efficiency that had been inconceivable just a few years before. Then, beginning in the 1920s, a transportation revolution for the average consumer arrived with the advent of the automobile age. Cars became an integral part of everyday life in the United States after becoming affordable for average Americans and not simply a toy for the rich. However, for many years, consumer rights and protections were not a significant feature of the automotive industry.

A substantial increase in the number of motorcars on the road every year brought a proportional increase in fatalities. In the mid-1960s, a young lawyer named Ralph Nader noted that auto accidents were a major cause of death in the United States. He believed the reason was that the *cars themselves* were dangerous due to the tendency of automotive manufacturers to seek profits over safety. Although he was opposed by the auto industry, Nader's work would make him a household name not only in automobile safety but also in the field of consumer rights and protections in general.

Similarly, when air travel became accessible to Americans of all income levels, greater numbers of passengers led to more flights, which led to an increase in aviation-related incidents. An air traffic "meltdown" during late 2022 resulted in members of Congress introducing a proposal for an Airline Passengers' Bill of Rights. Rail advocacy groups have called for the same level of consumer rights and protections for train travel.

American transportation made stunning advances in a matter of a few decades. Along with the transportation revolution came increasing demands for greater rights and protections for its consumers.

Q23: What role did Ralph Nader play in automotive consumer rights and protections?

Answer: Any look at consumer protections in the automobile industry must focus on Ralph Nader, who became a consumer rights icon beginning in the mid-1960s, remaining active into the twenty-first century. Credited with automotive consumer protection laws such as the National Traffic and Motor Vehicle Safety Act in 1966, Nader was both applauded and vilified, much as Harvey Washington Wiley had been when Wiley challenged the food industry. After the publication of Nader's book *Unsafe at Any Speed,* auto manufacturer General Motors hired private detectives to investigate Nader's private life. Nothing objectionable was found, and Nader won a substantial settlement for invasion of privacy. Just as Wiley became instrumental in food safety, many automotive protections for consumers that are taken for granted today can be attributed to one man: Ralph Nader.

The Facts: In 1910, Dr. Harvey Washington Wiley, who had fought for the passage of the Pure Food and Drug Act of 1906, bought one of the first automobiles in Washington, DC. For most of Wiley's life, transportation had been dominated by the horse. Therefore, it was ironic that almost immediately after he started driving his new car, it was damaged in an accident—with a horse-drawn wagon. Wiley described the incident as "a collision between the past and the future" (Blum 2018, 234).

Four years after Wiley died in 1930, Ralph Nader was born. Just as Wiley had been a household name in the early twentieth century for his efforts,

Nader became widely known as a leading consumer advocate. Although he has spearheaded efforts in other fields, Nader became synonymous for his battle over consumer rights and protections in the American automotive industry. In 1965, Nader was propelled into the spotlight with his bestselling nonfiction book, *Unsafe at Any Speed: The Designed-in Dangers of the American Automobile.*

After earning a law degree from Harvard, Nader was working as an attorney in his home state of Connecticut in 1959. He learned that auto accidents were the fourth leading cause of death in the United States, just after heart disease, cancer, and strokes. At the time, car owners had few consumer rights or protections. Studying auto injury cases, Nader became convinced that driver mistakes were too often the focus of laws, with little attention paid to the unsafe design of cars.

In *Unsafe at Any Speed,* Nader charged that American cars were generally risky to drive because automakers cut costs at the expense of safety. One car in particular, the Chevrolet Corvair, attracted Nader's attention. He researched legal case files on about 100 liability lawsuits against General Motors (GM), the American automaker that manufactured the Corvair. Nader claimed that due to its combination of a rear-engine layout and design flaw in its suspension system, the sporty vehicle was constructed with built-in hazards. Those alleged defects made the car susceptible to rolling over during sharp turns or abrupt movements like trying to avoid something unexpected in the road. In his book, Nader's chapter about the Corvair was titled "The One-Car Accident." According to automotive journalist Anita Leinert, "no official records exist of the number of people who died or were injured in the 1,695,765 Corvairs produced in the 1960s" (Lienert 1994). In any case, the Corvair's image was tarnished when Nader's book hit the bestseller lists.

Soon, Ralph Nader became a popular culture celebrity when it was discovered that GM had hired private detectives to discredit Nader through his politics, religion, and/or sex life "by tapping his phone in an attempt to uncover salacious information and, when that failed, hiring prostitutes in an attempt to catch him in a compromising situation" (Glass 2017). An inquiry ensued after Nader reported his suspicions of being followed to government officials. Under oath before a Senate subcommittee, the chairman of GM was forced to admit to those acts and apologize for this invasion of privacy, eventually paying Nader a $425,000 settlement (almost $4 million in 2022 dollars). Nader created a number of public interest groups with the awarded money.

In 1966, less than a year after *Unsafe at Any Speed* was published, Congress passed the National Traffic and Motor Vehicle Safety Act. The law mandated such requirements as seat belts, child safety seats, and safer brakes. In

Congress, Speaker of the House John McCormack said the passage of the act was due to the "crusading spirit of one individual who believed he could do something: Ralph Nader" (Lienert 1994). Not everyone was complimentary, however. Nader was criticized by corporate leaders and some politicians who said "such reforms made trial lawyers richer, drove up the cost of products, and created a lawsuit culture" ("How Ralph Nader Defined Consumer Rights" 2015).

In 1972, results were released of a study of the Corvair by the National Highway Traffic Safety Administration (NHTSA), a federal agency that was created in 1970. It concluded that "Chevrolet's 1960–63 Corvair models were at least as safe as comparable models of similar cars sold during in the same period" (Glass 2017). Nader fired back, calling the study "a shoddy, internally contradictory whitewash [using] biased testing procedures and model selection" (Glass 2017). After 1969, the Corvair was no longer being assembled. So by the time the 1972 NHTSA report came out, General Motors had already decided to halt development of the Corvair. Contrary to some public perceptions, automotive experts state that the decision was not made because of Nader but rather due to the enthusiastic response of car buyers to the sporty Mustang, which was introduced in 1964 by the Ford Motor Company. At GM, "development dollars were then shifted to make the Camaro because they wanted to create a car that could directly compete with the Mustang" (McGuire 2016). The Corvair "just couldn't compete with the muscle cars" (Lienert 1994).

Vehicles manufactured by Ford were not spared from Nader's scrutiny. Introduced in 1970, Ford's subcompact car called the Pinto was reported as having a tendency to explode into flames if a collision burst its gas tank. Lawsuits "by injured people and their survivors uncovered how the company rushed the Pinto through production and onto the market" (American Museum of Tort Law n.d.). After "an estimated 500 deaths and hundreds of injuries were linked to a faulty design that made the gasoline tank vulnerable to explosion after rear-end collisions" (Sherefkin 2003), more than one hundred lawsuits were filed against Ford. In 1981, a court found that the company knowingly endangered Pinto drivers by ignoring safety precautions that would have cost very little for the manufacturer to install.

Nader accused Ford of delaying a recall of Pintos when the problem was discovered. Substantiating Nader's claims, an investigation by the National Highway Traffic Safety Administration ultimately led to a recall in 1978 not only of Ford Pintos but also Ford's Mercury Bobcats and GM's Chevrolet Chevettes for fuel tank modifications. However, it was the image of burning Pintos that caught the attention of consumers. The perception was not helped by Ford advertisements that had initially included the line, "Pinto leaves you with that warm feeling" (American Museum of Tort Law n.d.). That sentence was eventually dropped from the ads.

There were complaints from automakers that Nader's criticisms would lead to government regulations that would hinder growth and stifle innovation. Henry Ford II, who headed the Ford Motor Company, said that minimum safety standards were "unreasonable, arbitrary, and technically unfeasible. If we can't meet them when they are published we'll have to close down" (Keller 2017). The company did meet the safety standards, and as of this writing, the Ford Motor Company is still in business.

Having spurred car safety features that are standard today such as airbags, antilock brakes, seatbelts, and padded dashboards, many people think of Ralph Nader exclusively in terms of consumer rights and protections involving the auto industry. However, Nader "went on to address a vast litany of issues: unsanitary food preparation, flammable clothing, avaricious sports franchises, [and] the limits of standardized testing. … The net result of all Nader's frenetic activity was a full-blown movement: consumerism" (Martin 2002, xiv). In addition, Nader "is a fierce proponent of openness on the part of government and corporations—in fact, he is the primary architect of [1967's] Freedom of Information Act" (Martin 2002, xiv). Nader was instrumental in the passage of more than two dozen landmark laws promoting consumer protection, including the Occupational Safety and Health Act (1970), Clean Water Act (1972), Consumer Product Safety Act (1972), Foreign Corrupt Practices Act (1977), and Whistleblower Protection Act (1989). His efforts also resulted in the creation of the Environmental Protection Agency (1970). According to the *Digital History* website, whose partners include the National Endowment for the Humanities, "Few Americans have ever compiled such a long and impressive list of legislative accomplishment" ("Ralph Nader and the Consumer Movement" 2021). Ralph Nader has been a polarizing force, inspiring both those who support his work (called "Nader's Raiders") as well as opponents ("Nader Haters").

According to biographer Justin Martin, "when a US president's term ends, another one is elected. … But there has only ever been one Ralph Nader" (Martin 2002, xiv). However, there may have been a fictional precursor to Nader in an 1882 play by Norwegian playwright Henrik Ibsen titled *An Enemy of the People*. In the drama, a man exposes a deadly secret when he finds that the water in the town's health spa is contaminated. He demands that it be shut down. Facing loss of profits if the spa is closed, the town labels him an enemy of the people, with disastrous results for him and his family. Yet, despite the consequences, he remains proud of standing alone against powerful foes. Some today might find the tale comparable to that of Ralph Nader.

Further Reading

American Museum of Tort Law. n.d. "Grimshaw v. Ford Motor Company, 1981." Accessed September 10, 2024. https://www.tortmuseum.org/ford-pinto/.

Blum, Deborah. 2018. *The Poison Squad: One Chemist's Single-Minded Crusade for Food Safety at the Turn of the Twentieth Century*. New York: Penguin, 234.

Glass, Andrew. 2017. "Federal Study Refutes Nader's Corvair Charges, July 20, 1972." *Politico*. Accessed November 28, 2024. https://www.politico.com/story/2017/07/20/federal-study-refutes-naders-corvair-charges-july-20-1972-240609.

"How Ralph Nader Defined Consumer Rights." 2015. *PBS NewsHour*. Accessed November 28, 2024. https://www.pbs.org/newshour/classroom/2015/12/how-ralph-nader-defined-consumer-rights/.

Keller, Jared Robert. 2017. "What Ralph Nader Taught Us About Car Safety—and the Virtue of Red Tape." *Enterprise*. Accessed November 28, 2024. https://thelongandshort.org/enterprise/ralph-nader-car-safety-regulation.

Lienert, Anita. 1994. "25 Years after Its Demise, Corvair Remains an Object of Derision and Devotion." *Chicago Tribune*. Accessed November 28, 2024. https://www.chicagotribune.com/news/ct-xpm-1994-11-13-9411130268-story.html.

Martin, Justin. 2002. *Nader: Crusader, Spoiler, Icon*. New York: Basic Books, xiv.

McGuire, Eva. 2016. "The Last Corvairs." *Corvair Society of America*. Accessed November 28, 2024. https://www.corvair.org/index.php/home/history-and-preservation/meet-the-makers/the-last-corvairs.

Nader, Ralph. 1965. *Unsafe at Any Speed: The Designed-in Dangers of the American Automobile*. New York: Grossman Publishers.

Nader, Ralph. 2000. *The Ralph Nader Reader*. New York: Seven Stories Press.

"Ralph Nader—An Unreasonable Man." 2006. *YouTube*. Accessed November 28, 2024. https://www.youtube.com/watch?v=9ycR36N68R8.

"Ralph Nader and the Consumer Movement." 2021. *Digital History*. Accessed November 28, 2024. https://www.digitalhistory.uh.edu/disp_textbook.cfm?smtid=2&psid=3351.

Ralph Nader: The Official Website of Ralph Nader. Accessed November 28, 2024. https://nader.org/.

Sherefkin, Robert. 2003. "Ford 100: Defective Pinto Almost Took Ford's Reputation with It." *Autoweek*. Accessed November 28, 2024. https://www.autoweek.com/news/a2099001/ford-100-defective-pinto-almost-took-fords-reputation-it/.

Q24: Do consumer rights and protections cover the automotive industry and car sales?

Answer: While many consumer protections in the automobile industry concern safety factors, there are also other elements of consumer rights for car buyers. Agencies such as the Federal Trade Commission and various state entities play significant roles in guaranteeing consumer rights in the auto-related field. This includes guarding against deceptive advertising and false claims in loan arrangements as well as monitoring warranty schemes, service contracts, and dubious financing plans that may not be in the best interest of the consumer.

The Facts: According to Derek Thompson, staff writer for *The Atlantic* magazine, there were about two million cars on the roadways of America when the Federal Trade Commission (FTC) opened its doors in 1915. However, there were not many actual roads outside major cities. "In 1915, 100 million people lived in the United States [equating to] about one car for every 50 people" (Thompson 2016). By 2015, one hundred years later, there were "more than 255 million registered vehicles in the United States" (Thompson 2016). By 2023, that number grew to about 290 million.

With the number of cars steadily increasing over the years, there came to be a need for greater consumer rights and protections regarding selling and maintaining autos, often one of the most expensive outlays in the life of the average consumer. For many, purchasing a car is one of their biggest expenditures, often ranking only behind buying a home in terms of cost, both in an initial down payment and fees associated with financing over the years. In addition, having a reliable auto is essential for most people in order to preserve their livelihoods and maintain their daily lives and those of their family.

Many areas of auto-related consumer rights and protections fall under the jurisdiction of the Federal Trade Commission. A large part of the consumer protections afforded by the FTC in the automotive trade involve investigating possible deceptive advertising as well as questionable practices in financing and warranties. Additional authority was granted to the FTC through the Dodd-Frank Wall Street Reform and Consumer Protection Act, passed by the US Congress in 2010. This federal law was aimed at overhauling financial regulation in the aftermath of a major recession that plagued the United States from 2007 to 2009. The economic turndown affected many other segments of the nation's economy, including the automotive industry. The Dodd-Frank Act gave the

FTC expanded authority regarding motor vehicle dealers that were already in place as well as new responsibilities in areas of oversight. "Since 2011, the FTC has been gathering information on possible consumer protection issues that may arise in the sale, financing, or lease of motor vehicles by seeking public comments" (Federal Trade Commission n.d.b). These include regulatory actions against "companies falsely promising to reduce auto loan payments, car dealers and others making deceptive advertising claims, telemarketers pitching bogus auto 'warranties' that are actually extended service contracts, and companies promoting illegal pyramid operations through lease offers" (Federal Trade Commission n.d.b).

The FTC is also responsible for enforcing the "Used Car Rule," formally known as the Used Motor Vehicle Trade Regulation Rule. It requires car dealerships to display a window sticker called the *Buyers Guide* on the used cars they offer for sale. These window stickers on pre-owned vehicles are meant to provide information for consumers as people decide whether to buy a car as well as determining who will pay repair costs if something goes wrong.

The possibility of something going amiss is the impetus for a number of consumer rights and protections in the automotive marketplace, especially when repairs will be costly to the buyer. This issue involves auto warranties, or a promise to the purchaser that the vehicle will perform as represented with no significant flaws that are unknown to the consumer. Prior to the passage of the Dodd-Frank Act, an earlier law called the Magnuson-Moss Warranty Act of 1975 covered warranties on cars as well as on other consumer items. The law does not require any products to have a warranty—most can be sold *if* the potential buyer knows it is being sold "as is." However, if the product does offer a warranty, that warranty must meet legal standards. The Magnuson-Moss Act was intended to protect consumers from deceptive warranty practices, addressing problems that arose when manufacturers used disclaimers on warranties that appeared to be presented in an unfair, misleading manner. While consumer products are not required to have warranties, if one is given, it must comply with the Magnuson-Moss Act. With a large purchase such as an automobile, the law is meant to make warranties more readily understood by the buyer. It enables the Federal Trade Commission to enforce the rule in order to better protect consumers.

Many car buyers believe there is a "cooling off period" in which they can return the vehicle. Some also believe there are "lemon laws" protecting consumers from buying cars that are defective. In fact, the right to return a car a few days after its purchase for a refund exists only if the dealer offers it to buyers. Consumer advocates encourage potential buyers to ask about the dealer's return policy, get it in writing, and read it carefully.

Although "lemon laws" can cover all types of consumer goods, they are most often considered in terms of the automotive marketplace because buying a car is generally a major expenditure for the average person. An automobile classified as a "lemon" is considered to be a vehicle with manufacturing or design defects that could impact its safety or value and cannot reasonably be repaired. The defect may be significant enough that the vehicle cannot serve its intended purpose, which is to provide safe, reliable transportation.

The Magnuson-Moss Warranty Act provides consumer protection by making it easier to file a breach of warranty claim after purchasing a "lemon." The Magnuson-Moss Act also enables consumers to recover attorney fees, court costs, and other expenses if they win in court. In addition to protections under the federal Magnuson-Moss Warranty Act, each state has its own version of lemon laws. The specifics vary from state to state, but most require an auto manufacturer to buy back a vehicle that has a defect so significant that the manufacturer is unable to repair it within a reasonable amount of time, generally after three or four repair attempts. Details vary according to state, such as whether a "loaner" vehicle would be provided so the consumer can get to work or meet other obligations during the extent of those three or four repair attempts. Websites such as "State Rankings of Lemon Laws" from the Center for Auto Safety provide details for each state as well as suggestions for consumers if there are unresolved issues. Often, recourse can be found by contacting their local Better Business Bureau, state attorney general, or Department of Motor Vehicles.

Along with issues in the automotive industry such as gas mileage and emission controls, safety remains a major factor regarding protection for consumers. Much of that can be traced back to the work of Ralph Nader, who argued that the auto industry knew about safety issues but ignored public safety. In 1966, Nader testified before the Senate Commerce Committee, which released a report supporting his allegations, finding "disturbing evidence of the automobile industry's chronic subordination of safe design to promotional styling" (Keller 2017). This report led not only to the creation of safety standards for car buyers under the National Traffic and Motor Vehicle Safety Act, but also to the founding of the National Highway Traffic Safety Administration, which established minimum safety standards for automobiles as well as their crashworthiness. There were objections by auto manufacturers and dealerships claiming that such consumer protection laws would hinder growth and innovation, but "regulations actually helped force innovation and American automakers to produce cars that were not only good for passenger safety and the environment, but for profits as well" (Keller 2017).

Further Reading

Center for Auto Safety. n.d. "State Rankings of Lemon Laws." Accessed September 20, 2024. https://www.autosafety.org/lemon-laws/.

Federal Trade Commission. n.d.a. "About the FTC." Accessed September 20, 2024. https://www.ftc.gov/about-ftc.

Federal Trade Commission. n.d.b. "The Auto Marketplace." Accessed September 20, 2024. https://www.ftc.gov/news-events/topics/consumer-finance/auto-marketplace.

Federal Trade Commission. n.d.c. "Automobiles." Accessed September 20, 2024. https://www.ftc.gov/business-guidance/industry/automobiles.

Federal Trade Commission. n.d.d. "Magnuson Moss Warranty-Federal Trade Commission Improvements Act." Accessed September 10, 2024. https://www.ftc.gov/legal-library/browse/statutes/magnuson-moss-warranty-federal-trade-commission-improvements-act.

Keller, Jared. 2017. "What Ralph Nader Taught Us about Car Safety—and the Virtue of Red Tape." *Enterprise*. Accessed November 28, 2024. https://thelongandshort.org/enterprise/ralph-nader-car-safety-regulation.

Thompson, Derek. 2016. "America in 1915: Long Hours, Crowded Houses, Death by Trolley." *The Atlantic*. Accessed November 28, 2024. https://www.theatlantic.com/business/archive/2016/02/america-in-1915/462360/.

USA.gov. 2022. "Car Complaints." Accessed November 28, 2024. https://www.usa.gov/car-complaints.

Q25: Are railroads accountable to consumer rights and protections?

Answer: For many years, the completion of the transcontinental railroad took precedence over consumer rights and protections in the rail industry. Even in the golden age of train travel during the early twentieth century, consumer rights and protections were not a high priority compared to the relative ease of transportation across the country. This would change somewhat in later decades, but for many years, most people were simply grateful for America's railroads, which united the country in ways that were previously unimaginable.

The Facts: One way or another, most societies depend on their systems of transportation not only to move people but also to carry foodstuffs, raw materials, and finished goods. Some modes of transport have had the power to transform an entire society. In the nineteenth century, the transformation of the United States was brought about by the railroad.

The nature of warfare was transformed by railroads during America's Civil War, as railroads were used to transport troops and supplies. After the war, as more railways were built, many Americans discovered the transformational nature of rail travel. Passenger travel was greatly improved. Trains could operate in all types of weather, moving people and goods at previously unheard-of speeds. For the first hundred years of the nation's history, the journey from New York to California took months; by rail in the late 1800s, it took a week. In addition, "the old sectionalism of our pre-Civil War politics eroded … [as] citizens spoke more often of a singular, 'this United States' instead of a plural, 'these United States'" (Smithsonian n.d.).

The emergence of America's railroads radically altered the nation's economic system. By the 1870s, after the completion of the transcontinental railway, the American economy expanded to an extraordinary degree, "growing almost tenfold in the last quarter of the 19th century" (Smithsonian n.d.). The country was revolutionized by railways in the space of a few decades. With the ability to ship raw materials and finished products quickly over long distances, the railroad transformed American society from an agrarian culture that had been based primarily on family farms to an industrial powerhouse. Small towns lived or died according to whether they had access to a railroad. Cities with rail terminals, such as New York and Chicago, grew into behemoths.

By the beginning of the twentieth century, there were "200,000 miles of track … more than any other country in the world" (Wolmar 2013). Most members of the American public were so enthralled by this revolutionary new means of transportation that few considered whether they had any rights and protections as railway customers. However, in some cases, the pressure to build quickly led to dangerous situations. Iron straps on the track occasionally came loose from the wooden planks, causing accidents that killed or injured passengers. Additionally, the rail cars themselves were not reinforced to withstand derailments. Few, if any, consumer rights or protections existed for maimed survivors or the next-of-kin of people killed in train accidents.

In 1862, in order to encourage the construction of transcontinental railroads, the federal government began offering land grants in the American frontier of the West to railway companies with the expectation that the land would ultimately be sold to white settlers, raising money to pay for more railroad construction. After laying track, rail builders could sell what remained of the lands that had been granted to them through generous deals from the federal government. The land was considered "public domain," and by 1871, more than a million acres were sold. There was little recourse for Native Americans whose lives were devastated when their traditional lands were considered public domain and taken from them. Railroad lines also cut Native Americans off from the bison herds that were crucial to their survival. Indigenous peoples had few rights or protections. Their options were generally limited to relocating to reservations where they were dependent on federal support.

Private individuals involved in building railroads often grew enormously wealthy and influential. By the latter part of the nineteenth and early twentieth centuries, there came a rise of "railroad barons" whose business practices inclined toward monopolies. This reduced rights and protections to consumers by limiting the option of taking their business elsewhere. These powerful men included American titans such as Jay Gould, Edward Harriman, George Pullman, Leland Stanford, and Cornelius Vanderbilt. Consumer rights were not the highest priority of such men and crossing them could be a risky business. "Railroads used their power to influence politicians and avoid infrastructure improvement and safety enhancements ... This arrogant attitude eventually led to extreme regulatory oversight" (Burns 2023).

The era considered to be the "Golden Age" of railroads lasted roughly from the 1880s until the 1920s. During the peak year of 1916, "railroads carried virtually 100% of all interstate traffic" (Burns 2023). However, by the middle of the twentieth century, automobiles and airplanes were steadily eroding the railroad's monopoly on transportation. In addition, after decades of a virtual free hand, the railroads found themselves caught in a rising spirit of progressivism. "Stifling government regulation beginning in the early 20th century eventually choked [railroads] to the point of desperation. Unable to set their own freight rates, abandon unprofitable routes, or rid themselves of money-losing passenger trains, many were on the brink of collapse by the 1970s" (Burns 2023).

Today, railways continue to be a major carrier of freight. Amtrak, which provides passenger service for the United States, "owns only 3% of the country's rail" (Black 2022). Apart from derailments and toxic spills by freight trains, it is therefore generally regarding Amtrak that questions of consumer rights and protections arise most frequently. In 2021, a bill was introduced in the US Congress to address what some lawmakers saw as an erosion of rights and protections that Amtrak riders had as consumers. According to the sponsoring legislators, Senator Richard Blumenthal of Connecticut and Representative Conor Lamb of Pennsylvania, in 2019, Amtrak implemented a class action ban policy, "specifically writing it to be 'as broad as legally permissible,' including discrimination and any personal injury claims" ("Blumenthal & Lamb" 2021). The ban also mandated forced arbitration in which, instead of going to court, a dispute is decided by one or more persons who serve as the final authority. Under forced arbitration, a company requires consumers to consider themselves bound by the arbitrator's decision as a condition of purchasing the product or service. The consumer therefore waives the right to sue, to participate in a class action lawsuit, or to appeal.

The Ending Passenger Rail Forced Arbitration Act of 2021 from Blumenthal and Lamb sought "to restore legal rights and protections to Amtrak riders who are currently prevented from seeking justice in the courts and joining together to seek accountability for their claims" ("Blumenthal & Lamb" 2021). Federal lawmakers claimed that Amtrak put the policy in place after incidents like a 2015 train derailment in Philadelphia and a 2017 derailment in Washington State, which resulted in multimillion-dollar settlements for the victims. After 2019, "if a similar incident were to happen today, passengers would not be able to file lawsuits" (Heck 2020). The legislators sponsoring the bill noted differences between protections available to consumers of rail transportation and those that are provided by the airline industry, stating that "airlines are already prohibited from using mandatory forced arbitration" ("Blumenthal & Lamb" 2021). Therefore, some consumer groups and railroad associations demand rights and protections in rail travel that would be equivalent to those available to airline passengers.

According to the Rail Passengers Association, a nonprofit advocacy organization for railway passengers in the United States, consumer protections for rail travelers should include the right to accurate information, frequent service, reliable on-time arrivals and departures, essential human services, and suitable food onboard. The group also calls for providing rights for passengers with disabilities and reduced mobility. In addition, the Rail Passengers Association calls for regulations ensuring that rail passengers have effective ways for complaints to be heard and to be resolved in a reasonable amount of time. In a letter to the author, Jim Mathews, president of the Rail Passengers Association, stated, "Every airline passenger has rights set out for them that they can leverage if they encounter any sort of problem while traveling. We believe rail passengers deserve the same protections" (Mathews n.d.).

Rail safety issues are also periodically debated, often in the wake of derailments or toxic spills. According to reporter Jacob Knutson, conservative groups oppose safety legislation for railway consumers, regarding both freight and passenger service. Their grounds are that such protection "would do little to improve safety while creating gross inefficiencies for thousands of businesses," also arguing that more stringent safety laws "would give the Transportation Department 'unimaginable authority'" (Knutson 2023).

Most observers would agree that railroads can be credited with building the United States into the world power we know today, at least until the middle of the twentieth century when airplanes and motor vehicles, including the trucking industry, began to replace railways in the transportation field. "Yet railroads still flourish in the United States and are a vital part of the infrastructure" (Wolmar 2013, xix) and as such, face continued calls as time passes for appropriate consumer rights and protections.

Further Reading

Black, Erin. 2022. "Why Freight Railroads Are So Successful in the U.S." CNBC. Accessed November 28, 2024. https://www.cnbc.com/2022/02/03/why-freight-railroads-are-so-successful-in-the-us.html.

"Blumenthal & Lamb Lead Introduction of Legislation to Restore Amtrak Riders' Legal Rights & Protections." 2021. Senate.gov. Accessed November 28, 2024. https://www.blumenthal.senate.gov/newsroom/press/release/blumenthal-and-lamb-lead-introduction-of-legislation-to-restore-amtrak-riders-legal-rights_protections.

Burns, Adam. 2023. "U.S. Railroad History." American Rails. Accessed November 28, 2024. https://www.american-rails.com/history.html.

Heck, Denny. 2020. "Blumenthal, Lamb, Heck Introduce Bill to Restore Amtrak Riders' Legal Rights and Protections." VoteSmart.org. Accessed November 28, 2024. https://justfacts.votesmart.org/public-statement/1408868/blumenthal-lamb-heck-introduce-bill-to-restore-amtrak-riders-legal-rights-and-protections.

Knutson, Jacob. 2023. "Conservative Groups Oppose Safety Bill Introduced after Ohio Derailment." *Axios*. Accessed November 28, 2024. https://www.axios.com/2023/03/14/conservative-groups-rail-safety-ohio-derailment.

Mathews, Jim. n.d. "Letter to Members." Rail Passengers Association. Washington, DC. Personal letter to author.

Smithsonian National Museum of American History. n.d. "American Railroads in the 20th Century." Accessed September 10, 2024. https://americanhistory.si.edu/america-on-the-move/essays/american-railroads.

Stanford University. n.d. "Rise of Monopolies: History of American Railroads." Accessed September 10, 2024. https://cs.stanford.edu/people/eroberts/cs181/projects/corporate-monopolies/development_rr.html.

US Government Accountability Office. 2019. "Rail Safety: Freight Trains Are Getting Longer, and Additional Information Is Needed to Assess Their Impact." Accessed November 28, 2024. https://www.gao.gov/products/gao-19-443.
Wolmar, Christian. 2013. *The Great Railroad Revolution*. New York: PublicAffairs Books, xix.

Q26: What consumer rights and protections cover air travel?

Answer: Air travel has evolved from being a luxury for a few wealthy people into a commonplace mode of transportation for the masses. For the first half of the twentieth century, the passenger experience aboard an airplane was usually loud, uncomfortable, unreliable, and expensive, with few—if any—consumer rights and protections. However, the years following the Second World War saw technological advances in airliners, increasing prosperity of average Americans, the deregulation of airlines in 1978, and a growing air travel consumer rights movement. The aviation industry has come under greater scrutiny, resulting in consumer-related proposals such as an Airline Passengers' Bill of Rights.

The Facts: In the 1920s and 1930s, during the early days of aviation, people who flew on airplanes were often secondary in status to sacks of mail, as postal transportation was the greater source of income for airlines. Little thought was given to passenger comfort, and even less to their rights and protections. Those who flew were usually businessmen or wealthy people, since the cost of a round trip coast-to-coast flight was "about half of the price of a new automobile" (Smithsonian n.d.). Early airliners were not pressurized and therefore had to fly at low altitudes where they were often buffeted by wind and stormy weather. Air sickness was commonplace, and crashes were not unusual. In the 1920s, 1930s, and early 1940s, most people still traveled by bus or train.

When the United States entered the Second World War in 1941, the number of civilians who flew by plane was only a small fraction of the American public. During the 1940s, civilian air travel was unpredictable due to wartime priorities. Delays and cancellations were relatively common, with passengers routinely being bumped off flights due to military precedence.

After the war ended in 1945, advances in airliners and postwar prosperity brought about a new world of passenger travel. Development of the jet engine for passenger aircraft in the postwar era was revolutionary. For average Americans, who now had more disposable income, jetting across the nation or around the world became affordable. "In 1955, for the first time, more people in the United States traveled by air than by train. By 1957 airliners had replaced ocean liners as the preferred means of crossing the Atlantic" (Smithsonian n.d.).

In its early years, the airline industry was regulated by the federal government. However, in 1978, Congress passed a law that deregulated airlines with a goal of stimulating competition. Airlines could now set their own fares and cancel unprofitable routes. As a result of deregulation, fares dropped, and the number of passengers grew. However, to offer competitive low fares, airlines often had to reduce amenities and services. As was the airlines' goal, cabins were often filled to capacity, but passengers lost some of the luxury and comfort of previous air travel. Many airlines still offered a more exclusive flight experience through limited premium seating for a higher price.

Particularly around the holidays in November, December, and January of each year, passengers are often at the mercy of unpredictable bad weather, overbooking, and delays on the ground. Amid passenger complaints, in December 2009, the federal Department of Transportation (DOT) issued a directive called "Enhancing Airline Passenger Protections." Along with addressing delays, cancellations, and overbooking, it required airlines to provide greater disclosure of information to consumers when they were choosing flights, plus an improved system of responding to customer complaints. An addendum in 2011 mandated airlines to disclose the total cost of a flight for consumers, including all fees and taxes. These rules were based on the Department of Transportation's authority to protect consumers from unfair or deceptive practices, as well as providing safe and adequate service. However, "the interpretation of the phrase 'unfair or deceptive' can significantly affect the scope of DOT's enforcement authority" (Tang 2016).

Despite a decline in bookings during the Covid-19 pandemic of 2020, the number of passengers rebounded after the pandemic was brought under control, with boardings continuing to grow each year. In 2022, "US airlines carried 853 million passengers, up from 658 million in 2021" (Bureau of Transportation Statistics 2023). Concurrently, media reports of passenger complaints seemed to increase while amenities, seating room, and space inside crowded cabins decreased.

Then came the Christmas holiday season at the end of 2022. Southwest, a low-cost airline that became the largest domestic carrier in the United States, experienced problems that many observers, including the Department of Transportation, saw as "disproportionate and unacceptable" (Harper 2022). "Severe weather, staff shortages brought on by the pandemic, and an outdated computer system caused the largest domestic airline in the US to cancel thousands of flights from December 21 to December 31" (Heyward 2023). During those ten days, Southwest cancelled about 16,700 flights. With each of the Boeing 737 aircrafts operated by Southwest carrying an average of 125 passengers, the cancelled flights affected more than two million passengers. The cancellations left not only individual travelers and families without transportation over the holidays but also caused airline staff to be stranded amid the chaos in airports. Some attributed the Southwest disruption in part to cost-cutting measures, such as not updating its information technology systems. Southwest Airlines claimed that the cancellations could cost the company $825 million.

In the wake of that event, several members of Congress sponsored a bill called the Airline Passengers' Bill of Rights. It included the requirement for airlines to give passengers a cash refund if the airline cancels or significantly delays their flight. Along with fee structures for compensation over flight delays and cancellations, it listed proposed consumer protections in such matters as reduction in the size of seats, less leg room, and narrower aisles. It also required that airlines provide drinking water free of charge and "sufficient functional lavatories" ("S.178" 2023). The bill was referred to the Senate Committee on Commerce, Science, and Transportation. As of mid-2024, no further action had been taken.

Meanwhile, in 2023, the federal Department of Transportation (DOT) released Fly Rights: A Consumer Guide to Air Travel. While not an actual bill of rights, it states that "while you do have certain rights as a passenger, your demands for compensation will probably be subject to negotiation and the kind of action you get often depends in large part on the way you go about complaining" (US Department of Transportation 2023c). The DOT's Aviation Consumer Protection website indicates that the types of complaints passengers may seek compensation for include issues related to air fares, baggage, delayed or canceled flights, frequent flyer programs, involuntary "bumping," passengers with disabilities or health problems, overbooking, safety and security, schedules, ticketing, and travel scams. *Air Travel Consumer Reports*, issued monthly by DOT's Office of Aviation Consumer Protection, provides consumers with access to information regarding the quality of services by the airlines.

The DOT also has the authority to levy fines against airlines if the agency feels they have not honored the rights of consumers. In the year 2022, domestic and foreign airlines and other travel-related companies were penalized $8.55 million in consumer protection fines, with the bulk of the fines arising from failure to comply with customer refund requirements during the Covid-19 pandemic in

2020. It was the highest total in fines levied for a single year. Enforcement by the DOT "led to the airlines eventually paying out more than $600 million in refunds that had previously been held back from customers" (Silk 2023).

Sharon Pinkerton of the industry group Airlines for America spoke to the Senate Committee on Commerce, Science, and Transportation on behalf of the aviation industry in early 2023. Pinkerton defended airlines regarding the delays and cancellations of Christmas 2022 by stating that air carriers take customer service seriously and "airlines have absolutely no incentive to delay or cancel flights and only do so when circumstances dictate" ("Strengthening Airline Operations" 2023). In response to calls in Congress for greater regulatory oversight of air travel, Pinkerton said that it is not necessary to impose additional regulations such as government-controlled pricing. Such proposals, she maintained, would lead to higher ticket prices, reduced services, and the kind of decreased competition that would "completely unravel the positive policy benefits that consumers have reaped via deregulation of the airline industry" ("Strengthening Airline Operations" 2023).

Both airlines and passengers are also affected by government involvement in security measures around air travel. Following the terrorist attacks of September 11, 2001, heightened security at airports, managed by the Travel Safety Administration (TSA), an agency of the US Department of Homeland Security, brought about screening procedures that were restrictive and time-consuming, often leaving passengers frustrated before they even boarded the aircraft. Writer Thomas Tacker, who holds a PhD in economics, argues against the cost of airport security. "It actually is quite possible that air travel is 'too safe,'" he claims. "We are pouring in so much money, time and human resources into safety in this area that some of our expenditures are generating more costs than benefits" (Tacker 2019). He concedes that "it is true that the United States has remained relatively safe from terrorism, and it may be that TSA activities have been helpful in that regard. But there is no sign that TSA airport screening itself can possibly justify its enormous cost" (Tacker 2019). Tacker's rationale is that air travel has become so unpleasant due to lost time at TSA checkpoints and what he calls "harassment" by airport security that people decide to travel by car, which statistically is a more dangerous mode of transportation.

It is difficult to determine how much consumer protection in aviation is too much or too little. Which consumer rights and protections in air travel will take off and which will be grounded is often dependent on changing political administrations.

Further Reading

Bureau of Transportation Statistics. 2023. "Full Year 2022 U.S. Airline Traffic Data." Accessed November 28, 2024. https://www.bts.gov/newsroom/full-year-2022-us-airline-traffic-data.

Harper, Karen Brooks. 2022. "Southwest Airlines' Holiday Meltdown Brings on Federal Investigation." *Texas Tribune*. Accessed November 28, 2024. https://www.texastribune.org/2022/12/27/texas-swa-southwest-airlines-cancellations-flights/.

Heyward, Giulia. 2023. "Southwest Airlines' Holiday Chaos Could Cost the Company as Much as $825 Million." NPR. Accessed November 28, 2024. https://www.npr.org/2023/01/06/1147445280/southwest-airlines-cancellations-costs-825-million.

"S.178—Airline Passengers' Bill of Rights, 118th Congress (2023–2024)." 2023. Congress.gov. Accessed November 28, 2024. https://www.congress.gov/bill/118th-congress/senate-bill/178/text.

Silk, Robert. "The DOT Will Start 2023 Levying a Big Fine." 2023. *Travel Weekly*. Accessed November 28, 2024. https://www.travelweekly.com/Travel-News/Airline-News/DOT-start-2023-big-airline-fine.

Smithsonian National Air and Space Museum. n.d. "The Evolution of the Commercial Flying Experience." Accessed September 10, 2024. https://airandspace.si.edu/explore/stories/evolution-commercial-flying-experience.

"Strengthening Airline Operations and Consumer Protections." 2023. Senate.gov. Accessed November 28, 2024. https://www.commerce.senate.gov/services/files/BF66F413-07BE-4144-B5E6-4FCA6B3C4BD3.

Tacker, Thomas. 2019. *Rethinking Consumer Protection: Escaping Death by Regulation*. Lanham, MD: Lexington Books, 121.

Tang, Rachel Y. 2016. "Airline Passenger Rights: The Federal Role in Aviation Consumer Protection." Accessed November 28, 2024. Congressional Research Service. https://sgp.fas.org/crs/misc/R43078.pdf.

US Department of Transportation. 2023a. "Air Travel Consumer Reports." Accessed November 28, 2024. https://www.transportation.gov/individuals/aviation-consumer-protection/air-travel-consumer-reports.

US Department of Transportation. 2023b. "Aviation Consumer Protection." Accessed November 28, 2024. https://www.transportation.gov/airconsumer.

US Department of Transportation. 2023c. "Fly Rights: A Consumer Guide to Air Travel." Accessed November 28, 2024. https://www.transportation.gov/airconsumer/fly-rights.

7

Consumer Rights and Protections in Finance and Technology

There are some who feel that consumer protections are not necessary in matters of finance and the technology it uses. Their rationale is that, while humans have a survival-based need for safe food products, consumers are not required to enter into financial transactions or invest their money. Responsibility for these voluntary activities, therefore, should rest on the consumer. The very concept of *caveat emptor* is derived from a longer phrase in Latin, dating back to financial matters in the days of ancient Rome: *Caveat emptor, quia ignorare non debuit quod jus alienum emit*, loosely translated as "Let the buyer beware, and not be ignorant about what he buys from another." The idea is that a careful buyer can choose to walk away from an unacceptable deal. Despite that advice from the ancients, in the centuries that followed, financial fraud was able to flourish in a monetary landscape that became more and more confusing for the average consumer. It is hard to imagine explaining junk bonds to the savviest toga-clad Roman or cryptocurrency to even a visionary like Benjamin Franklin. Franklin's era had its own fraudsters, however. In fact, it was an invention of Franklin's that gave rise to one of the most pervasive financial frauds of early America. His lighting rod was at the center of a swindle to bilk farmers out of their money.

As the United States grew, fraudsters found lucrative means to enrich themselves not only in the marketplace for products such as food and pharmaceuticals, but also in financial matters. Some fraudsters took advantage of uneducated, vulnerable people. The first steps toward true universal public education in the United States did not take place until the late 1800s and early 1900s, a time when millions of non-English-speaking immigrants arrived in America.

Over the years, financial crises decimated the savings of many average Americans. These ranged from the Panic of 1785 to the Great Depression of the 1930s, and from pyramid schemes of the early twentieth century to the "dot-com bubble" as the world entered the new millennium. Players included such notorious individuals as Charles Ponzi and Bernard Madoff, whose names became household words. Less well known was Sarah Howe, a precursor to both men.

In the 1980s, thousands of financial institutions failed during the Savings and Loan Scandal, which took on major political ramifications that proved expensive for taxpayers, although less so for the perpetrators. Subsequent to other costly financial crises in the 2000s such as the housing bubble, the Consumer Financial Protection Bureau (CFPB) was created in 2010 as an arm of the US government. Its mandate is to protect consumers—and taxpayers—by enforcing more than a dozen consumer financial protection laws covering institutions such as banks, brokerage firms, and insurance companies. The CFPB has the power to intervene in financial practices that are found to be deceptive or unfair in areas such as credit cards, debt collection, and financial technology.

Some feel that there is too much government intervention in the commercial marketplace as well as too many laws geared to providing consumer rights and protections in financial matters. However, some economists believe there could be unexpected monetary meltdowns in coming years that could conceivably call for more protections.

Q27: Are consumer rights and protections necessary in financial matters?

Answer: Some people feel that *caveat emptor* should be the rule of thumb in financial matters because activities such as investing in stocks are not mandatory for survival. They feel that a consumer has the right to buy stocks, bonds, land, or other investments with the hope of making a profit, but consumers also have the responsibility to judge the risk. Advocates of *caveat emptor* feel that if buyers do not understand the terms of the deal, they have the right not to accept it. However, there have been regular occurrences of disastrous financial crises from the earliest days of the nation with causes and implications that were beyond the scope of average consumers. Some people believe that a degree of regulation could have helped avoid wiping out the life savings of untold numbers of Americans over time. A number of laws and regulations have been approved in relatively recent years, offering greater consumer financial protections, especially when it can be proven that fraud or deceit were involved.

The Facts: Since the earliest days of the nation, there have been financial crises that wiped out people's savings. These events also damaged people's faith in themselves and in the country's economy, prompting them to ask what could have been done to protect them. While a few individuals may have profited from the misfortune, many consumers suffered.

It is unknown whether governmental regulation might have altered some of the financial crises that plagued the nation in the 1700s, 1800s, and 1900s. Many events were referred to by the term "panic," reflecting the sudden widespread scares about finances that result in costly losses. Often a panic is accompanied by bank failure when large numbers of frightened depositors, convinced that their assets are at risk, demand to withdraw their money all at once. The bank fails if it runs out of money and is unable to pay. In the United States, a sampling of such crises includes the Panic of 1785, the Panic of 1792, and the Panic of 1796–7.

The Panic of 1819 has been seen as the crux of America's first boom-to-bust economic cycle. One of the reasons that the 1819 financial panic was so severe was that it was not localized, but instead swept across the country, which had been steadily expanding westward. America's trade growth following the nation's victory in the War of 1812 suddenly slowed as a result of the Napoleonic wars in Europe. American agricultural prices fell, investment in western lands lagged, and there was widespread unemployment amid growing industrialization. People lost their homes and farms when mortgages were foreclosed due to nonpayment. At the time, banks were unregulated, offering no financial consumer protection. They tended to fail when large numbers of people demanded their savings at the same time, creating a vicious cycle. The Panic of 1819 was not the last time such a widespread financial spiral damaged consumers in the United States amid a lack of regulation.

As the country expanded its territory and grew more industrialized, financial crises became more severe, generating both recessions and depressions. In simple terms, a recession is about a year or two of slow—or no—economic growth, accompanied by a sharp rise in unemployment. A depression is basically an extreme form of recession that usually lasts three or more years, characterized by high unemployment and general financial distress.

Without regulation, anyone with a minimum amount of capital could start a bank and issue bank notes. Many failed, taking consumer savings with them. The Panic of 1837 prompted numerous bank failures and a five-year depression. Twenty years later, more bank failures accompanied the Panic of 1857. The Panic of 1873 led to still more bank failures and a four-year depression. The twentieth century saw the Panic of 1901 and Panic of 1907. An economic downturn following America's participation in the First World War (1917–18) was termed the Depression of 1920–1.

As bad as previous financial meltdowns were, those debacles paled in comparison to the Wall Street Crash of 1929 and the subsequent Great Depression of 1929–39. It was the worst economic disaster in modern history, not only in the United States but also around the world. During the grim era of the Great Depression, which lasted through the 1930s, there was a record unemployment rate and staggering loss of income for millions of Americans. Untold numbers of people lost their jobs, their savings, and their homes.

In 1932, Franklin Delano Roosevelt (1882–1945) was elected US president, with his administration departing from the government's traditional hands-off policy in financial affairs. A series of programs called the New Deal followed almost immediately after Roosevelt's inauguration, with the name based on his pledge to launch a "new deal for the America people." It was an attempt to stem the grip of the Depression from continuing to cause suffering for millions of Americans. The government under Franklin Roosevelt became more involved in consumer financial matters than any other administration ever before in the nation's history.

Dozens of programs were enacted. In its first few years alone, a few New Deal consumer protection measures to stabilize banking and reform the financial markets included the Emergency Banking Relief Act (1933) in which financial institutions were evaluated for their stability after being temporarily closed in a "bank holiday." Also in 1933, the Federal Deposit Insurance Corporation (FDIC) was created to insure consumers' savings against bank failure. Around the same time, the Securities Act of 1933 and the Securities Exchange Act in 1934 created the federal Securities and Exchange Commission (SEC). This act empowered the government to protect consumers by regulating stocks and bonds that were traded by public corporations. The Bankruptcy Reform Act (1934) helped consumers by setting up a greater degree of options in personal bankruptcy if they lost all their savings. In areas other than banking and the stock market, the Public Utility Holding Company Act (1935) protected consumers from certain rate increases in utilities like electricity. Also in 1935, the Social Security Act aided mothers with children, created a national pension plan for older Americans, and offered a means to provide unemployment insurance to help people who lost their jobs.

To some, the Depression years of the 1930s seemed like some sort of cosmic retribution for the excesses in the decade of the "Roaring Twenties." Then it got worse. In the midst of the Depression, another catastrophe struck: the Dust

Bowl, a severe drought suffered by the nation's breadbasket in the Great Plains between 1930 and 1940. In addition to the economic disaster of the Depression, the Dust Bowl left many American farmers watching helplessly as their topsoil dried up and blew away, heading for the Gulf of Mexico. With it went their ability to earn a living. The Dust Bowl years inflicted immense agricultural, economic, and personal damage across the nation. The image of hardscrabble farm families abandoning their land in mid-America to migrate westward in search of jobs as migrant workers is an indelible image of the Depression. In an attempt to help, the New Deal's Farm Security Administration was created in 1937 to provide low-interest credit and other aid to farmers in need.

During the New Deal era, dozens of laws and new programs were enacted in response to the times. Of those dozens of New Deal programs, "some are well known, some are not; some changed names or were amended in mid-course; some lasted only a few years, some still exist" (McKee n.d.). The entire concept of New Deal programs angered opponents who felt that the government had no place interfering with banking, the stock market, or other financial matters, even in the form of protections for American consumers. Opponents of the Roosevelt administration have stated that the New Deal has been overrated in its capacity to stem the Great Depression, claiming that it was only the coming of the Second World War that brought America out of its economic slump.

Critics also claim that FDR's New Deal overreached itself by its massive incursion into financial markets via the creation of federal regulatory agencies. However, in the view of financial writer Diana Henriques, "the dream of 'deregulating' American finance has never lost its appeal in America's conservative circles. … But no one who makes those arguments today has ever actually experienced an unregulated financial world in America. They have always had a 'cop on Wall Street' " (Henriques 2023, 19). With different political administrations coming and going since the 1930s, many financial consumer protections that remained from the New Deal era have been weakened or dismantled. However, popular New Deal agencies such as the Securities and Exchange Commission (SEC) and Federal Deposit Insurance Corporation (FDIC) have continued to protect the finances of innumerable American consumers for decades.

Other financial plans were introduced by various administrations over the years, including the implementation of "trickle-down economics" in the Ronald Reagan era of the 1980s. Under that system, claims were made that increasing the wealth of the richest Americans via tax cuts would gradually benefit the poorest.

Although government intervention in consumer financial affairs fluctuated with political administrations, a series of financial disruptions in the late twentieth century and early twenty-first century made some people feel that effective consumer financial protections were indeed necessary. Among those events was the savings and loan crisis of 1986–95, when a third of all savings and loan institutions in the nation failed. The country experienced a recession in the early 1990s and again in the early 2000s. The "dot-com bubble" (2000–2), the "housing bubble" (2003–11), and the subprime mortgage crisis (2007–10) all prompted what were called "stock market corrections," in which the value of average people's assets was usually "corrected" from high to low. Three official "Black Mondays," when the stock market collapsed, occurred in 1987, 2015, and 2020. The 2020 collapse was basically caused by the global Covid-19 pandemic and proved disastrous to the assets of many consumers of financial products. Although the lethal path of Covid-19 could not immediately be contained, some Americans whose savings were decimated felt there were not enough regulations to protect consumers.

Among federal lawmakers who advocated for consumer financial protection regardless of partisan politics was US Senator Elizabeth Warren (1949–) who proposed creating the federal Consumer Financial Protection Bureau (CFPB). Before the CFPB was established in 2010, existing laws and regulations—when they existed at all—were spread out among numerous governmental agencies so that many consumer financial issues fell through the cracks. "The CFPB was created to provide a single point of accountability for enforcing federal consumer financial laws and protecting consumers in the financial marketplace" (Consumer Financial Protection Bureau n.d.). The agency's goal is to "protect consumers from unfair, deceptive, or abusive practices and take action against companies that break the law" (Consumer Financial Protection Bureau n.d.).

When most people think of bank failures, their minds go to the 1930s, although there are modern-day examples that are often unknown to most consumers unless they are directly affected. "From 2001 to 2007, the US saw an average of … 3.57 bank failures per year" (Aldrich 2023). However, "this took a sharp turn after the US declared a recession in December 2007. From 2008 to 2012, bank failures shot up to an average of 93 per year" (Aldrich 2023). Then, in early 2023, Silicon Valley Bank (SVB) and Signature Bank both collapsed, followed closely by the collapse of the First Republic Bank. In what has been called the second biggest bank failure in US history, "the FDIC estimates the SVB failure will cost its deposit insurance fund $16.1 billion. The agency plans to recoup those losses by assessing fees on banks" (Egan 2023). Critics of the bailout predicted that one way or another, those costs would be passed on to consumers.

Like bank failures, financial crises can occur unexpectedly at any time, although many economic observers feel that the United States is probably not in danger of another Great Depression due to existing regulations that safeguard consumers in the financial marketplace. Some even see a bright side if recessions do occur, suggesting that consumers of financial products should monitor the status of such indicators as inflation data. "While recessions can lead to job losses and other financial difficulties for Americans, they have historically been excellent buying opportunities for long-term investors" (Duggan 2023).

A well-known story in Arkansas involves one of its wealthy citizens who went duck hunting at an isolated camp for two weeks in late October of 1929, carrying $87 in cash with him for possible incidentals. When he returned home, he found that the bank holding his fortune had failed and all the money he had left in the world was the $87 in his pocket. Most experts do not see that sort of scenario happening in the present day due to such consumer protection measures as the FDIC, which was established to guard against just such a debacle.

Further Reading

Aldrich, Elizabeth. 2023. "Failed Banks in the US: An Analysis by Year, Size and More." *Forbes*. Accessed November 28, 2024. https://www.forbes.com/advisor/banking/list-of-failed-banks/.

Consumer Financial Protection Bureau. n.d. "The CFPB." Accessed September 20, 2024. https://www.consumerfinance.gov/about-us/the-bureau/.

Duggan, Wayne. 2023. "Recession or Soft Landing: What's Next for the U.S. Economy?" *Forbes*. Accessed November 28, 2024. https://www.forbes.com/advisor/investing/is-a-recession-coming/.

Egan, Matt. 2023. "FDIC Accidentally Reveals Details about Silicon Valley Bank's Biggest Customers." *CNN Business*. Accessed November 28, 2024. https://www.cnn.com/2023/06/23/investing/svb-bank-fdic/index.html.

Henriques, Diana. 2023. *Taming the Street: The Old Guard, the New Deal, and FDR's Fight to Regulate American Capitalism*. New York: Random House, 19.

McKee, Brent. n.d. "New Deal Programs." *Living New Deal*. Accessed September 10, 2024. Accessed November 28, 2024. https://livingnewdeal.org/history-of-the-new-deal/programs/.

Q28: How has fraud been part of the evolution of financial consumer protections?

Answer: Fraudulent activities have been part of the human experience since antiquity. Only in relatively recent times have some consumer protections been put in place to address financial fraud through such agencies as the US government's Securities and Exchange Commission and the Federal Trade Commission. They are able to do so when they can root out the culprit and determine the damage, which is frequently a difficult task. Banking and securities frauds usually end in loss—not only in terms of financial damage but also loss of confidence by consumers in themselves. The embarrassment of having been deceived often leads to a reluctance to come forward and admit they were duped. For that reason, although there are more financial fraud protections for consumers today than in the past, innumerable scams still go undetected, allowing fraudsters to prey on still more unsuspecting targets.

The Facts: According to the Bureau of Consumer Protection at the Federal Trade Commission, a few types of fraud—also known as scams—that exist in today's world include elder exploitation, identity theft, imposter scams, malfeasance by financial advisers, and mail fraud. One technique perpetrators use, called "phishing," involves sending faked communications to consumers that appear to come from a legitimate source but that trick people into revealing personal information such as passwords or credit card numbers. In another method, called "spoofing," fraudsters disguise themselves as a trusted contact in an e-mail address, text message, website, or caller ID in order to gain access to personal information. Pyramid scams, also known as Ponzi schemes, appear to be legitimate investment opportunities for potential consumers who are lured in, but the deals tend to end badly.

Financial fraud is hardly new. One of the first recorded cases can be found in 300 BC when two merchants in ancient Greece tried to defraud investors who financed the men's cargo ship by collecting the money, sinking the ship as an "act of the Gods," and pocketing the money. When they were caught, one died trying to escape while the other faced the wrath of Athenian courts. This ploy "set a precedent for many such scams today [such as] businesses deliberately being sabotaged to redeem insurance money" ("The History and Evolution of Fraud" n.d.)

In early America, *caveat emptor* was the rule of thumb. One of the earliest examples of consumer fraud took place in colonial days. It was indirectly sparked by Benjamin Franklin (1706–1790), the eminent Founding Father who invented a practical lightning rod around 1750. The purpose of the device was to protect homes, barns, and public buildings from fire in an age of all-wood construction. A roaring blaze after being struck during electrical storms was a common occurrence. Many early Americans were farmers, with their survival dependent on protecting the agricultural equipment, seed, supplies, and livestock in their barns. The "lightning rod scam" involved a respectable looking "salesman" who would appear at an isolated rural homestead. He claimed that for a cash deposit, a lightning rod installer who was working on a nearby farm would soon follow. The installer never arrived because he did not exist; the salesman and the cash were gone. To avoid the risk being seen as a sucker, the farmer was often too embarrassed afterward to report the fraud, so other farmers inevitably fell for the same trick.

Many others were also taken in by slick salesmen in the absence of consumer protections. Scammers took advantage of the fact that women in early America had few opportunities to make a living, especially if they were unmarried, widowed, or had been abandoned. Having few ways to support themselves, women were targeted by "work-at-home" schemes, in which alleged money-making tasks could be performed without needing to leave the house while caring for children. Fraudsters, working from a post office box address, enticed women to purchase a sample embroidery pattern. The women were to replicate the sample and return the item to the company. They were told that if their embroidery was good enough, they would be offered steady employment. Even if the women who responded had outstanding embroidery skills, they were informed by postcard that their work was inferior, embarrassing them into keeping their experience (and so-called poor embroidery skills) to themselves. Usually, however, the women heard nothing back at all. The scammers made money by selling their victims the high-priced patterns before moving to a new town under a new name. In the absence of mass communication and social media to spread the word, these fraudsters were rarely detected.

With the country growing tremendously in the nineteenth century, people often moved away from their extended families, long-time friends, and customary environment to seek work in the city. Unfortunately, being strangers in unfamiliar situations, they were vulnerable. In addition, another vulnerable group—non-English-speaking immigrants—flooded in from abroad. Due to the success of targeting these populations, "arguably, the 1800s were the Golden Age of schemes. The term 'confidence man' or 'con man' was probably coined midcentury and, according to the *New York Times*, the Brooklyn Bridge was sold more than once to unsuspecting folks in the 1880s and 1890s" (Weeks 2015). A "confidence man" was someone who relied on just that: building *confidence* that the fraudster was honest. The vulnerability of victims often came down to basic human nature: "Our senses, and our assumptions about how the world operates, are exactly what can be manipulated against us—even when we know that and are primed for it" (Weeks 2015). No doubt there was an element of greed involved with some victims; others were simply being human. Consumer protections for vulnerable people, even for the nastiest frauds, were virtually unknown. It was simple for swindlers to disappear as they changed their names and moved from town to town, practicing their deceptive and often cruel tricks without getting caught.

It was simple for swindlers to disappear as they changed their names and moved from town to town, practicing their deceptive and often cruel tricks without getting caught. Furthermore, "confidence men took inordinate pride in the structured nature of their profession" (Reading 2013). Many felt that since they were not committing physical violence, they were of a higher class than common criminals. They felt they were simply using people's own weaknesses against them, specifically the lust for easy money. Confidence men, also known as grafters or grifters, tended to downplay the desperation of victims they defrauded, such as the women who were victimized in the embroidery scam. Their attitude was that the victims should have known better. American popular culture "has retained a soft spot for charismatic grafters and oily-tongued salesmen, evincing admiration for their audacity, ingenuity, and capacity to land on their feet" (Balleisen 2017, 5). This has been especially true of the elaborate, multi-phase ploy called the "big con." These intricate frauds inspired such popular films as *The Grifters*, *American Hustle*, and especially *The Sting*.

It is difficult to know the full story of financial fraud over the years because "no formal or written record ever existed of the thousands of cons which occurred" (Reading 2013). However, as the nation progressed through the industrial revolution and technological age, fraudsters also kept up with the times in order to take advantage of a victim's gullibility and/or greed. One of the most popular gambits was the fake stock market deal. Stocks and bonds have traditionally been among the few ways that an average citizen might enjoy a significant financial gain. It was an attractive idea; therefore, many people invested. News media of the day highlighted thrilling stories of "stock market plungers" such as Jesse Livermore (1877–1940), who made a fortune trading securities. A popular confidence trick was to convince the victim that the stock market was controlled by "insiders" who blocked the "little guy" out of the best deals. By investing in a con man's proposed venture, the victim had the chance to join the ranks of those who made a big score. After pocketing the victim's investment money, the fraudster made a quick exit, heading for a new town under a new name. Even if consumer protections had been in place, the victim might well have been too embarrassed to report being duped.

According to best-selling financial writer Maria Konnikova, "the best confidence games remain below the radar. They are never prosecuted because they are never detected [or] they are detected but the embarrassment is too great" (Konnikova 2017, 16). What was true of farmers in colonial America remains true today—many victims of fraud keep quiet, hoping to avoid ridicule for their gullibility. "Thus, in 1985, the *New York Tribune* surmised that a full 90 percent of fraud cases remained hidden from public view" (Balleisen 2017, 55). Swindlers continue to rely on the presumption that most victims will stay silent; thus, more unsuspecting people are victimized.

Konnikova states that "when it comes to the con, everyone is a potential victim" (Konnikova 2017, 13), including—or perhaps especially—those who feel they are too smart to fall for it. She cites statistics from the Federal Trade Commission as part of the agency's efforts to provide protection for consumers: "Between 2011 and 2012—the last period surveyed by the Federal Trade Commission—a little over 10 percent of adults, or 25.6 million, had fallen victim to fraud. The total number of fraudulent incidents was even higher, topping 37.8 million" (Konnikova 2017, 10). Consumer fraud increased by more than 60 percent between 2008 and 2012. "In 2012 alone, the Internet Crime Complaint Center reported almost three hundred thousand complaints of online fraud. The total money lost: $525 million" (Konnikova 2017, 10).

The Federal Trade Commission states that it attempts to stop fraud "by collecting reports from consumers and conducting investigations, suing companies and people that break the law, developing rules to maintain a fair marketplace, and educating consumers and businesses about their rights and responsibilities" (Federal Trade Commission n.d.). While the FTC cannot resolve individual cases, the agency uses reports from consumers "to investigate and bring cases against fraud, scams, and bad business practices" (Federal Trade Commission n.d.). Many consumers feel that in our modern, technology-driven world, the FTC can protect them through computerized scrutiny, although "millions of Americans get scammed every year. In 2018, nearly 3 million claims of fraud and scams were reported to the FTC's Consumer Sentinel Network, an uptick from 2017" (Exley 2019).

In fact, technology such as cyber security has not been shown to protect consumers—it is often the exact tool that is used to victimize them. Frank Abagnale (1948–), a former con man who was portrayed by Leonardo DiCaprio in the movie *Catch Me If You Can*, now works with consumer protection authorities to try to prevent fraud, but it is a big job. According to Abagnale, modern technology has made it easier for scammers to operate, adding "What I did 50 years ago is 4,000 times easier to do today" (Exley 2019).

A contemporary case that exemplifies fraud in the age of technology is that of Elizabeth Holmes (1984–). She billed herself as a biotechnology entrepreneur, creating a blood-testing company, Theranos, which she founded in 2003 at age nineteen. By late 2014, she and Theranos were valued at hundreds of millions of dollars by claiming the ability to use cutting-edge technology to test for such medical conditions as diabetes or cancer from just a few drops of blood. The photogenic Holmes was lauded in the media, attracting large investments from venture capitalists and private investors. However, in 2015, the *Wall Street Journal* began publishing a series of articles regarding Holmes's blood-test technology at Theranos, "and the dominoes fell from there" (O'Brien 2022). In 2018, Holmes and other Theranos executives were indicted for massive long-term fraud based on federal charges of "allegedly engaging in a multi-million dollar scheme to defraud investors, as well as a scheme to defraud doctors and patients" (O'Brien 2022). Holmes was fined millions of dollars before being sentenced to eleven years in prison, which she began serving in 2023.

Many observers of the Holmes case echoed the old maxim that if something seems too good to be true, it probably is. The difference between this case and examples of fraud from the past is that with the coming of often-confusing implements of the technological age, "con games [have passed] into the realm of big business" (Maurer 1999). Contemporary frauds are often not discovered for years, having indeed become big business. The huge financial fraud perpetrated by Bernard Madoff, which went undetected for at least twenty years, was only identified when his sons turned him in. By the time Madoff made headlines after his arrest in 2008, his type of financial fraud was already timeworn, having basically replicated a swindle operated a century earlier by a man named Charles Ponzi, who became synonymous with the scam, known as the Ponzi scheme (see Question 29 for more information). Even in our current age of greater consumer protections against financial abuses, history tends to repeat itself.

Further Reading

Balleisen, Edward. 2017. *Fraud: An American History from Barnum to Madoff.* Princeton, NJ: Princeton University Press, 5, 55.

Exley, Robert, Jr. 2019. "Real-life 'Catch Me If You Can' Con Artist Says You Should Never Post These Three Things on Social Media." CNBC. Accessed November 28, 2024. https://www.cnbc.com/2019/11/14/frank-abagnale-from-catch-me-if-you-can-talks-about-social-media.html.

Federal Trade Commission. n.d. "Bureau of Consumer Protection." Accessed September 10, 2024. Accessed November 28, 2024. https://www.ftc.gov/about-ftc/bureaus-offices/bureau-consumer-protection.

"The History and Evolution of Fraud." n.d. Fraud.com. Accessed September 10, 2024. https://www.fraud.com/post/the-history-and-evolution-of-fraud.

Konnikova, Maria. 2017. *The Confidence Game: Why We Fall for It … Every Time.* New York: Penguin Books, 10, 13, 16.

Maurer, David. 1999. *The Big Con: The Story of the Confidence Man.* New York: Anchor Books, 11.

O'Brien, Sara Ashley. 2022. "The Rise and Fall of Elizabeth Holmes: A Timeline." CNN. Accessed November 28, 2024. https://www.cnn.com/2022/01/04/tech/elizabeth-holmes-rise-and-fall/index.html.

Reading, Amy. 2013. *The Mark Inside: A Perfect Swindle, a Cunning Revenge, and a Small History of the Big Con.* New York: Vintage Books, 8.

Weeks, Linton. 2015. "How Scams Worked in the 1800s." NPR. Accessed November 28, 2024. https://www.npr.org/sections/npr-history-dept/2015/02/12/385310877/how-scams-worked-in-the-1800s.

Q29: What roles did Charles Ponzi, Bernard Madoff, and Sarah Howe play in financial consumer protections?

Answer: When *Forbes*, a business magazine, listed the ten biggest financial frauds in recent US history, nine of the ten were carried out by major corporations. However, there was one individual on the list: Bernard Madoff, with a type of fraud known as a "Ponzi scheme." Some people do not realize that Charles Ponzi was an actual person in the 1920s. Both Ponzi and Madoff practiced a fraudulent financial activity that is also often called a pyramid scheme. In the 1800s, before the time of men such as Ponzi and Madoff, a notorious perpetrator of several costly pyramid schemes was a woman: Sarah Howe. Despite millions of dollars lost by average investors in all three cases, enacting financial consumer protections to guard against such fraudulent schemes has proved difficult at best.

The Facts: In 2013, ten of the largest, most costly financial frauds in America's recent history were itemized in *Forbes* magazine, a publication focusing on American business. Its findings were based on the cumulative effect of each, looking at "investor losses, Securities and Exchange Commission and Department of Justice enforcement actions, and private lawsuits, as well as societal impact" (Jacobs 2013). In the top spot, amid allegations of massive accounting fraud in 2001, the giant energy company Enron "wiped out $78 billion in stock market value ... [and] a class action settlement of $7.185 billion was the largest of all time" (Jacobs 2013). Listed third was the large investment banking firm Lehman Brothers, followed by World Com, Qwest Communications, and HealthSouth, all huge multibillion-dollar corporations. Their demise, usually due to accounting fraud, sent shock waves throughout the economy. The fraudulent actions of these corporations had a disastrous ripple effect not only on those who invested in the companies, wiping out the savings of many, but also on many average consumers across the country. Holding second place on the list, between Enron and Lehman Brothers, was not a vast corporation but a single man: New York money manager Bernard Madoff. His "$65 billion Ponzi scheme [was] the largest fraud ever by an individual" (Jacobs 2013).

In 2024, *U.S. News & World Report* ran an updated list of the biggest financial fraud cases in recent history, an infamous roll call that included not only those taking place in the United States but also China and Germany. In the eleven years since the *Forbes* article, collapsed cryptocurrency trading platform FTX joined the list along with the fraudulent biomedical testing company, Theranos. Yet, even with massive frauds perpetrated globally in more than a decade since the *Forbes* list, the same individual appeared: Bernie Madoff. He held a top spot in the rogues' gallery by virtue of still being "the mastermind behind the biggest Ponzi scheme ever recorded" (O'Connell 2024).

Sometimes called a pyramid scheme or simply "robbing Peter to pay Paul," a Ponzi scheme can appear legitimate as long as there are new investors to contribute fresh money, and as long as most shareholders do not demand full payment of their investment. When the pyramid scheme crashes, unsuspecting consumers who bought into the plan as latecomers are often ruined. The ripple effect of such a collapse spreads across other parts of the economy, affecting consumers who never invested in the scheme. When the word gets out about a Ponzi scheme, mainstream financial markets can be disrupted by diminishing trust in legitimate investment opportunities. Economic growth and stability are slowed. Average consumers who own stocks can find that the value of their portfolio drops, resulting in decreased spending by virtue of having less discretionary income.

Meanwhile, many people are reluctant to buy securities when stock prices fall—normally a good strategy in a "buy low/sell high" market environment—because they have less confidence in the financial market. Potential investors are averse to running the risk of inadvertently entering into a fraudulent scheme.

The now-familiar Ponzi scheme began with a most unlikely person, the Italian-born Carlo Pietro Giovanni Guglielmo Tebaldo Ponzi (1882–1949). According to his recounting of the tale, 21-year-old Ponzi arrived in Boston as an immigrant in 1903, having nothing but $2.50 in his pocket after betting away his savings during the voyage to America. Changing his first name to "Charles," he learned English and slept on the floor of the restaurant where he was employed. There, he worked his way up from dishwasher to waiter before being fired for alleged theft and shortchanging customers.

Ponzi then devised an investment scheme based on international postage stamps, recruiting fellow immigrants to invest with a promise of high returns. Soon, he began diverting money from new investors to make payments to earlier ones—and to himself. The word got out about his unusually high returns, not only attracting new investors but also sparking attention from the news media. Reporters noted that Ponzi was conducting a very public luxurious lifestyle including "a 12-room mansion in upscale Lexington; servants; a couple of automobiles, including a custom-built limousine; fine clothes and gold-handled Malacca canes for himself, and diamonds and other baubles for [his wife] Rose. He purchased commercial and rental properties all over Boston and acquired stock in several banks" (Darby 1998).

The sort of media coverage that at first built him up eventually led to his downfall. Discussing his booming business in a front-page article in the July 24, 1920, issue of the *Boston Post*, Ponzi said he was wealthy enough that he had no need for more investors. But he would continue accepting their money "so they could join him and his family in savoring the finer things in life" (Zuckoff 2006, 7). The reporter accepted Ponzi's claims about his financial expertise "at length and without challenge … Ponzi explained his business in broad, confident terms" (Zuckoff 2006, 6). And, added the reporter, "authorities have not been able to discover a single illegal thing about it" (Zuckoff 2006, 7–8). The paper ran the story, but its editors were suspicious, bringing in financial experts who said Ponzi's returns were not possible. Closer investigation revealed Ponzi's fraudulent activities. Less than a month after its original, glowing story, the *Boston Post* stated that Ponzi had been convicted in the past of forgery. The next day, Ponzi surrendered to federal authorities. Most sources estimate that investors lost about $20 million, or about $225 million in today's dollars.

Ponzi was eventually convicted on federal charges of violating the Mail Fraud statute, which had been passed by Congress in 1872. After Ponzi's arrest, no consumer protection laws were passed to guard against such pyramid schemes, with consumers of financial products simply being advised to be cautious in their investments. After serving three and a half years in prison, Ponzi later went back to jail on various charges including a Florida land scam. Upon his release, he left the United States, never having become an American citizen. In 1949, Ponzi died in Brazil with what was said to be only $75 to his name. It was used to pay for his burial. Before his death, however, he wrote an upbeat autobiography called *The Rise of Mr. Ponzi*, which was published in 1938. It was the same year that saw the birth of a man who could be called Ponzi's spiritual son: Bernie Madoff.

Bernard Lawrence "Bernie" Madoff (1938–2021), was born to middle-class parents on Long Island, near New York City. His father worked as a plumber before starting an investment company that was eventually shut down by the Securities and Exchange Commission (SEC) for failing to file financial reports. Unlike Charles Ponzi, Bernie Madoff never slept on restaurant floors. He lived a comfortable suburban existence, graduating from New York's Hofstra University in 1960. That year, he began dealing in low-level stocks before eventually founding the firm of Bernard L. Madoff Investment Securities.

Like Ponzi before him, Bernie Madoff was charming, handsome, and well-dressed, radiating confidence. The two men were also alike in attracting what are called affinity groups, people with similar ethnic or religious backgrounds to their own, making investors feel they have something in common. Madoff became highly regarded in the financial industry, earning the prestige of serving on SEC advisory committees. For several years, Madoff was chairman of NASDAQ (National Association of Securities Dealers Automated Quotations), a major electronic financial system that handles billions of dollars in securities transactions around the world.

Also like Ponzi, Madoff did not avoid the spotlight—he enjoyed it. In interviews, Madoff invoked Ponzi's strategy of appearing reluctant to take new investors, making people even more eager to give him their money. "His investment advisory business attracted a devoted legion of clients, including A-list celebrities, rewarding them with steady returns that defied market fluctuations" (Gordon and Associated Press 2021). Or so it appeared. Actually, "his clients' funds were simply deposited into … Madoff's bank account [which] received $150 billion in transfers and deposits, and maintained a balance between three and five billion dollars" (Eren 2017).

In 2000, "an analyst named Harry Markopolos handed the SEC a report [about Madoff] that said 'The World's Largest Hedge Fund is a Fraud,' [but] they didn't nail Madoff" (Rosenbaum 2016). It took until 2009 for it to all come crashing down, after Madoff's sons contacted the FBI. Madoff was charged with federal crimes that violated New Deal-era consumer protection laws such as the Securities Act of 1933, the Securities Exchange Act of 1934, and the Advisers Act of 1940 for offenses including mail fraud, money laundering, securities fraud, wire fraud, and perjury. When the scheme collapsed, some analysts noted that "Madoff's scam wasn't terribly sophisticated or high-tech, utilizing phony account statements sent to clients, for example. But it wiped out thousands of people's life savings" (Gordon and Associated Press 2021).

After being sentenced to 150 years in prison, Madoff gave an interview, saying "it never entered the SEC's mind that it was a Ponzi scheme" (Gordon and Associated Press 2021). Noting that examiners never sought basic records, he said that the financial experts did not ask the right questions. After entering a guilty plea, in 2009 Bernie Madoff went to prison, where he died in 2021 at age eighty-two. Innumerable commentators were prompted to ask how Madoff fooled regulators for so long with such a huge crime.

Although Ponzi and Madoff came from different backgrounds—one, a penniless immigrant and the other, a middle-class, college-educated suburbanite—they had important similarities, especially being men who were attractive and charming. The unlikely precursor to both men was actually a *woman*: Sarah Howe. This little-known figure ran major Ponzi schemes before Charles Ponzi was even born.

If Ponzi was Bernie Madoff's spiritual father, Sarah Emily Howe (*c.*1826–1892) might be said to have been Ponzi's spiritual mother. By the time Ponzi was born in 1882, Sarah Howe was already in jail for fraud, with another year to go on her three-year sentence. She had been convicted of running the same type of pyramid scheme that was later named for Ponzi.

Little is known of Sarah Howe's early life, such as the exact date and place of her birth. She was said to have lived in various locales around New England, and to have been married several times. She was described as either beautiful *or* unattractive *or* plain but respectable, depending on the source. Ultimately adopting the last name of Howe, by the mid-1870s she was single, working as a fortune-teller in Boston. Her first known brush with the law came in 1875 when she was jailed for taking out several loans secured by the same collateral. When the conviction was overturned, Sarah Howe foresaw good fortune for herself.

In 1879, Howe opened what she called the Ladies' Deposit Company. It was billed as a savings bank that only accepted money from unmarried women. Promising a high rate of interest, Howe referred to it as a bank for women, run by women. She claimed it was funded by a Quaker charity that wanted to help single ladies of modest means. However, there was no such charity, and the so-called high rate of interest from the "bank" was paid by the funds deposited by new clients. Generally, the women who trusted Howe with their life savings tended to reinvest their alleged earnings rather than withdrawing them, so she was able to keep the scam going.

New clients sought out Howe through word of mouth. They included women who struggled to get by, such as housekeepers, teachers, and widows. Howe is said to have "dressed in the finest clothes, enticed ladies to join, and encouraged them to spread the news among their friends and family. … Money came in from Buffalo, Chicago, Baltimore, Pittsburgh, and Washington, all without Howe taking out a single newspaper advertisement" (Eveleth 2019). There are no records of how much Sarah Howe took in through the Ladies' Deposit Company, but sources generally claim at was "at least $250,000 from 800 women … [while] some estimate that Howe collected more like $500,000, the equivalent of about $13 million today" (Eveleth 2019).

Hearing stories of Howe's success, the *Boston Daily Advertiser* took notice, but not in a good way. Much of the newspaper's antagonism stemmed from what they saw as an offense against nature by a woman taking on a man's role through her work as a banker. Their ire was made worse when reporters—all male—were not allowed to enter the bank's lobby. One intrepid reporter is said to have dressed as a woman to get in the door so he could pursue information. The reporter struck pay dirt. In 1880, "the *Boston Daily Advertiser* began a series of stories that exposed Howe's bank as a fraud. Her 8 percent returns were too good to be true" (Eveleth 2019). This led to a run on the bank by terrified depositors; the pyramid scheme collapsed as it quickly ran out of money. Howe was sentenced to three years in prison.

Unlike Ponzi who fled to Florida after his conviction, Sarah Howe stayed in Boston after her release. She boldly opened a new venture called "Woman's Bank" that was in business from 1884 to 1886, "offering depositors 7 percent interest and gathering at least $50,000, although historians think the number might be far higher" (Eveleth 2019). When Howe was again arrested, she was not convicted because depositors were unwilling to come forward. Newspaper editorials relied on a blame-the-victim mentality, asserting that women who lost everything should have known better than to enter into a man's game like investing their money, and doing so in an institution run by another woman, no less.

There were reports that Howe opened another firm called Ladies Provident Aid in Chicago, but eventually she returned to Boston where she resumed fortunetelling and lived in poverty. However, her bold endeavors in the women's banking scams had made her enough of a celebrity that when she died in 1892 at age sixty-five, she earned an obituary in the prestigious *New York Times*.

Charles Ponzi was ten years old and living in Italy at the time Sarah Howe died, but both had important similarities such as preying on affinity groups—immigrants and women respectively—and operating their scams in the city of Boston. Another important similarity was that even after their notorious frauds were exposed, there were no noticeable financial consumer protection laws being passed to guard against such scams in the future. *Caveat emptor* remained in place. In financial matters, consumers were told they simply needed to beware.

There were very few financial regulations in Howe's day. Like anyone else who could get away with it, Sarah Howe was able to start her own bank, and in the 1800s, many did. "As much as people love to point fingers at Howe, very rarely do people consider the complete lack of oversight that allowed her to prey upon these women" (Eveleth 2019). The *caveat emptor* pattern continued even after Ponzi's rise and fall in 1920. The passage of any new legislation was superseded by advice to use caution in investments, and that if something seems too good to be true, it probably is. It would take the Stock Market Crash of 1929 and the catastrophe of the Great Depression in the 1930s to arouse the kind of government intervention over *caveat emptor* in finances that took place in the New Deal era of the 1930s.

By the time of Madoff's conviction in 2009 in the glare of twenty-first-century mass media, Americans had become used to demanding consumer protections, and they wanted action. When it became known that the Securities and Exchange Commission (SEC) had been warned for years about Madoff, public pressure resulted in the SEC making rule changes. "The most significant were changes in how the agency carries out inspections of investment advisers and brokerage firms" (Gordon and Associated Press 2021). The SEC and the stock exchanges were given more oversight in monitoring how brokerage firms manage clients' funds. Firms were required to submit more information, and inspections focused more on investor risk. To help detect fraud, the SEC established an electronic reporting system for gathering tips and complaints for investigators to pursue. The SEC's enforcement division was reorganized to include specialized units, and experts in the financial industry were hired to support the agency's attorneys and accountants.

Today, those who are accused of running Ponzi schemes and other types of investment fraud can be charged with such crimes as commodities fraud, conspiracy, filing false statements with the SEC, investment adviser fraud, mail fraud, money laundering, perjury, securities fraud, theft, and wire fraud. Penalties are both civil and criminal, with long prison sentences attached. Fraudsters may be ordered to pay restitution to their victims, although usually there is very little money to do so.

Even with increased oversight, "2019 saw the largest number of Ponzi schemes since the Great Recession. Authorities uncovered 60 alleged Ponzi schemes totaling $3.25 billion in investor funds" (Harvey 2023). It remains unknown how many more are in operation, partly because often the victims are too embarrassed to come forward. Even at this point in the twenty-first century, Howe, Ponzi, and Madoff might feel right at home.

Further Reading

Darby, Mary. 1998. "In Ponzi We Trust." *Smithsonian.* Accessed November 28, 2024. https://web.archive.org/web/20131022204902/http://www.smithsonianmag.com/people-places/In-Ponzi-We-Trust.html.

Eren, Colleen. 2017. *Bernie Madoff and the Crisis: The Public Trial of Capitalism.* Stanford, CA: Stanford University Press, 6.

Eveleth, Rose. 2019. "The No. 1 Ladies' Defrauding Agency." *Longreads.* Accessed November 28, 2024. https://longreads.com/2019/07/02/the-no-1-ladies-defrauding-agency/.

Gordon, Marcy, and the Associated Press. 2021. "How Ponzi King Bernie Madoff Conned Investors and Seduced Regulators." *Fortune.* Accessed November 28, 2024. https://fortune.com/2021/04/15/how-ponzi-king-bernie-madoff-conned-investors-and-seduced-regulators/.

Harvey, Eric. 2023. "Ponzi Schemes." *FindLaw.* Accessed November 28, 2024. https://www.findlaw.com/criminal/criminal-charges/ponzi-schemes.html.

Jacobs, Deborah. 2013. "The 10 Biggest Frauds in Recent U.S. History." *Forbes.* Accessed November 28, 2024. https://www.forbes.com/pictures/efik45ekdjl/our-take-on-the-10-biggest-frauds-in-recent-u-s-history-2/?sh=21eff769775a.

O'Connell, Brian. 2024. "9 of the Biggest Financial Fraud Cases in History." *U.S. News & World Report.* Accessed November 28, 2024. https://money.usnews.com/investing/articles/biggest-corporate-frauds-in-history.

Rosenbaum, Ron. 2016. "Richard Dreyfuss on Being Bernie Madoff." *Smithsonian*. Accessed November 28, 2024. https://www.smithsonianmag.com/arts-culture/richard-dreyfuss-bernie-madoff-180957679/.

Zuckoff, Mitchell. 2006. *Ponzi's Scheme: The True Story of a Financial Legend*. New York: Random House, 6, 7, 8.

Q30: How did the Savings and Loan Scandal affect consumer financial protections?

Answer: In the 1980s and 1990s, there was a severe financial crisis involving America's savings and loan industry, commonly known as "S&Ls" or "thrifts." Economists cite numerous factors that combined to create the S&L crisis, including competition, deregulation, and outright fraud. Amid public outcry about the staggering losses being incurred in the S&L Scandal, Congress passed a consumer protection law called the Financial Institutions Reform, Recovery, and Enforcement Act of 1989 (FIRREA). Lawmakers also placed thrifts under the authority of the Federal Deposit Insurance Corporation (FDIC) to protect future consumers. However, those measures came too late for those who lost their savings. Along with direct losses to S&L customers, the Federal Reserve estimates that the crisis ultimately cost taxpayers more than one hundred billion dollars.

The Facts: During the financial crisis known as the Savings and Loan Scandal, an often-repeated joke was: "I went to the ATM at my savings and loan today, and it asked to borrow twenty bucks." For many S&L customers as well as taxpayers, however, it was no laughing matter.

The basic difference between S&Ls and what are called commercial banks is that while both offer such products as checking, savings accounts, and personal loans, S&Ls primarily focus on lending money, particularly for home mortgages. Savings and loan associations originated in the early 1800s as a way to enable average Americans to become homeowners. According to the Federal Reserve, the first one was established in 1831 at Frankford, Pennsylvania, which is now a neighborhood in Philadelphia. During the early era of S&Ls, they were organized by groups of people who wanted to buy their own home but did not have the money to do so, since banks did not lend money for home mortgages at that time. The group members pooled their savings, enabling them to lend sufficient funds to other members to finance a home. When those homebuyers repaid the money, it could be lent to other members.

As S&Ls evolved into the kind of standard financial institutions that are common today, they were generally smaller than commercial banks but were successful in their own right for many years. "In 1980, there were almost 4,000 thrifts with total assets of $600 billion, of which about $480 billion were in mortgage loans. That represented half of the approximately $960 billion in home mortgages outstanding at that time" (Robinson 2013). However, from the mid-1980s to the mid-1990s, the picture changed. Between 1986 and 1995, about a third of America's S&Ls failed nationwide. The most commonly accepted statistic is that more than a thousand savings and loans across the country closed by 1995. Along with actual losses of consumer savings that were held in S&Ls, there came the price tag in tax dollars for the federal bailout. The eventual cost to American taxpayers was estimated to be more than one hundred billion dollars. Some pundits declared that "thrifts" had been anything but thrifty.

The S&L Scandal ran its course during the terms of three US presidents: Ronald Reagan (in office 1981–9), George H. W. Bush (1989–93) and Bill Clinton (1993–2001). Along with the astronomical financial costs of the S&L crisis itself and the shaken consumer confidence that accompanied it, there would also be a political fallout that cost taxpayers additional millions of dollars.

In 1982, Ronald Reagan signed the Garn-St. Germain Depository Institutions Act. It relaxed regulations on the way savings and loan institutions could invest money so S&Ls could better compete with financial firms such as commercial banks. Within this new relaxed environment, some S&Ls began investing in risky real estate deals, hoping to increase profits. According to financial writer Will Kenton, "if those returns didn't materialize, it would be taxpayers through the Federal Savings and Loan Insurance Corporation (FSLIC)—not the banks or S&L officials—who would be left holding the bag. That's exactly what eventually happened" (Kenton 2021). Law professor and economist William K. Black states, "It was more than greed and incompetence that brought down the US financial sector and plunged the economy in recession—it was fraud. … We now know what happens when you destroy regulation" (Moyers 2009). Some S&Ls hired "accommodating accountants, appraisers and attorneys, [creating] a 'fraud friendly' corporate culture by hiring yes-men" (Black 2013).

During the Reagan administration, there were budget cuts to the regulatory staff at the Federal Home Loan Banking Board (FHLBB), diminishing its ability to protect consumers by investigating risky conditions at S&Ls. In addition, "certain states also passed laws that allowed savings and loans to invest in speculative real estate, which should not have been allowed" (Kenton 2021), eventually further impacting consumers in the states where that practice took place. As the effects of practices by some S&Ls began to spiral out of control, affecting consumers across the nation, Texas, where at least half of S&Ls were based, was hit particularly hard. "Texas banks, such as Empire Savings and Loan, took part in criminal activities that further caused the Texas economy to plummet. The bill for Empire's eventual default cost taxpayers about $300 million" (Kenton 2021).

Before long, the line between *millions* and *billions* of taxpayer dollars began to blur. In 1993, the estimated cost to taxpayers, "not counting the interest payments on government bonds sold to finance the industry's bailout, is $150 to $175 billion. If interest over the next thirty years is added to this tab, the cost approaches $500 billion" (Calavita, Pontell, and Tillman 1999, 1). Most consumers had a hard time understanding the mechanics of the S&L crisis, but they knew staggering numbers when they saw them. Many demanded to know where the money went, who was responsible, why the culprits were not in jail, and whether consumers could somehow get their money back. According to criminologists Kitty Calavita, Henry Pontell, and Robert Tillman, "government officials often pleaded ignorance, claiming they did not have adequate information to answer these questions" (Calavita, Pontell, and Tillman 1999, 3).

Most of the people responsible were never prosecuted. A few went to jail, including Charles Keating, head of California-based Lincoln Savings and Loan, which failed in 1989, resulting in a $3 billion government bailout in addition to customer losses. Sentenced to twelve years in prison, Keating was ordered to pay about $120 million in restitution to the government (i.e., the taxpayers), but he said he had no assets to sell. After serving four years in prison, Keating was released after his conviction was overturned on technical grounds.

Political ramifications of the S&L crisis included what came to be called the Keating Five Scandal. Five US Senators from both political parties accepted more than a million dollars in campaign contributions from Charles Keating. The five senators were Alan Cranston, Dennis DeConcini, John Glenn, John McCain, and Donald W. Riegle. The lawmakers were accused of "pressuring the Federal Home Loan Banking Board (FHLBB) to overlook suspicious activities in which Keating had participated" (Kenton 2021), improperly interfering with the investigation of Lincoln Savings. The senators who were part of the Keating Five were reprimanded, but all retained their Senate seats.

Arkansas banker James McDougal was also convicted, and his actions initiated a ripple effect with political ramifications that would themselves cost taxpayers further millions of dollars. In 1982, McDougal bought Madison Guaranty Savings and Loan, based in Little Rock, Arkansas. Through Madison Guaranty, McDougal financed a real estate deal for about $200,000 (around $650,000 in

2024 dollars). It was called the Whitewater Development Corporation, which was intended to be subdivided into lots for vacation homes on the White River in northern Arkansas. McDougal's partners in the development of Whitewater were his old friend, Arkansas Attorney General Bill Clinton, and Clinton's wife Hillary. The Whitewater project failed because the lots did not turn out to be suited for construction. Ultimately, Madison Guaranty collapsed. It was seized by federal regulators in 1989, costing taxpayers millions of dollars in FDIC funds.

Bill Clinton was inaugurated as US president in 1993; McDougal was sentenced to prison in 1997. By 1998, when McDougal died in jail, an investigation into the Clintons' finances and personal affairs that had started in 1994 was costing taxpayers millions of dollars. The proceedings, which were led by independent counsel Kenneth Starr, lasted seven years. Ultimately, no criminal charges against the Clintons were filed. The Whitewater investigation cost more than $70 million, "the most costly independent counsel investigation ever, according to a General Accounting Office report" (Adams 2000).

The fallout from the S&L Scandal of the 1980s and 1990s made it the largest banking crisis since the Great Depression, costing hundreds of billions of dollars to American taxpayers. However, there were some gains for consumers. In the wake of the S&L crisis, "the resulting public backlash translated into meaningful reform" (Breslow 2013). In 1989, Congress passed the Financial Institutions Reform, Recovery, and Enforcement Act (FIRREA). Funded by $50 billion, FIRREA was enacted to overhaul S&L regulations, hopefully sparing consumers from similar catastrophes in the future. Today, savings and loans still exist in the United States, although they have been greatly reduced in number, 659 in 2019, down from 3,371 in 1989 (Kenton 2021). According to financial writer Will Kenton, banking reforms such as FIRREA were "not enough so to avoid another crisis [the housing bubble] that occurred between 2007–2008, leading to the Great Recession. Lessons are still being learned from the S&L crisis and further regulations in the banking industry are needed" (Kenton 2021).

Further Reading

Adams, Lorraine. 2000. "$52 Million Starr Probe Costliest Ever." *Washington Post*. Accessed November 28, 2024. https://www.washingtonpost.com/archive/politics/2000/04/01/52-million-starr-probe-costliest-ever/3be88582-f0ee-4673-ac0c-f66c87326e82/.

Black, William K. 2013. *The Best Way to Rob a Bank Is to Own One: How Corporate Executives and Politicians Looted the S&L Industry.* Austin: University of Texas Press, 2.
Breslow, Jason. 2013. "Were Bankers Jailed in Past Financial Crises?" *Frontline.* Accessed November 28, 2024. https://www.pbs.org/wgbh/frontline/article/were-bankers-jailed-in-past-financial-crises/.
Calavita, Kitty, Henry Pontell, and Robert Tillman. 1999. *Big Money Crime: Fraud and Politics in the Savings and Loan Crisis.* Berkeley: University of California Press, 1, 2, 3.
Dumas, Ernest. 2023. "Whitewater Scandal." *Encyclopedia of Arkansas.* Accessed November 28, 2024. https://encyclopediaofarkansas.net/entries/whitewater-scandal-4061/.
Kenton, Will. 2021. "Savings and Loan Crisis (S&L): What Happened and Aftermath." *Investopedia.* Accessed November 28, 2024. https://www.investopedia.com/terms/s/sl-crisis.asp.
Moyers, Bill. 2009. "William K. Black: CSI Bailout." *Bill Moyers Journal.* Accessed November 28, 2024. https://www.pbs.org/moyers/journal/04032009/profile.html.
Pizzo, Stephen, Mary Fricker, and PaulMuolo. 1989. *Inside Job: The Looting of America's Savings and Loans.* New York: McGraw-Hill.
Robinson, Kenneth. 2013. "Savings and Loan Crisis 1980–1989." *Federal Reserve History.* Accessed November 28, 2024. https://www.federalreservehistory.org/essays/savings-and-loan-crisis.

Q31: How has the Consumer Finance Protection Bureau affected consumers?

Answer: American consumers were not completely without financial protections before the Consumer Financial Protection Bureau (CFPB) was established in 2010. For instance, there were more than a half-dozen different agencies of the US government, such as the Federal Trade Commission, that covered various areas of consumer financial issues. There were also countless state laws at any given time. However, this situation produced a confusing maze for the average person to navigate. With the creation of the CFPB, areas of financial oversight that were scattered among different federal entities were combined under one "umbrella" agency. The CFPB's focus is not only to protect consumers but also to serve the interests of honest businesses. It aims to ensure that the marketplace is fair and equitable by determining when unfair and/or deceptive business practices are hurting both consumers and ethical companies that play by the rules. Although it has been criticized for being "overprotective," the CFPB claims that in the years since it was founded, its efforts have served millions of American people and businesses, providing hundreds of billions of dollars in compensation to those who were harmed.

The Facts: The Consumer Financial Protection Bureau (CFPB) was created by the US Congress in 2010 under the Dodd-Frank Wall Street Reform and Consumer Protection Act, commonly abbreviated as Dodd-Frank. Its enactment stemmed from catastrophic losses on mortgage-related financial assets that began in 2007, when the Federal Reserve declared that the US economy had officially entered a recession, which is defined as a general economic decline. The nation's economic situation worsened in 2008, "becoming deep enough and protracted enough to acquire the label 'The Great Recession'" (Weinberg 2013). It bottomed out in 2009, although economists note that recovery from that point was unusually slow.

Much of the problem was due to what was called a "bubble" in the housing market. A bubble in real estate is an abnormal increase in prices that is usually fueled by demand and speculation. As with soap bubbles, housing bubbles will grow larger and larger until they eventually burst, causing a decline in prices when demand decreases after the bubble collapses.

According to the Federal Reserve, "average home prices in the United States more than doubled between 1998 and 2006, the sharpest increase recorded in US history" (Weinberg 2013). Amid the nation's robust economy at the time, which was fueled by the "dot-com" boom (a rapid increase in online companies), many prospective homeowners eagerly sought to borrow money for mortgages before prices rose even more. Mortgage loans were granted by some financial institutions to consumers who barely qualified or would not have qualified at all under traditional circumstances. To observers, much of the problem appeared to be employees at financial institutions making risky decisions. Certain practices were described as blatantly unscrupulous, such as bank staffers approving loans for unqualified borrowers in order to improve their numbers and qualify for bonuses. Many loan recipients ultimately could not pay back what they had borrowed. When they defaulted, they lost their homes.

The result was devastating to millions of Americans. "The collapse of the housing market during the Great Recession displaced close to 10 million Americans as rising unemployment led to mass foreclosures. In 2008 alone, 3.1 million Americans filed for foreclosure, which at the time was one in every 54 homes" (Boyle 2021). While those figures were disruptive enough to the economy, the ripple effect spread even to those consumers who did not buy a home during the housing bubble or suffer the loss of a job. The consequences, not only direct but also indirect, were widespread and far-reaching. "The effect of the Great Recession and subsequent events was that the so-called American Dream [of home ownership] is no longer attainable for many, and optimism has been largely replaced by skepticism" (Boyle 2021).

When masses of consumers began defaulting in the crisis of 2007–8, large financial institutions such as AIG, Bank of America, Bear Stearns, Citigroup, and Lehman Brothers found themselves in trouble. They sought government support from the Federal Deposit Insurance Corporation, Federal Reserve, and the US Treasury, which sent ripples across financial markets. According to the Federal Reserve, the financial crisis of 2007–8 caused America's gross domestic product to fall to the degree that it was the worst, and longest, recession since the Second World War. "The unemployment rate more than doubled, from less than 5 percent to 10 percent" (Weinberg 2013).

In 2007, a Harvard Law School professor named Elizabeth Warren proposed creating a federal agency to provide consumer protection in such areas as mortgages, student loans, and various other financial products. Responding to the financial crisis of 2007–8, Congress passed the Dodd-Frank Wall Street Reform and Consumer Protection Act in 2010. One of its provisions incorporated Warren's proposal by creating the CFPB as a governmental agency. It was funded by the Federal Reserve, with a mission of establishing and enforcing regulations in matters of consumer finance. In addition, the CFPB was authorized to conduct investigations, issue subpoenas, and file lawsuits in federal court on behalf of consumers and honest businesses.

Prior to the establishment of the CFPB, such matters had been spread out among various governmental entities including the Federal Deposit Insurance Corporation, Federal Reserve System, Federal Trade Commission, Office of the Comptroller of the Currency, and Securities and Exchange Commission. As part of its mission, the CFPB aims to be an "umbrella" agency, the focal point for helping consumer financial markets work in the best interests of consumers as well as for the welfare of responsible providers and the US economy as a whole. The agency provides information to aid consumers in making intelligent, informed decisions by understanding the terms of a financial transaction, evaluating their options, and having sufficient information to "shop around." It also accepts consumer complaints and monitors financial markets to keep an eye out for new risks to consumers.

At the end of 2023, the CFPB released a "By the Numbers" summation of its efforts on behalf of American consumers since its creation in 2010. Some of its findings include the following:

> $20.2 billion+: Amount of monetary compensation, principal reductions, canceled debts, and other consumer relief resulting from CFPB enforcement and supervisory work.
>
> 205 million+: Estimated number of consumers or consumer accounts eligible to receive relief from the CFPB's enforcement and supervisory work.
>
> $4.1 billion+: Civil money penalties imposed by the CFPB on companies and individuals that violate the law. Civil money penalties are deposited into the CFPB's victims relief fund (also known as the civil penalty fund), which provides compensation to consumers who have been harmed by violations of federal consumer financial protection law.
>
> $5.5 billion: Estimated amount consumers will save every year due to recent changes in banks' overdraft and non-sufficient funds (NSF) fee policies. The CFPB's most recent analysis found that the decision of most large banks to eliminate NSF fees will save consumers nearly $2 billion annually.
>
> 4.6 million+: Consumer complaints sent to companies for response, including 2.8 million+ complaints about credit reporting, 76,000+ complaints about medical debt collection, and 81,000+ complaints about student loans.
>
> 60.1 million+: Approximate number of users who have accessed answers to hundreds of common financial questions via the CFPB's 'Ask CFPB' database. (Consumer Financial Protection Bureau n.d.)

The CFPB also cites a specific area of interest: US veterans and active members of the armed services. The agency claims to have dispersed $175 million in "monetary relief resulting from 39 public enforcement actions that involved harm to service members and veterans" (Consumer Financial Protection Bureau 2023). It also invited public input on "junk fees, resulting in tens of thousands of people sharing … complaints about unnecessary and potentially illegal fees in consumer financial services" (Consumer Financial Protection Bureau 2023). In addition, the CFPB claims that it handles an average of 3,000 complaints each day, and that it provides consumer-oriented materials translated into eight languages including Arabic, Chinese, Haitian Creole, Korean, Spanish, Tagalog, and Vietnamese. "Consumers can also submit a complaint on the phone in more than 180 languages" (Consumer Financial Protection Bureau n.d.).

Another provision of the Dodd-Frank Wall Street Reform and Consumer Protection Act spurred cooperation between the CFPB and other governmental entities such as the Federal Trade Commission (FTC). In this way, the agencies can avoid duplicating efforts, coordinate enforcement activities, and ensure that regulatory treatment of consumer financial products and services are consistent. The FTC has traditionally held regulatory powers under such federal laws as the Consumer Leasing Act (passed in 1976), Credit Repair Organizations Act (1996), Fair Credit Reporting Act (1970), Fair Debt Collection Practices Act (1978), Electronic Funds Transfer Act (1978), Equal Credit Opportunity Act (1974), Home Ownership and Equity Protection Act (1994), and the Truth in Lending Act (1968). By cooperating with the CFPB, the efforts of both agencies were strengthened under existing laws.

One of the areas in which there is interagency cooperation is "payday lending." The CFPB states that "while there is no set definition of a payday loan, it is usually a short-term, high cost loan, generally for $500 or less, that is typically due on your next payday" (Consumer Financial Protection Bureau 2022). Borrowers seeking a payday loan typically must write a postdated check for the full balance plus fees or authorize the lender to electronically debit the funds from their bank account. If the borrower does not repay the loan by the due date, the lender can cash the check or electronically withdraw money from their account. "Your ability to repay the loan while meeting your other financial obligations is generally not considered by a payday lender" (Consumer Financial Protection Bureau 2022).

Along with efforts by the CFPB to monitor payday loans, there are many state laws that set a maximum amount for payday loan fees, which usually range from $10 to $30 for every $100 borrowed. "A typical two-week payday loan with a $15 per $100 fee equates to an annual percentage rate (APR) of almost 400 percent. By comparison, APRs on credit cards can range from about 12 percent to about 30 percent" (Consumer Financial Protection Bureau 2022). The CFPB works to prevent payday lenders from attempting to collect payments from a person's bank account in ways that may generate excessive fees for the consumer or to deviate from what the borrower expects.

The CFPB also has broad regulatory authority over financial institutions with assets of over $10 billion and is permitted to take action to enforce consumer protection laws. In one high-profile case, "Wells Fargo was fined $185 million in 2016 after CFPB and federal regulators found that some of the bank's employees had opened more than one million accounts and applied for nearly 600,000 credit cards without authorization from clients" (Bush 2017).

Since its inception, there has been a continuing political debate about the CFPB. In 2013, Elizabeth Warren, who first proposed the agency, was elected to the US Senate and has fought to keep its authority intact in the face of conservatives who want to eliminate the CFPB or limit its power. Democrats believe there is a great need for the CFPB, while conservatives believe the agency is "another example of government overreach that stymies consumer choice and economic growth" (Bush 2017).

Further Reading

Boyle, Michael J. 2021. "How the 2008 Housing Crash Affected the American Dream." *Investopedia*. Accessed November 28, 2024. https://www.investopedia.com/ask/answers/062515/how-was-american-dream-impacted-housing-market-collapse-2008.asp.

Bush, Daniel. 2017. "What Is the Consumer Financial Protection Bureau, Anyway?" *PBS NewsHour*. Accessed November 28, 2024. https://www.pbs.org/newshour/economy/making-sense/what-is-the-consumer-financial-protection-bureau-anyway.

Consumer Financial Protection Bureau. n.d. "The CFPB." Accessed September 20, 2024. https://www.consumerfinance.gov/about-us/the-bureau/.

Consumer Financial Protection Bureau. 2022. "What Is a Payday Loan?" Accessed November 28, 2024. https://www.consumerfinance.gov/ask-cfpb/what-is-a-payday-loan-en-1567/.

Consumer Financial Protection Bureau. 2023. "Twelve Years of Protecting Consumers and Honest Businesses." Accessed November 28, 2024. https://www.consumerfinance.gov/about-us/blog/twelve-years-of-protecting-consumers-and-honest-businesses/.

Federal Trade Commission. n.d. "Consumer Finance." Accessed September 20, 2024. https://www.ftc.gov/news-events/topics/consumer-finance.

Weinberg, John. 2013. "The Great Recession and Its Aftermath." *Federal Reserve History*. Accessed November 28, 2024. https://www.federalreservehistory.org/essays/great-recession-and-its-aftermath.

Q32: Do consumer protections cover emerging technologies such as cryptocurrency and artificial intelligence?

Answer: In 2009, a peer-to-peer digital currency called Bitcoin introduced the concept of decentralized finance, usually called cryptocurrency, crypto-assets, or simply crypto. Some consumers wondered if they could use it legally and if their funds would be safe under existing consumer finance protection laws. Officials around the world have been debating how to control this new type of money, or even if it could be called "money." In addition, the wide-ranging introduction of artificial intelligence, or "AI," in recent years has added to the mix of confusion in consumer financial matters. Cryptocurrency and AI have attracted widespread attention in America, not only from consumers but also from the US Congress, Department of Justice, Department of the Treasury, Internal Revenue Service, and the Securities and Exchange Commission. In some ways, these new technologies are a return to the days of *caveat emptor*: buyer beware.

The Facts: In the early years of the twenty-first century, many American consumers had to learn a new financial language with terms such as Bitcoin, cryptocurrency, and digital assets. However, it was not the first time Americans have had to deal with new forms of money. Their ancestors had a similar problem after the American Revolution ended in 1783. A consumer trying to buy bread in the marketplace might be using British shillings, French guineas, Spanish doubloons, or even the Prussian thaler (pronounced "TAH-luhr"), which is said to be the origin of the word "dollar." To add to the mix, at the time, each state in the United States printed its own money. Many people avoided using "continentals," the new money being printed by the fledgling government of the United States starting in 1775, with its first plates being made by Paul Revere. No one was entirely sure what the exchange rate of the continental was, although converting into Spanish currency came the closest.

The Mint Act of 1792 was passed after the US Constitution was ratified, establishing the dollar to be America's principal unit of currency. Through the 1800s, various units of money such as Treasury Notes and Silver Certificates were issued, along with several thousand varieties of money printed by private banks as "state bank notes." In 1886, the Martha Washington One Dollar Certificate was issued, making her "the first and only woman to grace the primary portrait of US paper currency" (National Credit Union Administration n.d.). Finally, in 1914, Federal Reserve notes began to be issued as "the only currency still being manufactured today by the Bureau of Engraving and Printing" (National Credit Union Administration n.d.).

Although American consumers have historically encountered changes in legal tender, many people feel that the emerging field of cryptocurrency is something quite different. In its most basic terms, crypto is digital currency that exists electronically. It is accessed through a website or an app on electronic devices, as well as at cryptocurrency ATMs located in places such as airports, malls, restaurants, or retail stores. The purchase of crypto is instantaneous and is sent directly to the buyer's digital "wallet." Bitcoin is currently a well-known cryptocurrency, although new ones have also been created. According to the Federal Trade Commission, many Americans hold crypto-assets as an investment, although in some cases, people might use cryptocurrency for other reasons, such as "quick payments, to avoid transaction fees that traditional banks charge, or because it offers some anonymity" (Federal Trade Commission 2022).

As opposed to funds in banks that are protected by the Federal Deposit Insurance Corporation (FDIC), if something should happen to a person's digital wallet—for example, if the exchange goes out of business or the digital wallet is hacked or stolen—"you're likely to find that no one can step in to help you recover your funds" (Federal Trade Commission 2022). According to the CFPB, "there is no government agency or financial regulator that insures crypto-assets" (Consumer Financial Protection Bureau 2022). The lack of FDIC coverage or other government back-up adds to the element of *caveat emptor* for consumers of crypto in which the buyer must beware.

In addition, depending on many factors such as supply and demand, cryptocurrency values can change rapidly, even hour-to-hour. "Cryptocurrencies tend to be more volatile than more traditional investments, such as stocks and bonds. An investment that's worth thousands of dollars today might be worth only hundreds tomorrow. And, if the value goes down, there's no guarantee it will go up again" (Federal Trade Commission 2022). One case in point was exemplified in what became known as the Crypto Bowl, a series of ads from various sellers of cryptocurrency during the 2021 Super Bowl. One of the most talked-about featured movie actor Matt Damon (*Good Will Hunting*, *The Martian*). His tagline for Singapore-based Crypto.com was "Fortune Favors the Brave." However, investors who were inspired by Damon's ad to be brave lost about two-thirds of their money as Bitcoin's price "dropped by 64 percent since that fortuitous fall" (Pahwa 2023). Other forms of crypto experienced similar drops, and there was no government bailout or FDIC protection. Lawsuits alleging fraud were filed against the crypto companies and their celebrity promoters.

In the unregulated environment of crypto, "perhaps unsurprisingly for a currency designed with anonymity and lack of control in mind, Bitcoin [along with others] has proven to be an attractive and lucrative target for criminals" (Marr 2017). Although it has no regulatory power over cryptocurrency, the Federal Trade Commission has attempted to aid consumers by identifying a number of common fraudulent activities involving crypto including faked celebrity endorsements, investment scams, and promises of free money. There have also been cases of scammers impersonating well-known companies such as Amazon, FedEx, or the consumer's bank by calling, e-mailing, or texting to say there is a fraud alert on the consumer's account and their money is at risk. "To fix it, you need to buy crypto and send it to them. … If you click the link in any message, answer the call, or call back the number on the pop-up, you'll be connected to a scammer" (Federal Trade Commission 2022).

While the CFPB has no regulatory power over cryptocurrency, the agency attempts to protect consumers by regularly publishing complaint bulletins related to crypto-assets based on problems reported to the CFPB. Along with consumer complaints of being victimized by account hacks, fraud, theft, security holds, identity verification issues, and inability to access their account due to platform failures, "poor customer service is a common theme across crypto-related complaints" (Consumer Financial Protection Bureau 2022).

In 2024, American crypto entrepreneur Sam Bankman-Fried was convicted of fraud after the US Department of Justice filed criminal charges against him. In the highly publicized case, Bankman-Fried was sentenced to twenty-five years in federal prison for defrauding customers and investors in his failed crypto exchange, FTX. The judge agreed with prosecutors who claimed that Bankman-Fried was propelled in his financial crimes by the desire to become politically influential. Bankman-Fried was ordered to forfeit more than $11 billion, to be paid to the government from his assets plus a monthly sum over time. There was no immediate restitution for his customers or investors because the court stated it would be impractical with so many victims. When Bankman-Fried's verdict was handed down, US Attorney General Merrick Garland stated that there are serious consequences for financial fraud, adding "Anyone who believes they can hide their financial crimes behind wealth and power, or behind a shiny new thing they claim no one else is smart enough to understand, should think twice" (US Department of Justice 2024).

The Financial Crimes Enforcement Network (FinCEN) at the US Department of Treasury has been monitoring cryptocurrency for criminal activity. The Internal Revenue Service (IRS), also in the Department of Treasury, categorizes Bitcoin as property and taxes it accordingly. Outside of the United States, several countries allow the use of Bitcoin and have regulations regarding it, including Denmark, Germany, Japan, Spain, Switzerland, and the United Kingdom. Other countries have either banned it outright or cut off support from their banking and financial systems, including China, Egypt, Morocco, and Qatar. The world of cryptocurrency is evolving, according to futurist Bernard Marr. He states, "whatever your opinion on Bitcoin and cryptocurrency—and educated commenters have described them as everything from the future of money to an outright scam—it seems they are here to stay. [Will it] replace government-controlled, centralized money [and be] controlled by nothing besides market forces? … We are unlikely to know the answer for some time yet" (Marr 2017).

Concerns regarding the uncertain future of cryptocurrency may seem relatively minor compared to those surrounding the steady expansion and possible consequences of artificial intelligence (AI). At this time, consumers are not forced to buy digital assets such as crypto. However, AI, with very few consumer protections and the potential for abuses, may be well on its way to inserting itself into all aspects of life.

Basically, AI is the result of the creation of machines that can learn to think like humans. Unlike humans, AI technology can quickly process large amounts of data such as recognizing recurring patterns. After doing so, it can make decisions and formulate judgments on whatever it has been programmed to do. According to the Federal Trade Commission, with AI, "there are opportunities for public progress by enhancing human capacity to integrate, analyze, and leverage information. But also, perhaps in larger part … AI presents new layers of uncertainty and risk" (Fondrie-Teitler and Jayanti 2023). In addition, the FTC states that artificial intelligence is "changing the mechanics by which we go about our daily lives. That can be unsettling, especially when the harms brought about by that change are tangible and felt by everyday consumers" (Fondrie-Teitler and Jayanti 2023).

As millions of consumers interact with AI products, the FTC is examining the kinds of concerns and experiences people are having in the marketplace. Some of those concerns include how AI is built, as its "fuel" is based on mining personal data. Copyright and intellectual property issues are also being studied.

In addition, there are concerns about voice recordings that can be used to generate "voice prints," capturing the unique characteristics of a person's speech. Consumers have expressed reservations to the FTC about making customer support calls after hearing the standard message indicating the call may be recorded "for quality control purposes." The fear is that "the recording could then be used to train an AI using their voice" (Fondrie-Teitler and Jayanti 2023), utilizing it to deceive others. However, there is often no other form of contact for consumers needing help other than making customer support calls. To maximize corporate profit, "this often means reducing the number of humans involved, leaving consumers to engage with their AI replacements" (Fondrie-Teitler and Jayanti 2023). Consumer complaints to the FTC have already included voice cloning, in which the speech of family members was exploited for financial gain, such as the faked "grandchild-in-jail" telephone scam. Other malicious uses of

AI include phishing emails, disguised as coming from legitimate companies, and romance scams leading to financial fraud by tricking the consumer into providing money to help the new paramour.

According to the Federal Trade Commission, the FTC attempts to monitor the marketplace and the business practices of companies as more AI uses emerge. If abuses and offenders are identified, they could possibly be addressed under existing laws. But at this point, there are few ironclad consumer protection laws that can be applied across the board regarding AI. The technology behind artificial intelligence involves qualities of being too new, too confusing, and too pervasive, all of which combine to make it difficult to stem the malicious acts of fraudsters.

However, one aspect of artificial intelligence *does* currently qualify for regulatory oversight under existing laws: gender and racial bias. This may take place through AI algorithms that determine such things as decisions about employment or whether to approve consumer credit. According to technology writer Rebecca Heilweil, "humans are error-prone and biased, but that doesn't mean that algorithms are necessarily better. Still, the tech is already making important decisions about your life [and] we frequently don't know how a particular artificial intelligence or algorithm was designed, what data helped build it, or how it works" (Heilweil 2020).

Heilweil states that some areas of bias reported to consumer financial protection agencies and the Equal Employment Opportunity Commission involve gender bias and racial discrimination. She cites an example in which job applicants were screened with a bias toward men by factoring in data called "gender proxies" such as whether the applicant attended a women's college. Another case of gender bias involved a credit application from a husband and wife in which their finances were identical. The husband received a much higher credit limit than the wife, which became obvious when they compared their respective lines of credit. Racial bias could also be built into an application for credit, employment, or housing. This could take place if the algorithm is trained to detect a degree from a historically Black college or university, or a current address in what it recognizes as a predominantly minority neighborhood.

The Equal Employment Opportunity Commission looks into cases of alleged algorithmic discrimination in hiring practices, and legislation has been proposed that would require company AI systems to be cleared for bias by the FTC. The government is also trying to determine how to balance regulations on AI in a way that does not discourage technological innovation. "That raises the challenge of whether the government is prepared to study and govern this technology, and figure out how existing laws apply" (Heilweil 2020). At this time, governmental entities are still on a learning curve.

In 2023, the White House issued an Executive Order on the development of AI. The stated purpose was to make sure that AI complies with federal laws and to protect consumers "against unlawful discrimination and abuse, including in the justice system and the Federal Government" (White House 2023). The Executive Order cited consumer protections as being particularly important in certain critical fields. These areas include education, financial services, healthcare, housing, law, and transportation "where mistakes by or misuse of AI could harm patients, cost consumers or small businesses, or jeopardize safety or rights" (White House 2023).

The Federal Trade Commission recognizes the potential benefits of AI. These include the ability of AI to assist in medical diagnosis, automate repetitive tasks like data entry, boost productivity, enhance customer service, help in decision-making, improve efficiency, increase corporate revenue, offer 24/7 availability, provide data analysis, and reduce human error. However, cybersecurity remains a concern even for the most enthusiastic proponents of AI. The power of AI has implications for both consumer protection and competition in the marketplace, including "risks around consumer privacy as well as risks from consolidation of power in the form of data aggregation and access of AI tools" (Fondrie-Teitler and Jayanti 2023).

The CFPB has been looking at emerging forms of technology including both AI and cryptocurrency, stating that they have "hosted trainings and briefings for enforcement agencies on numerous consumer financial protection topics, including emerging practices in biometrics and how to address algorithmic harms" (Meyer 2023). The CFPB is not limiting its consumer protection efforts to the federal level. The agency has also involved entities such as "state attorneys general and state insurance commissioners—to sharpen our combined efforts to ensure consumers are protected" (Meyer 2023).

However, technology writer Heilweil questions whether any level of government is prepared to learn enough to oversee the technology, much less to determine what existing laws and/or new laws might apply. She states that there are people who "understand [emerging technology] very well, and that would be technologists ... and a group of people who don't really understand it at all, or have minimal understanding, and that would be policymakers" (Heilweil 2020). This situation could pose a challenge to both lawmakers and consumers. Consumer protections in the United States for emerging technology like cryptocurrency and artificial intelligence are very much in a state of transition as the nation looks to the future, which many Americans feel is already here.

Further Reading

Bajpai, Prableen. 2023. "Countries Where Bitcoin Is Legal and Illegal." *Investopedia*. Accessed November 28, 2024. https://www.investopedia.com/articles/forex/041515/countries-where-bitcoin-legal-illegal.asp.

Consumer Financial Protection Bureau. 2022. "CFPB Publishes New Bulletin Analyzing Rise in Crypto-Asset Complaints." Accessed November 28, 2024. https://www.consumerfinance.gov/about-us/newsroom/cfpb-publishes-new-bulletin-analyzing-rise-in-crypto-asset-complaints/.

Federal Trade Commission. 2022. "What to Know about Cryptocurrency and Scams." Accessed November 28, 2024. https://consumer.ftc.gov/articles/what-know-about-cryptocurrency-and-scams.

Fondrie-Teitler, Simon, and Amritha Jayanti. 2023. "Consumers Are Voicing Concerns about AI." Federal Trade Commission. Accessed November 28, 2024. https://www.ftc.gov/policy/advocacy-research/tech-at-ftc/2023/10/consumers-are-voicing-concerns-about-ai.

Heilweil, Rebecca. 2020. "Why Algorithms Can Be Racist and Sexist." *Vox*. Accessed November 28, 2024. https://www.vox.com/recode/2020/2/18/21121286/algorithms-bias-discrimination-facial-recognition-transparency.

Marr, Bernard. 2017. "A Short History of Bitcoin and Crypto Currency Everyone Should Read." *Forbes*. Accessed November 28, 2024. https://www.forbes.com/sites/bernardmarr/2017/12/06/a-short-history-of-bitcoin-and-crypto-currency-everyone-should-read/?sh=249fe8523f27.

Meyer, Erie. 2023. "Bringing Tech Enforcers Together to Protect Consumers." Consumer Financial Protection Bureau. Accessed November 28, 2024. https://www.consumerfinance.gov/about-us/blog/bringing-tech-enforcers-together-to-protect-consumers/.

National Credit Union Administration. n.d. "History of United States Currency." Accessed September 10, 2024. https://mycreditunion.gov/financial-resources/history-united-states-currency.

Pahwa, Nitish. 2023. "If You Bought Crypto Because of Larry David and Matt Damon, I'm Sorry." *Slate*. Accessed November 28, 2024. https://slate.com/technology/2023/02/super-bowl-ads-crypto-ftx-larry-david-coinbase-matt-damon.html.

US Department of Justice. 2024. "Samuel Bankman-Fried Sentenced to 25 Years for His Orchestration of Multiple Fraudulent Schemes." Accessed November 28, 2024. https://www.justice.gov/opa/pr/samuel-bankman-fried-sentenced-25-years-his-orchestration-multiple-fraudulent-schemes.

The White House. 2023. "Executive Order on the Safe, Secure, and Trustworthy Development and Use of Artificial Intelligence." Accessed November 28, 2024. https://www.whitehouse.gov/briefing-room/presidential-actions/2023/10/30/executive-order-on-the-safe-secure-and-trustworthy-development-and-use-of-artificial-intelligence/.

Index

About the Author

Nancy Hendricks holds a doctorate in education and is an award-winning author whose books include *Women's Equality in America: Examining the Facts* (Bloomsbury, 2024).